advancing learning, changing lives

Edexcel GCE History

Britain, 1830–85: Representation and Reform

Rosemary Rees   David Wilkinson
Series editors: Martin Collier   Rosemary Rees

Unit 2 Student Book

A PEARSON COMPANY

Published by Pearson Education Limited, a company incorporated in
England and Wales, having its registered office at Edinburgh Gate,
Harlow, Essex, CM20 2JE. Registered company number: 872828

www.pearsonschoolsandfecolleges.co.uk

Edexcel is a registered trademark of Edexcel Limited

Text © Pearson Education Limited 2011

First published 2011

12 11 10

10 9 8 7 6 5 4 3 2 1

British Library Cataloguing in Publication Data
A catalogue record for this book is available from the British Library

ISBN 978 1 846905 02 5

Disclaimer

This material has been published on behalf of Edexcel and offers high-quality support for the delivery of
Edexcel qualifications. This does not mean that the material is essential to achieve any Edexcel
qualification, nor does it mean that it is the only suitable material available to support any Edexcel
qualification. Edexcel material will not be used verbatim in setting any Edexcel examination or
assessment. Any resource lists produced by Edexcel shall include this and other appropriate resources.
Copies of official specifications for all Edexcel qualifications may be found on the Edexcel website:
www.edexcel.com

Acknowledgements

We are grateful to the following for permission to reproduce copyright material:

Text

Extract 2.i from *Forging of the Modern State*, 3rd edition, Longman (Evans, E.J. 2001) pp.267–268,
copyright © Pearson Education Ltd; Extract 3.g from *'Chartism in Manchester'* by Donald Read published
in Chartist Studies, St Martins Press (ed Briggs, A. 1959) reproduced with permission of Palgrave
Macmillan; Extracts 3.n, 3.v from *Popular Radicalism*, Longman (Wright, D.G. 1988) copyright © Pearson
Education Limited; Extract 3.u from *'Chartism in Manchester'* by Donald Read published in Chartist
Studies, St Martins Press (ed Briggs, A. 1959) reproduced with permission of Palgrave Macmillan;
Extract 4.a from *'Chartism'* by Alex Wilson published in *Popular Movements 1830–1850*, Macmillan
(ed Ward, J.T. 1970) p.132, reproduced with permission of Palgrave Macmillan; Extract 4.c from *Chartism*,
2nd edition, Longman (Royle, E. 1986) p.30, copyright © Pearson Education Limited; Extract 4.t from
'London in the Age of Reform' by Large, D. published in London in the *Age of Reform*, Wiley-Blackwell
(ed Stevenson 1977) reproduced by permission of Wiley-Blackwell; Extract 4.v from *Chartism*, 2nd edition,
Longman (Royle. E. 1986) p.45, copyright © Pearson Education Limited; Extract 5.c from *The Birth of
Modern Britain 1780–1914*, Longman (Evans, E. and Culpin, C. 1997) copyright © Pearson Education
Limited; Extract 5.p from *Forging of the Modern State*, 3rd edition, Longman (Evans, E.J. 2001) pp.437,439,
copyright © Pearson Education Ltd; Extract 6.f from *'Wellington and Peel'* by Norman Gash, published in
The Conservative Leadership 1832–1932, Macmillan (ed Southgate, D. 1974) reproduced with permission
of Palgrave Macmillan; Extract 6.g from Sir Robert Peel and the Conservative Party, 1832–1841: A Study
in Failure?, *The English Historical Review*, Vol. 98 (388), pp.529–557 (Ian Newbould 1983), Copyright
© 1983, Oxford University Press; Extract 6.h from *Peel and the Conservative Party 1830–1850*, 3rd edition,
Longman (Adelman, P. 1989) pp.24–25, copyright © Pearson Education Limited; Extract 6.j from *Forging of
the Modern State*, 3rd edition, Longman (Evans, E.J. 2001) pp.338–339, copyright © Pearson Education Ltd;
Extract 6.m from *Peel and the Conservative Party 1830–1850*, 3rd edition, Longman (Adelman, P. 1989)
p.79, copyright © Pearson Education Limited; Extract 7.b from *Gladstone, Disraeli and Later Victorian
Politics*, 3rd edition, Longman (Adelman, P. 1997) p.4, copyright © Pearson Education Limited; Extract 7.f
from *The Tories and the People 1880–1935*, Wiley-Blackwell (Pugh, M. 1985) reproduced by permission of
Wiley-Blackwell; Extract 7.m from *Democracy and Reform 1815–85*, Longman (Wright, D.G. 1970) p.88,
copyright © Pearson Education Limited; Extract 7.p from *Gladstone, Disraeli and Later Victorian Politics*,
3rd edition, Longman (Adelman, P. 1997) p.54, copyright © Pearson Education Limited; Extract 7.q from
The Extension of the Franchise 1832–1931, Heinemann (Whitfield, B. 2001) p.243, copyright © Pearson
Education Limited

In some instances we have been unable to trace the owners of copyright material, and we would
appreciate any information that would enable us to do so.

Picture Credits

The publisher would like to thank the following for their kind permission to reproduce their photographs:
(Key: b – bottom; c – centre; l – left; r – right; t – top)

Alamy Images: Mary Evans Picture Library 11, 74, 89, 100, 125, 157, World History Archive 36, 70;
Bridgeman Art Library Ltd: 43, Newport Museum & Art Gallery, South Wales 58, Private Collection 65;
Getty Images: Hulton Archive 12, 53; © **The Trustees of The British Museum. All rights reserved**: 7,
25; **TopFoto**: 73

Cover images: *Front*: **www.CartoonStock.com**

All other images © Pearson Education

Every effort has been made to trace the copyright holders and we apologise in advance for any
unintentional omissions. We would be pleased to insert the appropriate acknowledgement in any
subsequent edition of this publication.

Sections written with the assistance of Alan Marshall-Hicks

In memory of David Wilkinson

Contents

Introduction

Will you vote in the next general election? If you are over eighteen years old on polling day and you, or your parents, have registered you as an elector, then you can. So who is entitled to vote in United Kingdom general elections? To vote you must be:

- over 18 years old and registered to vote
- resident in the UK
- a British citizen, a Commonwealth citizen or a citizen of the Republic of Ireland

It really does seem that simple, as those who can't vote in UK general elections are:

- members of the House of Lords
- European Union citizens, even those are living in the UK
- convicted prisoners serving a prison term (although the EU is trying to change the British government's mind on this)
- those guilty of corrupt or illegal practices in connection with an election

It would seem, then, that most men and women over the age of eighteen may vote in general elections. Indeed, in the UK general election of 2010 just over 45.5m people, out of an estimated population of around 62m, were entitled to vote and to have a say in how they were governed.

However it was not always like this.

If you were eighteen years old in 1830, when the coverage of this book begins, you most certainly would not have been entitled to vote. For a start, you had to be over 21 years old, and, most importantly, you had to be a man. If you lived in a county, you had to own a substantial amount of property; if you lived in a borough, (a one-time important town within a county) there were all sorts of different regulations that applied before a man could vote. The result was that, from a total population of around 24m, about 439,000 people were entitled to vote. It was this relatively small group of people who decided who sat in the House of Commons and therefore ultimately decided on the people who enacted the laws that applied to everyone.

If you were eighteen years old in 1885, when this book ends, you still wouldn't be able to vote although many more people could. You had to be

Discussion point

Why are these four groups of people forbidden from voting in UK general elections?

Do you think this is fair?

a man and over 21 years old, this was the same as in 1830. But in 1885, your only 'qualification' to be granted the vote was that you had to be a householder, and to have occupied your house or lodgings for at least twelve months. Indeed, by 1885 two men out of every three were entitled to vote in general elections. The story of this book is the story of the ways in which these enormous changes came about; of how the members of the House of Commons were persuaded to give up some of their privileges and allow more and more of the people they governed to form the electorate and vote for those who governed them. There were two significant changes that came later. The Representation of the People Act in 1918 gave the vote to all adult males over the age of 21 and to some women over the age of 30. Ten years later, women were given the vote on equal terms with men.

It is important to realise, however that it was the years 1830-1885 that laid the foundations of what came later. It was these years that saw a shift in attitudes from the belief that the country should be run by a landowning elite elected by those who owned property, to the belief that the 'respectable' working class should be allowed to have a say in who governed them and made the laws by which they had to live. It was these shifting attitudes that led, finally, to the Representation of the People Act in 1969 that gave the vote to all those over the age of eighteen.

Important milestones in representation and reform 1830–1885

1832 Reform Act

- 1 in 5 adult males entitled to vote in general elections
- Some seats re-distributed to enable the large manufacturing towns of the midlands and north to be represented.

1867 Reform Act

- 1 in 3 adult males entitled to vote in general elections
- Some further redistribution of seats.

1872 Ballot Act

- Voting in general elections became secret

1883 Corrupt and Illegal Practices Prevention Act

- Wiped out the more severe forms of bribery and coercion at elections.

1884 Representation of the People Act

- 2 in 3 males entitled to vote in general elections

1885 Redistribution of Seats Act

- Seats re-distributed to more fairly reflect the population distribution

These changes were brought about by people who discussed and argued, petitioned and marched, rioted, fought and sometimes died to change the electoral system in the UK to make it more representative. Reflect on this whenever a general election is called.

Discussion point

Should voting in twenty-first century general elections be made compulsory?

1 The old order challenged: from repression to reform

What is this unit about?

In 1796, a Member of Parliament (MP) named Edmund Burke described the governance of Britain as: 'The King, and his faithful subjects the lords and commons of that realm – one triple cord which no man can break.' Burke, and those who thought like him, saw this 'triple cord' as being the great strength of the British political system. The monarch, the members of the House of Lords and the members of the House of Commons all played different, but equally important, parts in the government of Great Britain. This unit is about that triple cord; about the ways in which it worked well, and about the ways in which it increasingly ceased to serve a country that was rapidly changing. In the past, the old interests, based on land and property, had run Great Britain, confident that they had the right and the ability to do so. However, the industrial revolution had brought great changes, not only to the economy of Great Britain, but also to British society. Industrial towns grew and flourished; manufacturing became an important element in the economy, and those controlling this manufacturing base were not represented in the parliament that governed them. This unit considers the effectiveness of the old system, the challenges it met and examines the pressures that brought about the Reform Act of 1832.

Note: In order to understand the impact of the Reform Act of 1832, you need to know about the ways in which the electoral system worked before that date. You need to know, too, that protest against the system, and demands for reform, happened before 1830. However, in the examination you won't be asked any direct questions on protest before 1830, although the background information will be useful.

Key questions

- How effective was the British political system before 1832?
- What were the pressures that brought about change?

Timeline

1815	**End of Napoleonic wars against France**
1816	**Spa Fields Meeting, London** Calls for reform ended in riots and looting
1817	**Pentridge Rising** Failure of attempt to capture Nottingham castle by unemployed textile workers
	The Blanketeers A march to London by unemployed Manchester workers to present a petition to the Prince Regent broken up by troops
1819	**Peterloo** Meeting in St Peter's Field, Manchester, to demand parliamentary reform, broken up by force, killing 11 people and wounding many more
	The Six Acts The government makes peaceful protest difficult

1829–30	**Distress in towns and countryside** High poor rates and high unemployment
1829	**Birmingham Political Union founded** Pressure group to focus and lead reform movements Many political unions formed throughout Britain
1830	**Many leading London and provincial papers in favour of parliamentary reform** **General election returns Tory government** Majority greatly reduced (Wellington PM); ministry later defeated on civil list vote and Wellington resigns King asks Grey (a Whig leader) to form a government Grey becomes Prime Minister
1831–32	**Cholera epidemic hits Britain** Roughly 32,000 people die
1831	**First Reform Bill** Passed Commons by one vote. Parliament dissolved and general election held **General election** Whigs returned with majority of 130 **Second Reform Bill** Passed Commons easily but thrown out by Lords Country erupts in violence **Third Reform Bill** Passes Commons easily but Lords employ delaying tactics Grey asks King to create pro-reform peers; King refuses Grey resigns Country erupts in violence Wellington fails to form a government Grey back as PM and King agrees to create pro-reform peers Threat enough and Bill passes through Lords
1832 June	**Reform Bill becomes Reform Act**

Source A

The County of Yorkshire, which contains near a million of souls, sends two county members [to the House of Commons] and so does the County of Rutland, which contains not a hundredth part of that number. The town of Old Sarum, which contains not three houses, sends two members; and the town of Manchester, which contains upwards of sixty thousand souls, is not admitted to send any. Is there any principle in these things?

From Tom Paine, *Rights of Man*, published in 1791

Source B

Borough of Gatton

Proprietors	ONE	Sir Mark Wood, Bart., MP
Magistrates	ONE	Sir Mark Wood, Bart., MP
Churchwardens	ONE	Sir Mark Wood, Bart., MP
Overseers of the Poor	ONE	Sir Mark Wood, Bart., MP
Vestrymen	ONE	Sir Mark Wood, Bart., MP
Surveyors of the Highways	ONE	Sir Mark Wood, Bart., MP
Collectors of Taxes	ONE	Sir Mark Wood, Bart., MP
Candidates at the last election	TWO	Sir Mark Wood, Bart., MP
		His son, Mark Wood Esq., MP
Voters at the last election	ONE	Sir Mark Wood, Bart., MP
Representatives returned at the last election	ONE	Sir Mark Wood, Bart., MP

From *The Reformists Register and Weekly Commentary*, published 15 March 1817

SKILLS BUILDER

Read Sources A and B. What can you learn from them about the electoral system before 1832? What criticisms are they making of the electoral system?

The parliamentary system before 1832

In the eighteenth and early nineteenth centuries, governments were concerned with matters such as raising taxes, dealing with disorder, maintaining the army and navy, conducting foreign policy and fighting wars. It was not the job of government to become involved in providing education or health services, or to deal with matters such as housing, poverty or unemployment.

The Crown

The monarch appointed the ministers of state, and in this way ensured the Crown had a major influence on government policies. Parliament, however, had control of finances, and so the King's wishes (for it had been a king since the death of Queen Anne in 1714) could only be carried out if they had the support of parliament. In particular, support of the Commons was necessary because they, and not the Lords, could introduce financial measures. The king controlled a section of the Commons because over 100 MPs were 'placemen', dependent on the Crown for their seats. However, these were not sufficient in number for the monarch to be certain his policies would be carried out if a majority of MPs opposed them. On the other hand, MPs could not insist that the Crown appoint ministers acceptable to them. There had to be a balance.

The House of Lords

Most government ministers sat in the Lords, as did leaders of the army, civil service and Church of England. Most of the great landowners were peers, and sat in the Lords, too. Not only did they own vast estates, but

Definitions

County

Britain is divided into **counties**. Until 1832, each English county sent two MPs to parliament. The exception was Yorkshire, which returned four.

Borough

A **borough** was a town that, at some point, had been given a royal charter. These charters allowed the town to levy tolls at their market, to hold a court that dealt with civil and some criminal matters, and send a representative to the House of Commons. Most boroughs sent two MPs to Westminster. So boroughs were contained within counties. Some boroughs, known as 'rotten boroughs', had so few voters that they were easily bought or bribed to vote for a particular candidate. Other boroughs were also under the control of a single powerful person or family. These 'pocket boroughs' would nearly always return the influential person's choice of candidate.

Question

What were the strengths, and what were the weaknesses, of this system of government?

also many controlled constituencies that sent MPs to the Commons. Even so, with about 111 MPs owing their seats to the influence of the aristocracy, there were not enough of them to ensure the Commons would always support the Lords and the monarch's ministers. Neither was it enough to guarantee that the measures proposed by the Commons would always be supported by the Lords. It was quite usual for the House of Lords to join with the King in opposing a measure that had been passed by the House of Commons.

The House of Commons

The House of Commons consisted of 658 MPs, all of whom were elected in some way or another. Electors did not vote for a political party or a national programme, as now; instead, they voted on personal and local issues. There were no nationally organised parties with published manifestos. Indeed, there were no formal parties at all. There were groups of MPs called 'Whigs' and 'Tories', but these were usually made up of politicians who organised themselves into groups based on family and friends, or on a very general sharing of ideas and attitudes. However, the vast majority of MPs were independent members who could afford to spend time doing this unpaid job of work because they thought it important. They were not bound to ministers and the government by the need for an income, and they were not necessarily bound to either the Whigs or the Tories by ties of family. No government could be certain of the support of all these independent MPs, or even of a large proportion of them. Yet all governments needed their support if they were to survive for long.

SKILLS BUILDER

Using the information about the parliamentary system before 1832:

(a) Create a spider diagram to show how the three elements – Crown, Lords and Commons – inter-related.

(b) What were the checks and balances within this system that made sure no one element dominated? Build these into your spider diagram. How effective do you think they were?

Constituencies: counties and boroughs

All MPs represented one of two kinds of constituency: **county** or **borough**.

- Each county in England and Wales, no matter how small or how large, returned two MPs to parliament with one exception. Most Scottish counties returned one MP.

- Many counties contained towns, which, because they had been important ports or markets, had in the past been made 'parliamentary boroughs'. This meant that they, like the counties, could send two representatives to parliament. In Scotland, the burghs were grouped in fours, with each group being entitled to one MP.

This would seem to be a pretty straightforward system. But it threw up some apparently strange anomalies.

- Old Sarum had been an important place to the Normans, and from the reign of Edward II in the fourteenth century, the borough elected two members to the House of Commons. However, by 1831 it had 11 voters (although none of them lived there) and still sent two MPs to the Commons.

- Dunwich had been a bustling Suffolk port in the thirteenth century, when it was granted the status of 'borough'. By 1831, however, with only 44 houses, it had clearly lost its early importance. Yet it was still entitled to 'borough' status, and to two MPs.

- Six Cornish boroughs, with hardly 1,000 inhabitants each, were entitled to send, between them, 12 representatives to parliament.

Boroughs like these were called 'rotten boroughs'. Many of the early boroughs had been created in the six southern counties that bordered the English Channel. In 1801, one-third of England's MPs came from these counties, yet only 15 per cent of the population of England lived there.

In contrast, large northern towns such as Manchester with 182,000 inhabitants in 1831 and Leeds with 123,000 inhabitants, and midland towns like Birmingham with 144,000 inhabitants, did not have a single representative in the House of Commons. This was because, in medieval times, when boroughs were first created, towns like these were unimportant small villages, which did not merit borough status and their own MPs.

The Franchise: who could vote?

The right to vote went with certain qualifications, which were mostly to do with ownership of land. Whether or not a man was allowed to vote in a parliamentary election depended on where he lived and what he owned.

- If he lived in a county, and owned freehold land or property that was worth at least £2 a year, then he had the right to vote.

- If he lived in a borough, the situation was more complicated. Whether or not he had the right to vote depended on the ancient rights and customs of that borough. For example, in 'burgage' boroughs, voting rights were handed down from father to son; in 'pot-walloper' boroughs, it was enough to own a hearth and not to be claiming **poor relief**. In many boroughs, only members of the local town corporation were entitled to vote. 'Scot and lot' boroughs, on the other hand, allowed all men who paid certain ancient taxes the right to vote. All this variety meant that, in some boroughs, nearly all the adult men could vote; in others, only one man in a hundred could do so.

Definition

Poor relief

Help given to poor people by the parish in which they lived. This could be in the form of goods or money.

Throughout the whole country, the actual number of people who could vote was, in fact, very small. In 1831, out of a population of 24 million people fewer than 500,000 were entitled to vote. None of these were women.

Elections

Legally, there had to be a general election at least every seven years. However, in constituencies where there were the same number of candidates as there were seats, there was no point in holding an actual election. Indeed, in the hundred years before 1832, no more than 11 county seats and 82 borough seats were actually contested in general elections. If a landowner supported a candidate, there was often no point in anyone else trying to get elected to that seat. In these 'pocket boroughs', where one landowner owned enough property to be able to control the election, it would be a brave elector who voted against his candidate! An angry landowner might well turn such a voter out of his home, off his land or refuse to give him work.

Elections, when they happened, were usually very lively affairs. The polls were open for several days. In this way, everyone who was qualified to vote had the opportunity to do so. The candidates paid for the cost of transporting the electors, and for the board and lodging of those they thought were going to vote for them. A successful candidate (or candidates) usually had to pay for vast banquets and other sorts of celebrations as well.

The vote was not secret. Each voter walked on to a platform, called the **hustings**, and called out the name of the person for whom he was voting. This was noted down in a poll book (which was later made public) and the voter was given a certificate, which he could later use to claim back whatever he had been promised by his candidate. Sometimes money was promised that could not be paid. A pamphlet, *The Extraordinary Blue Book*, written in 1831 by **radicals** who wanted to change the system, reported that: 'At Hull, one of the sitting members dared not appear before his constituents – not for any defalcation [fault] of duty in parliament, but because he had not paid the "polling money" from the last election.'

Definitions

Hustings

A platform from which parliamentary candidates were nominated and addressed electors, and on which voters shouted out the name of the person for whom they were voting.

Radical

A person who wanted to change the whole political system right from its roots.

Source C

I was unanimously elected by one elector to represent this ancient borough in parliament. There was no other Candidate, no Opposition, no Poll demanded. So I had nothing to do but thank the said Elector for the Unanimous Voice with which I was chosen. Then we had a great dinner at the castle, and a famous ball in the evening. On the Friday morning I shall quit this triumphant scene with flying colours and a noble determination not to see it again in less than seven years.

From Sir Philip Francis, writing about his election in 1802 as MP for Appleby

Source D

Some seats are private property; the right of voting belongs to a few householders, and these are votes commanded by the owner of the estate. The fewer they are, the more easily they are managed. Where the number of voters is greater, the business is more difficult and expensive. The candidate must deal individually with the constituents, who sell themselves to the highest bidder. At Aylesbury, a bowl of guineas stood in the committee room, and the voters were helped out of it. The price of votes varies according to their number. In some places, it is as low as forty shillings; in others it is thirty pounds.

From Robert Southey, *Letters from England*, published in 1807

Source E

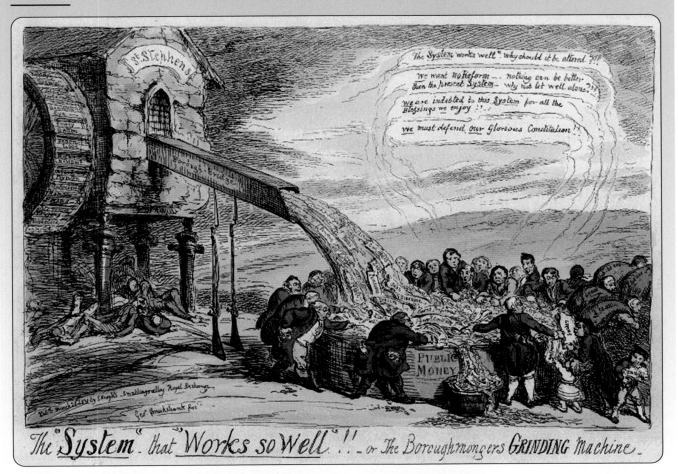

A cartoon drawn by George Cruikshank, published in 1831. The water mill, called St Stephens, represents the House of Commons; the paddles on the mill wheel have the names of rotten boroughs on them; the mill is pouring gold and notes into a huge bowl, from which people are filling their pockets and some are even carrying it away in sacks! The people under the mill represent those struggling and suffering because they do not have the vote.

Source F

(a) What is clear is that the people who used the system generally thought that it worked, but that their conception of how it worked was very different from our own. The modern parliamentary system is seen as representing an electorate which is, to all intents and purposes, the adult population; the eighteenth century parliament was conceived of as representing different '**interests**' that constituted the nation. These might be economic interests, such as the woollen interest in East Anglia, or the farming interest, or it might be the Church of England or the armed forces.

It was very important that all major interests should be represented in parliament, but it was by no means necessary for them to be represented directly. As long as there were people in parliament – in either House – to speak up for each particular interest, it did not matter which constituencies any of them happened to represent.

When radicals complained that huge sections of the population were not represented in parliament, either because they did not have the vote or because they had no MP, the answer was that they did not need to be directly represented because they were virtually represented.

(b) Having open hustings was a safeguard against corruption. Voters were held to be answerable not to their landlords or patrons, but to the **unenfranchised** community as a whole, who had a right to know which way their 'representatives' were casting their votes. Elections were communal events, notoriously robust, not to say violent, and it was a foolish candidate (or voter) who ignored the crowd just because they did not have the vote; a wise patron would spend a lot of money on free beer and food for all and sundry.

From Sean Lang, *Parliamentary Reform 1785–1928*, published in 1999

Definitions

Interests

An influential and powerful group of people who have the same aims, or support the same causes, the success of which is important to them personally or professionally.

Unenfranchised

A person who doesn't have the right to vote.

SKILLS BUILDER

1 Read Sources C and D. What can you learn from them about elections before 1832? Now read Source F(b). How far does this source explain what is happening in Sources C and D?

2 Study Source E. Is the source critical of, or in support of, the pre-1832 electoral system? Explain your answer.

3 Study Sources E and F(a). How far does Source F(a) support the view of the electoral system shown in Source E?

Early reform movements: from Spa Fields to Peterloo

Peace at the end of the wars with France in 1815 did not bring prosperity. Soldiers returning from the wars could not find work; workers who had been employed in war supplies lost their jobs; manufacturers could not find markets for the goods they were producing; the high price of corn kept the price of bread high; and the government was so much in debt that it had to put a tax on such things as candles and tea. Many suffered hardship and distress: there were bread riots and demonstrations against high taxation. Many radicals hoped to channel this discontent into support for parliamentary reform.

Ideas and some action

Throughout the time Britain was at war with France (1799–1815), various people kept the idea of parliamentary reform alive.

John Cartwright (1740–1824)

An ex-naval officer and major in the Nottinghamshire militia, Cartwright was removed from his position because of his political views. Believing Britain would only be the true home of freedom if the parliamentary system was reformed, specifically giving the vote to all adult men and holding annual elections, Cartwright began a series of whistlestop tours in the Midlands and North of England. He set up a series of clubs (the Hampden Clubs) for his supporters and these spread rapidly throughout the country. By March 1817, there were 40 Hampden Clubs in the Lancashire cotton towns alone.

William Cobbett (1763–1835)

In 1802, Cobbett, the son of a Surrey farmer, began a weekly newspaper, the *Political Register*, which, from about 1810, was urging parliamentary reform. In 1816, Cobbett found a loophole in the **stamp duty** that put the price of such newspapers out of the reach of ordinary people, and was able to reduce its price from just over one shilling (12 pence) to 2 pence. His enemies nicknamed his paper the *Twopenny Trash,* but in the first two months of its reduced price, 200,000 copies were sold.

Henry Hunt (1773–1835)

A prosperous Wiltshire farmer, Henry Hunt became a familiar figure at political meetings, speaking out strongly in favour of parliamentary reform. Known as 'Orator' Hunt, radicals often invited him to front their meetings. Imprisoned after the Peterloo Massacre (see page 10), Hunt turned to writing and later was to oppose the 1832 Reform Act because he believed it did not go far enough.

Once the wars with France were over, the ideas of men like Cartwright, Cobbett and Hunt became popular again and influenced much of the early agitation for reform.

The Spa Fields Meetings 1816

A group of extreme reformers, followers of Thomas Spence who wanted to nationalise land and abolish all taxes except income tax, held what turned out to be a large-scale meeting on Spa Fields, Islington, London. Henry Hunt addressed the meeting, adding his call for parliamentary reform to an already inflamed situation. Almost inevitably, part of the crowd rioted and marched on the City of London. All this was easily stopped by the military, but the government used it as an excuse to suspend the **Habeas Corpus Act** for one year.

Definitions

Stamp duty

A tax imposed by the government on newspapers. It was first levied in 1712 and gradually increased until in 1815 the tax was 4d a copy. This put the price of newspapers out of reach of ordinary people.

Habeas Corpus Act

This is still a very important law. It literally means 'to have the body produced' and meant that everyone imprisoned had to be brought to trial within a certain length of time. It prevents people from being imprisoned indefinitely without being charged of a crime.

The Pentridge Rising 1817

The government's use of spies and informers paid off when one undercover agent known as 'Oliver' reported back on a threatened mass revolt in the north of England. Although a meeting in Huddersfield broke up before anything significant happened, in Derbyshire it was another matter. Unemployed textile workers, led by Jeremiah Brandreth, set out to link up with other (actually, non-existent) groups and capture Nottingham castle. The whole episode was completely mismanaged: 'Oliver' had alerted the authorities and troops were waiting to arrest the marchers. Brandreth and two of his fellow conspirators were tried and hanged; 14 were transported and others imprisoned.

The Blanketeers 1817

Unemployed workers – mainly weavers – from Manchester planned a march to London, where they were to present a petition to the **Prince Regent** demanding the reform of parliament, the restoration of Habeas Corpus and help for their distress. Carrying blankets in which to sleep overnight (hence the nickname 'Blanketeers') they did not get very far. A huge meeting held in St Peter's Fields, Manchester, to cheer them on their way was broken up by troops and the leaders arrested. Groups of marchers who had already started were chased, caught, arrested and thrown into prison without trial. Very few marchers got further than Macclesfield and only one got through to London.

Peterloo 1819

On 16 August 1819, around 60,000 men, women and children gathered in St Peter's Field in Manchester carrying banners on which were slogans 'Liberty and Fraternity', 'Reform or Death' and 'Votes for All'. They had come to listen to Henry Hunt criticise the government and demand parliamentary reform. Expecting trouble, the local magistrates called out 400 special constables and the Manchester **Yeomanry**. Standing ready, too, were the regular cavalry in case the yeomanry could not cope. Although Hunt, sensing trouble, offered to give himself up, the magistrates preferred him to begin addressing the crowd. When well into his speech, the magistrates took fright and came to the conclusion that Manchester was 'in great danger' and ordered the Deputy Constable, Joseph Nadin, to arrest Hunt and the other speakers. Nadin replied that he and his constables could not do this without the help of the military. The yeomanry therefore moved in to help. In the uproar that followed, the cavalry had to force their way through the crowd to rescue the badly trained yeomanry. The results were terrible. Eleven people were killed and hundreds seriously injured, including many women and children.

The outcry in the country was tremendous: British troops had charged and killed their own people. Radicals nicknamed the massacre 'Peterloo' in mocking remembrance of the British victory over Napoleon at Waterloo. Publicly, the government seemed well pleased: the Home Secretary,

Biography

Prince Regent (1762–1830)

The Prince Regent was George Augustus Frederick, the eldest son of King George III. He acted in the King's place from 1811 during his father's bouts of mental illness. When King George III died in 1820, the Prince Regent became King George IV and reigned until his own death in 1830.

Definition

Yeomanry

Militia recruited from local businessmen, farmers and lesser gentry.

Lord Sidmouth, congratulated the magistrates and Hunt was imprisoned for two years. Privately, however, the government blamed the magistrates for over-reacting.

Source G

An anonymous poster entitled 'Manchester Heroes', published in 1819

The Six Acts

There had been nothing illegal about holding the meeting in St Peter's Field. The government, however, was determined that such a meeting would never happen again. By passing the Six Acts, the government showed its determination to end all possibilities of peaceful protest. Meeting for the purpose of presenting a petition were limited to the inhabitants of the parish in which the meeting was held. Stamp duty was extended to all papers and periodicals of a specific size, which was a great blow to all kinds of protest literature and particularly to Cobbett's *Political Register*. Magistrates were given wide powers to search private homes for political pamphlets, and the power to try certain cases that previously had to be tried by a judge and jury. Finally, private military training and amassing firearms was forbidden.

SKILLS BUILDER

Study Source G. What can you learn from Source G about attitudes of the radicals towards the authorities?

Question

Were the early attempts at parliamentary reform defeated only because of the strength of the government?

Altogether, the Six Acts were a very powerful attack on the radical movement. Legal protest was virtually impossible and, by 1820, parliamentary reform seemed a long way off.

Pressure for reform: people, political unions and press

Source H

The Reformers' Attack on the Old Rotten Tree; or, the Foul Nests of the Cormorants in Danger. Pub. by E. King, Chancery lane.

A cartoon drawn by E. King, published in 1832

SKILLS BUILDER

Look carefully at Source H. What is being criticised here? What is being praised? What further questions would you need to have answered before you can understand the cartoon more fully? (Keep a note of these questions, because they should be answered in the next two sections, and we'll come back to them later.)

By 1832, as you can see from Source H, the 'old rotten tree' of parliament was again under attack. This time the attack was much more powerful. It was organised and included different groups of people.

The manufacturing interest

The manufacturing towns of the Midlands and North were well established by 1815. Gradually, the realisation grew among those who owned and ran the cotton mills and iron foundries, shipyards and nailworks, that their own particular interests were not being represented in parliament. Some took matters into their own hands. For example, in 1812 Birmingham manufacturers tried to influence the Warwickshire county election so that the man of their choice was elected. They were unsuccessful, but the idea that they should be represented had taken root. Seven years later, on 10 July 1819, a local paper, the *Edmonds Weekly Recorder and Saturday Advertiser*, firmly stated: 'The people of Birmingham have a right to choose a member or members to sit in the Commons House of Parliament.' Industrialists and manufacturers did not find the situation satisfactory, and the belief spread that for them to try to influence an election was only a temporary measure. Reform of the whole system was needed.

British elections and revolution in France

The general election of 1830 coincided with a revolution in France. Although the revolution didn't directly influence British politics, it helped to keep excitement and interest in politics at fever pitch. Nowhere was this more evident than in Yorkshire, where the manufacturers and merchants worked together with Edward Baines, the editor of the *Leeds Mercury* newspaper, to overturn the influence of the local landowner, Earl Fitzwilliam. They were successful, and Henry Brougham was elected to represent the county.

Distress in the towns and countryside

Bad harvests in 1829 and 1830, and a sudden trade slump in 1830 hit rich and poor alike, in towns and in the countryside. The cholera epidemic of 1831–32 made a bad situation worse. Throughout the period 1830–32, there were reports from town and country of high **poor-rates**, high unemployment, poor trade and low wages when employment could be found. In the first three months of 1830, 22 county meetings were held to protest about distress or taxation, or both. In February **Earl Grey** admitted that the country was in a 'state of distress such as never before pressed on any country'.

Source I

Nothing can be more fit than that the manufacturing and commercial interests of this Great County should have a representative of their own choice to do their business in parliament. We don't live in the days of Barons, thank God – we live in the days of Leeds, of Bradford, of Halifax and of Huddersfield – we live in the days when men are industrious and desire to be free; and not when they are lazy and indolent and deserve to be trampled on and dominated over. Therefore you are bound to have your rights and choose your representative.

From one of Henry Brougham's electioneering speeches as reported in the *Leeds Mercury*, 27 July 1830

Definition

Poor rates

A parish tax levied on property and landowners in order to provide for parish paupers.

Biography

Earl Grey (1764–1845)

Born into a notable Northumbrian family, Charles Grey was elected to parliament in 1786 and soon became an important member of the Whig Party. He was a strong supporter of **Catholic emancipation** and a long-time campaigner for parliamentary reform, being a founder member of the Society for the Friends of the People, a group committed to more equal representation of people in parliament. He introduced an unsuccessful franchise Bill in 1797. In 1807, on the death of his father, Charles Grey went to the House of Lords as the 2nd Earl Grey. He remained in opposition until the 1830 election, when the Whigs were returned to power. With Grey as Prime Minister, the Reform Act was passed in 1832, and slavery was abolished throughout the British Empire in 1833. In 1834, Grey withdrew from public life and spent his last years in retirement on his estates in Howick.

Definitions

Catholic emancipation

In 1829, the Roman Catholic Relief Act gave Roman Catholics the right to vote in British general elections and to stand for election to the House of Commons.

Source J

It will be asked, will the reform of parliament give the labouring man a cow or a pig, will it put bread and cheese into his satchel instead of infernal cold potatoes; will it give him a bottle of beer to carry to the field instead of making him lie down on his belly and drink out of the brook? Will parliamentary reform put an end to the harnessing of men and women by a hired overseer to draw carts like beasts of burden; will it put an end to the system which causes the honest labourer to be worse fed than the felons in the jails? The enemies of reform jeeringly ask us, whether reform would do all these things for us; and I answer distinctly THAT IT WOULD DO THEM ALL.

Written by William Cobbett in the *Political Register*, early 1832

Political unions

The Birmingham Political Union (BPU), founded in 1829 by the banker Thomas Attwood, was intended to operate as a **ginger group** to focus and lead local reform movements by way of petitions and public meetings. Some 15,000 people attended the first meeting of the Birmingham Political Union in January 1830. By May 1832, around 100,000 people were attending meetings of the BPU, one-quarter of whom were fully paid-up members.

Political unions sprang up all over the country. However, while the BPU was able to unite masters and men in one organisation, this was not possible elsewhere. Leeds, for example, had three political unions:

- Edward Baines, the editor of the *Leeds Mercury*, led the Leeds Association
- Joshua Bowers, a glassblower, led the Leeds Political Union
- the printers Mann and Frost organised the Leeds Radical Political Union.

Definition

Ginger group

A small pressure group within a larger organisation that strongly presses for action on a particular issue.

Not all the political unions wanted the same kind of reform, which was a further complication. In London, Francis Place, a tailor from Charing Cross, organised the National Political Union. This union simply wanted the manufacturing interests to be represented in the House of Commons. On the other hand, William Lovett (a cabinet maker – see page 65) and Henry Hetherington (the editor of the *Poor Man's Guardian* – see page 43) wanted nothing less than the vote for every man. Together, they established the National Union of Working Classes.

Clearly, the political unions wanted different kinds of parliamentary reform. However, what united the unions was that they all focused public opinion on reform, and in doing so helped to create that public opinion; they showed how this public opinion could be expressed without breaking the law, and they managed to keep public enthusiasm for reform alive and active.

Source K

The honourable House [of Commons] in its present state, is evidently too far removed in habits, wealth and station [position] from the wants and interests of the lower and middle classes of the people, to have any close identity of feeling with them. The great aristocratic interests of all kinds are well represented there. But the interests of Industry and of Trade have scarcely any representatives at all.

From the *Declaration of the Birmingham Political Union*, published in 1830

SKILLS BUILDER

1 Read Sources I and J. Are Henry Brougham and William Cobbett demanding the same thing? Are their reasons for demanding the reform of parliament the same?

2 Now read Source K. How far does this source support the views expressed in Sources I and J?

The press

Was the press supporting parliamentary reform? By 1830, many leading London papers were certainly in favour of some kind of reform. The *Times* and the *Examiner* insisted that parliamentary reform was the 'great issue of the moment'; the *Globe* and the *Westminster Review* ran a very full discussion on the British electoral system, while the *Morning Chronicle* was completely in favour of some kind of reform of both the distribution of seats and of the franchise.

It was, however, in the provinces that newspapers were the most powerful in channelling local pressure for reform. Parliamentary debates and important speeches by ministers were fully reported, along with comment from the provincial editors, and would both reflect and lead local opinion.

By 1830, some of the larger provincial papers had supported reform for over a generation. Fathers, and now their sons, had written rousing articles and editorials for more than 20 years. Men such as Edward Baines and his son (also called Edward) in the *Leeds Mercury,* Thomas and James Thompson in the *Leicester* Chronicle, and Charles and Richard Sutton in the *Nottingham Review* all thundered against a system that did not allow for proper representation from the manufacturing districts. It was the same on Tyneside, with the *Newcastle Chronicle,* on Merseyside with the *Liverpool Mercury* and in Sheffield with the *Sheffield Independent.*

The provincial newspapers were important, not just for their impact on local opinion, but for their links with the political unions. The BPU, which set the pattern for others to follow, stated quite clearly that it was the duty of members 'to consider the means of organising a system of operations whereby the Public Press may be influenced to act generally in support of the public interests'.

By 1830, all the indications were clear. The press, political unions and people were clamouring for a reform of parliament. Would those inside parliament listen? Would members of the Lords and Commons vote to reform themselves?

Question

Which do you think was the strongest and most influential pressure outside parliament?

The struggle in parliament for reform

It was one thing for voices to be raised outside parliament for reform, but quite another for parliament to take any notice. In the end, for reform to happen, parliament – and in particular the two main political parties, Whigs and Tories – had to want it.

What were the attitudes of the Whigs and Tories to reform?

At the beginning of 1827, Lord Liverpool remained firmly in control of the Tory government. Repression, as you have already seen, was the order of the day. However, Lord Liverpool suffered a massive stroke in February that year and retired from politics. The Tories who had held together (more or less as a party) under his leadership, fragmented. Loyalties were not entirely fixed and there were considerable factional variations within the loose groupings that could be said to resemble political parties. Nevertheless, it is possible to outline some key ideas and attitudes that separated Tories from Whigs by this time.

Tories traditionally defended the rights of the monarch and the status of the Church of England as the established Church, and advocated strong measures to maintain law and order – especially against radical agitation or riots caused by economic distress.

Whigs sometimes used softer language about radical or popular unrest, but in practice acted as vigorously as most Tories when their own interests or property were threatened. However, in the 1820s the leader of the Whigs in the Commons, **Lord John Russell**, led a campaign there for parliamentary reform, and (as you will see later) in 1830 the Whigs enthusiastically embraced the cause of parliamentary reform – much to the horror of the Tories.

In some respects leading Whigs only differed tactically from the Tories. Both wished to preserve the power and status of the landowning classes and both were determined to prevent revolution. By 1830 the Whigs had come to believe that the best means of gaining these ends would be to enact a substantial measure of parliamentary reform. The Tories had not, as shown by their repressive response of the Six Acts.

The 1830 election

King George IV died in the summer of 1830 and, as always happened when a monarch died, a general election was held. Look back to page 13 for a reminder of the tensions that surrounded this election, and the success of the reformers in Yorkshire. Many MPs (like the Whig Henry Brougham) who opposed the policies of the Prime Minister, the Duke of Wellington, were elected. However, there were not enough of them to bring about a change of government, and the Tories continued in power.

Tories out: Whigs in

Disaster struck the government on Tuesday 2 November. The Duke of Wellington was well into a speech in the House of Lords when he suddenly

Biography

Lord John Russell (1792–1878)

Born into a powerful Whig family as a younger son of the 6th Duke of Bedford, he was a Whig MP from 1813. A strong supporter of parliamentary reform, he was largely responsible for drafting the 1832 Reform Act. In 1834 he became leader of the Whigs in the Commons, where he continued to hold reformist views. As Home Secretary in the late 1830s, he played a large part in bringing democracy to the government of British cities through the Municipal Corporations Act of 1835. In the following years he was responsible for several new reforms, including the establishment of the registration of births, deaths and marriages, and the legalisation of the marriages of non-Church of England worshippers in their own chapels. He was Home, and then Colonial, Secretary in Melbourne's government (1835–41). A supporter of the repeal of the **Corn Laws**, he combined forces with the Tory Prime Minister, Robert Peel, to bring about their repeal in 1846. Lord John Russell was twice Prime Minister (1846–52 and 1865–66), resigning in 1866 when his proposals for further reform of the franchise were defeated.

Definition

Corn Laws

Controversial legislation introduced in 1815, and variously amended until finally abolished in 1846. The Corn Laws were designed to protect the price of British wheat and other types of 'corn' against foreign competition. For radicals, both middle class and working class, the Corn Laws represented a great evil of the unreformed system. The landed interest was, it was argued, using its parliamentary influence to protect itself against cheaper imported corn that would otherwise benefit the rising urban population. Such blatant aristocratic self-interest aroused intense resentment, leading to the formation of the Anti-Corn Law League in 1838.

began defending the current electoral system: 'The legislature and the system of representation possesses the full and entire confidence of the country . . .'

The Prime Minister seemed to be ignoring the political unions, the great reform rallies and the thundering articles in the press. Above all, he seemed to be ignoring the results of the summer general election. Wellington concluded that not only was the present system good, but also he had no intention of changing it. 'I am not only not prepared to bring forward any measure of this nature [reform], but I will at once declare that I shall always feel it my duty to resist such measures when proposed by others.'

The Duke of Wellington had hoped to rally his supporters against the reform of Parliament. The speech had the opposite effect. Tories who had been anxious before 2 November 1830 were now desperately worried. They joined the Whigs. The fall of the government was now certain. A few weeks later, on a minor financial matter, the Tory government of the Duke of Wellington was defeated.

No other Tory leader could form a government that would have the support of the majority of MPs. The new King, **William IV**, therefore asked the Whig leader, Earl Grey, to become Prime Minister and form a new government. Ironically, this Whig government had more aristocrats in it than had the previous Tory administration. Yet the Whigs had always seen themselves as reflecting the true interests of the country. Many of them, despite being aristocrats, were involved in trade or business. And, perhaps as importantly, the Whigs were very aware of public pressure to introduce far-reaching parliamentary reforms.

From 1830–32, the Lords strenuously opposed parliamentary reform, and in this they were backed and encouraged by the King. However, realising the country was in uproar, he finally agreed to Grey's demand that he would create enough pro-reform peers to get the Reform Bill through the House of Lords. The threat to create new peers was enough, but in making it, William started a process that changed the constitutional relationship between Crown and parliament. Two years later, when William replaced Peel with Melbourne as Prime Minister, he became the last monarch to try to choose a Prime Minister in opposition to the wishes of parliament.

The first Reform Bill

On 31 March 1831, the government's proposals were introduced into the Commons by Lord John Russell. The proposals were an attempt to shift the balance of representation away from the landowners and towards the middle classes:

- 61 boroughs were to lose both their MPs
- 47 boroughs were to lose one MP
- MPs were to be reduced in number from 658 to 596

Biography

William IV (1765–1837)

William Henry, the third son of King George III and younger brother and successor to King George IV, was King of the United Kingdom of Great Britain and Ireland from June 1830 to June 1837. Having two elder brothers, he was not expected to inherit the throne, and was sent into the Royal Navy when he was 13. By 1789 William had risen to the rank of Rear Admiral. However, the deaths of his two elder brothers, who were without children, meant that the throne passed to him. As King, his most important public act related to the crisis surrounding the passing of the Reform Act in 1832. When William died in June 1837, the throne passed to his niece, Victoria.

- 46 seats were to be given to the large industrial towns of the Midlands and the North

- there was to be only one voting qualification: that of owning or renting a house worth more than £10 a year; and, of course, to be a man.

Outside the Commons, these proposals were met with enthusiasm. Only Henry Hetherington, the editor of the *Poor Man's Guardian* sounded a note of caution, urging working people to oppose the proposals. He saw that, while low wage earners like shopkeepers and tradesmen would probably be given the right to elect their MP, most working men would not have that privilege. Nail makers, spinners, weavers and farm labourers simply did not live in houses worth £10 a year or more. However, other working-class leaders such as Bronterre O'Brien and John Doherty believed the Reform Bill was the first step towards the kind of electoral reform they wanted, and urged their followers to support it.

That said, it was what happened inside the Houses of Parliament that mattered if the Bill was to become law. The debate in the House of Commons was heated. Tories and Whigs spoke against the Bill, and Whigs and Tories spoke in favour. At the end of the debate, the Bill was passed by just one vote. At this point, the Bill would move to the committee stage, where a small number of MPs would study it in detail and recommend changes that would amend the Bill before it came back to the Commons again.

Earl Grey was uneasy. A majority of one was not enough. Those opposing the Bill would be able to get **amendments** agreed that would wreck it completely. He was right. The first amendment that was passed objected to the reduction of the number of MPs. Grey acted swiftly. He persuaded the King, William IV, to dissolve parliament and hold a general election.

> **Question**
>
> Should a measure be supported because it is a step in the right direction, or opposed because it doesn't go all the way?

> **Definition**
>
> **Amendment**
>
> An amendment to a parliamentary Bill is a change that an MP, or group of MPs, would like to make to a Bill. Then, as now, MPs vote on the amendments before they vote on the actual Bill.

Source L

I oppose universal suffrage because I think it would produce a destructive revolution. I support this measure because I am sure that it is our best security against revolution.

I support this measure as a measure of reform; but I support it still more as a measure of conservation. That we may exclude those whom it is necessary to exclude, we must admit those whom it may be safe to admit.

We say, and we say justly, that it is not by numbers, but by property and intelligence that a nation ought to be governed. Yet, saying this, we exclude from all share of government vast masses of property and intelligence, vast numbers of those who are the most interested in preserving tranquillity and who know best how to preserve it. We do more. We drive over to the side of revolution those whom we shut out from power. Is this a time when the cause of law and order can spare one of its natural allies?

Turn where we may – within, around – the voice of great events is proclaiming to us, 'Reform, that you may preserve'.

From a speech by Thomas Babington Macaulay, the Whig MP for the rotten borough of Calne, defending the Reform Bill, March 1831

Question

Are you surprised that an MP representing a rotten borough should support parliamentary reform?

SKILLS BUILDER

Read Sources L and M. How far does Source M challenge Source L?

Source M

The measure proposed is an effective one. It cuts off obvious and disgusting abuses.

No one can deny that whatever is in the Bill is good.

To the House we should say, 'Pass it, pass it.' To the people, 'Urge in every way the passing of the Bill; call for it, press it forward.'

Let the public cast their eyes over the list of rotten boroughs, as contained in Lord John Russell's speech. Their mock representatives will not much longer insult the commonsense of all mankind, by retaining seats in a British House of Commons to pass laws which are to bind the men of England.

From the leading article in *The Times*, 2 March 1831

Commons vs Lords vs people

The 1831 general election proved a great triumph for the reformers. Earl Grey, the Whig Prime Minister, had a majority of 130 seats in the newly elected House of Commons. He did not have to fear wrecking amendments in Committee; neither did he have to fear defeat in the Commons. A second Reform Bill, very like the first, was introduced into the House of Commons in July 1831; it went through all its stages very quickly and on 22 September passed its third reading in the Commons by 109 votes. It was then sent to the Lords. And that was a very different story.

The majority of members of the House of Lords were known to be against reform. On 8 October 1831, after a fiery debate lasting five days and nights, the Lords voted on the Reform Bill. They threw it out by 41 votes. The reaction in the country was violent.

- There were riots in Bristol, Derby, Nottingham and other cities, and in small towns like Blandford in Dorset and Tiverton in Devon.
- The windows of the Duke of Wellington's London home were smashed.
- Radical, reforming newspapers appeared with black borders as a sign of mourning.
- New political unions were formed in towns that had not previously had one and the older unions were strengthened.
- The Church of England was attacked in the press; 26 bishops sat in the House of Lords and all but five of them voted against reform.
- Everywhere there were protest marches, and property belonging to anti-reform lords was attacked by stone-throwing mobs.

Source N

I have been uniformly opposed to reform on principle, because I was unwilling to open a door that I saw no prospect of being able to close. I will continue my opposition to the last, believing, as I do, that this is the first step, not directly to revolution, but to a series of changes which will affect the property, and totally change the character of this country. We may establish a country full of energy – splendid in talent – but in my conscience I believe fatal to our liberty, our security and our peace.

From a speech by Sir Robert Peel during
the debate on the Reform Bill, 17 December 1831

SKILLS BUILDER

Read Sources M and N. Set up a debate between the editor of *The Times* and Robert Peel. Use your knowledge of the issues to inform the debate on each side. Who will win the argument?

The Reform Bill again

In December 1831, Lord John Russell presented a third Reform Bill to the House of Commons. Again, it passed smoothly through all the necessary stages and, again, it was sent to the Lords. To Grey's exasperation, his fellow lords started employing delaying tactics. Many ministers thought the only way out of the situation would be for the King to create new peers who would be chosen because they supported reform. The King refused to do so and on 14 April 1832, Grey's Whig government resigned.

The days of May

Once again, the country erupted into riots and rallies. Men like Thomas Attwood and Francis Place (see page 15) were determined to stop any likelihood of the Tory leader, the Duke of Wellington, being able to form a government. Westminster was flooded with anti-Tory petitions; the Birmingham Political Union announced that 200,000 men would march on London and stay there until the Bill became law. Francis Place suggested that investors should withdraw all their money from banks at the same time, thus creating an enormous financial crisis. 'Stop the Duke!' and 'Go for gold!' were slogans shouted in the streets of London and the provinces. The *Leeds Mercury* gloomily reported:

> A great Calamity has befallen England
> The **Boroughmongers** have triumphed
> The Reform Bill has been strangled
> The King has refused to make Peers and
> The Grey and Brougham administration has resigned

Definition

Boroughmonger (Boromonger)

A person who buys or sells parliamentary seats in a borough.

In desperation, the King asked Wellington to investigate the possibility of forming an administration that would be pledged to limited reform. When Sir Robert Peel, the leader of the Tories in the Commons, refused to serve under him, Wellington knew his task was impossible. William IV, who had never formally accepted Grey's resignation, asked Grey to take over again. This time, he promised to create as many reforming peers as Grey needed to get his Bill through the Lords.

Question

How far do you agree with the view that parliamentary reform came about in 1832 only because of popular pressure?

The Bill becomes law

In the event, the threat to create new peers was enough. Once new peers were created, they would be there for always. There would, therefore, always be a Whig majority in the Lords. The Tory Lords could not contemplate this possibility. When the Reform Bill came up for its final reading in the Lords, most of those who opposed it simply stayed away and the Reform Bill was passed by 106 votes to 22. King William IV signed the Bill on 7 June 1832. The Reform Bill became the Reform Act of 1832.

Unit summary

What have you learned in this unit?

You have learned that the balance of Crown, Lords and Commons, by which Great Britain was governed, was coming under increasing criticism in the late eighteenth and early nineteenth centuries. In particular, the constituencies that sent MPs to parliament, and the franchise, which laid down the qualifications a person had to have before being allowed to vote in general elections, were being seen by some as being no longer fit for purpose. You have understood that those who defended the old system did so on the basis of habit and custom and through fear of revolution. More significantly, you have learned that different interests were represented – not who elected the MPs, nor which constituency they represented. Those who attacked the system, you have learned, did so on the basis of fairness of representation, because the growing industrial towns of the Midlands and the North were not directly represented in the House of Commons. You have seen how the pressure for change grew outside parliament, how the government initially repressed all demands for reform and how, with the Whigs forming a government under Grey in the Lords and Russell in the Commons, reform became a real possibility. You have understood how Grey and Russell manipulated the monarch so that, eventually, the Reform Act became law in June 1832.

What skills have you used in this unit?

You have used your skills of comprehension and inference to demonstrate an understanding of the apparent inadequacies of the pre-1832 electoral system. You have used information to create a spider diagram showing linkages and checks and balances in that old system that had worked for so long. Working with primary sources, especially political cartoons, you have cross-referenced for support and challenge regarding attitudes of contemporaries to the pre-1832 franchise and to acts of repression by the government to movements for radical reform.

You have cross-referenced secondary sources with contemporary ones in order to demonstrate your understanding of the strengths of the pre-1832 franchise, and the importance that was felt at the time of interests being represented as opposed to specific numbers of people. You have worked with contemporary sources in order to understand that pressure for change to the electoral system came from a range of institutions and individuals and for a variety of different reasons.

Finally, you have analysed major speeches by Macaulay and Peel – one in favour of reform and one against – in order to understand the attitudes of articulate and committed parliamentarians to the whole question of reform.

SKILLS BUILDER

Study Sources H, L and M. How far do Sources L and M support Source H about the need for parliamentary reform?

Exam tips

The Skills Builder above is the sort of question you will find appearing on examination papers as an (a) question.

Here are some tips for answering these questions.

- **Don't** bring in a lot of your own knowledge. All (a) questions focus on the analysis, cross-referencing and evaluation of source material. Your own knowledge won't be credited by the examiner and you will waste valuable time writing it out.
- **Do** remember that the only knowledge you should introduce will be to put the sources into context. This means, for example, when analysing Source L that you know what a rotten borough is, but you should not go on to compare these with pocket boroughs.
- **Don't** describe, or even re-write, the sources. The examiner will have a copy and to do this will waste your time.
- **Do** draw inferences from the sources; in this example to show how they could be used to support Source H.
- **Do** reach a supported judgement about how far the Sources L and M support Source H by careful cross-referencing and evaluation.

RESEARCH TOPIC

Where do you live? In which parliamentary constituency is your home (or your school)? Find out what the situation was before 1832 and who represented it in the House of Commons. Did anything change as a result of the 1832 Reform Act?

2 'Reform that you may preserve': change and continuity after 1832

What is this unit about?

This unit focuses on the consequences of the 1832 Reform Act for the electoral system. The passage of the Reform Bill through parliament sharpened the differences between Whigs and Tories and those who supported them, giving the appearance of a two-party system. The enlarged electorate meant that politicians had to pay closer attention to the policies they were supporting if they wanted to get elected. However, politics was still not that clearly divided along party lines, and politicians still grouped and regrouped within and between the main groups of Whigs and Tories – depending on the matters being debated and the Bills under discussion. In many ways, after 1832 elections were similar to those conducted before 1832. There were still parliamentary seats that were strongly influenced by the local landowner, and there were still complaints about bribery and corruption. This unit looks at what had changed and what remained the same as the result of the 1832 Reform Act.

Key questions

- What impact did the 1832 Reform Act have on the electoral system?
- How different was the membership of the reformed House of Commons from that of the unreformed one?

Timeline

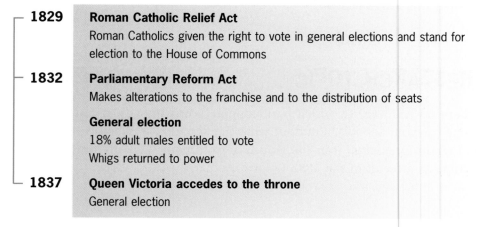

1829	**Roman Catholic Relief Act** Roman Catholics given the right to vote in general elections and stand for election to the House of Commons
1832	**Parliamentary Reform Act** Makes alterations to the franchise and to the distribution of seats
	General election 18% adult males entitled to vote Whigs returned to power
1837	**Queen Victoria accedes to the throne** General election

Source A

A cartoon entitled *Taking the Boromongers Home*, published in June 1832 (the month in which the Reform Act was passed); it shows the devil carrying off a group of politicians

Discussion point

Look carefully at Source A. What point is the cartoonist making?

What were the specific details of reform?

Three separate Acts were passed to reform parliamentary representation in the United Kingdom, with different acts passed for England and Wales, Scotland and Ireland. However throughout the United Kingdom the effects were the same, with corrupt boroughs being disenfranchised, the seats redistributed and the electorate extended as new members of society were given the franchise.

England and Wales

Disenfranchisement

- 56 rotten and pocket boroughs returning 111 MPs lost their representation.
- 30 boroughs with fewer than 4,000 inhabitants lost their MP.
- Weymouth and Melcombe Regis lost two of their four MPs.

Redistribution

- 65 seats were given to the counties.
- 44 seats were given to the boroughs – including Birmingham, Manchester, Leeds and Sheffield.
- 21 smaller towns were given one MP each, including two new Welsh single member seats, although some Welsh boroughs were still grouped in order to return one MP.
- Scotland was given eight more MPs.
- Ireland was given five more MPs.

Franchise

In the counties, the vote was given to adult males:

- owning freehold property worth at least 40 shillings (£2) a year
- holding a copyhold (a special kind of lease) on land worth at least £10 a year
- leasing or renting land worth at least £50 a year.

In the boroughs, the vote was given to adult males:

- owning, or living in, property worth at least £10 a year, provided they had lived there for at least a year and did not owe any taxes on the property, and that they hadn't received poor relief in the previous year
- who had had the vote under the old qualifications but didn't qualify under the new ones.

Question

Reflect on the debates surrounding the passage of the Reform Bill through parliament. Which would MPs at the time have considered to have been the more important reform – the redistribution of seats or the extension of the franchise? Why?

What was the immediate significance of the 1832 Reform Act?

Source B

Whereas it is expedient to take effectual measures for correcting diverse abuses that have long prevailed in the choice of members to serve in the Commons House of Parliament, to deprive many inconsiderable places of the right of returning members, to grant such privilege to large, populous and wealthy towns, to increase the number of knights of the shire, to extend the elective franchise to many of His Majesty's subjects who have not heretofore enjoyed the same, and to diminish the expense of elections . . .

From the **Preamble** to the 1832 Reform Act for England and Wales

Disenfranchising boroughs

The most dramatic change brought about by the 1832 Reform Act was the abolition of 56 rotten or pocket boroughs, including Aldeburgh, Dunwich, Ilchester, Old Sarum and St German's (see Unit 1). These were well known to reformers who used them as examples of what was wrong with the old system. These boroughs were entirely disenfranchised. In other words, they lost the right to send a representative to the House of Commons.

There had been lengthy debates in parliament over the details of the Reform Act. The Whig ministry had stuck to certain basic principles, such as the complete disfranchisement of some boroughs, and the partial disfranchisement of others. Yet the status of various individual boroughs had shifted as part of the manoeuvring within and between the main political groups. But not all small boroughs were disfranchised. Thetford, Reigate, Westbury and Calne all survived, even though none had more than 200 voters. About 60 or 70 MPs were still directly dependent on patronage for their seats.

How were seats redistributed?

Increasing county representation

One important feature of the Reform Act was the sizeable increase – from 92 to 144, or 76 per cent – in the number of MPs who represented English counties. This was viewed favourably by most of the gentry and aristocracy – both Tories and Whigs – who frequently praised county MPs for being less corrupt, more independent and motivated by the best interests of the nation. It seems that not all the redistribution of seats was intended to help the great industrial towns of the Midlands and North to be represented in parliament!

Enfranchisement of small and large towns

Many seats were now available for redistribution (see page 26) and as a result the great industrial towns of the Midlands and North were

Definition

Preamble

The opening section of an Act, which sets out the purpose of the legislation.

SKILLS BUILDER

1 Read Source B. List the main purposes of the Reform Act.

2 Now study Sources C and D opposite. Which parts of the Preamble to the Act are being addressed here? How successfully do you think they are being met?

Source C

Boroughs that were completely disenfranchised

Source D

Boroughs that gained one or two MPs

represented in parliament for the first time. However, seats were also given to relatively small towns because they represented particular interests such as Frome (wool), Walsall (iron and leather), Whitby and Sunderland (shipping). The motives behind these changes reflected continuity between the unreformed and the reformed system. There was still a continuing belief that it was interests that should be represented in parliament rather than numbers of people. Also, the enfranchisement of cities such as Birmingham and Manchester certainly did not spring just from their size. Industrial towns were generally included because their interests as a whole were under-represented. It was not considered necessary to give parliamentary seats to all large towns.

How significant was the increase in the size of the electorate?

It is difficult to estimate the size of the electorate before 1832 because there was no register of voters. Votes were recorded in poll books when contests took place. Yet this only gives figures for those who actually voted and not for those who were qualified but who, for whatever reason, did not vote. Moreover, there were numerous uncontested elections, which meant that no poll was taken. Nevertheless, detailed research in recent decades has improved our understanding of size and behaviour of the electorate before and after the Reform Act. Generally, it seems that the number of people eligible to vote rose from one in ten of the male population before the 1832 Reform Act, to one in five after the Act was passed.

Source E

	1831	1833	% increase 1831–33
Counties	239,000	370,379	55%
Boroughs	200,000	282,398	41%
Combined	439,000	652,777	49%

The electorate in England and Wales 1831–66

Source F

1831	1833
12.7%	18%

Adult males entitled to vote in England and Wales 1831–33

The percentage increases were significant, but it is important to note that the overall proportion of voters among adult males remained low. Just under one in five adult males was entitled to vote in 1833. Although there were no further changes to the franchise in England and Wales until 1867, a combination of inflation and rising population resulted in a slight proportional increase over time.

SKILLS BUILDER

How far do Sources E and F challenge the claims of Source G?

Source G

The revolution is made – that is to say that power is transferred from one class of society, the gentlemen of England, professing the faith of the Church of England, to another class of society, the shopkeepers, being **Dissenters** from the Church. A new democratic influence has been introduced into elections [and is] formidably active against the aristocratic influence of the landed gentry. The mischief of the Reform is that, whereas democracy prevailed heretofore in some places, it now prevails everywhere. There is no place exempt from it. In the great majority it is preponderant.

From a letter by the Duke of Wellington to John Wilson Croker, dated 6 March 1833. In 1808 Croker became an MP and rose to be Secretary to the Admiralty; a staunch Tory, he opposed parliamentary reform vowing he would never sit in a reformed House of Commons – he resigned his seat in 1832

Definition

Dissenter

A person who refuses to accept the authority, doctrines or practices of the Church of England, preferring instead to belong to a non conformist church such as the Methodists or Presbyterians.

The electorate in Scotland

In Scotland, changes to the franchise and voting system in urban areas, together with an increased rural electorate, made a significant impact. Under the unreformed system the entire Scottish representation of 45 MPs had been shaped by powerful patrons, local rivalries and the manipulation of a tiny electorate. Before 1832 only about one Scottish male in 50 could vote; after reform this increased 14-fold to about one in eight.

There were 30 Scottish county seats in total, as before, but now comprising:

- 27 counties with one seat
- three groups of two counties, each group with a single seat.

There were 23 Scottish burgh (borough) seats – an increase of eight seats:

- one extra seat for Edinburgh, giving it two seats
- one extra seat for Glasgow, which now had two seats and was no longer part of a group of burghs
- 14 seats for groups of smaller towns, as previously but minus Glasgow, with each group having a single seat
- five additional seats for individual towns.

Franchise

Scottish counties

- £10 property owners
- £10 long-term leaseholders and £50 medium-term leaseholders
- £50 tenants
- Previous voters, not otherwise qualified, retained franchise during their lifetimes.

Scottish burghs

- £10 householders/occupiers (subject to one-year's residence without claiming poor relief)
- The old system, of indirect voting in groups of towns, was abolished; previously each burgh had elected only a single delegate, who then voted at the election.

One man in eight could now vote.

The electorate in Ireland

In Ireland, an important change had taken place in 1829. As part of the process of Catholic emancipation, the county franchise had been raised from £2 (40 shillings) to £10. This slashed the county electorate from about 216,000 to 37,000. Most English politicians, in the period before and after the Reform Act, were unwilling to increase the size of the Irish electorate, fearing the rise of Catholic influence. In 1832 only a minor change – the enfranchisement of certain leaseholders – was conceded.

Voter qualification in Ireland

Political parties did attempt to increase their own support by registering voters under the new Irish system. This raised the total to 60,000 or thereabouts, which still meant that only about one in 20 Irish men had the vote. The system of registration was confused and uncertain. Sometimes qualified county voters were stopped from voting because they had not been properly registered, and the unqualified allowed to vote because they had been wrongly registered. Further complications arose because landlords increasingly refused to grant long leases, for motives that were mainly economic but partly political. In County Waterford, for example, the electorate was halved between 1832 and 1841; and in County Meath landlords deliberately granted leases that were shorter than required to qualify to vote. In 1840 only about 7 per cent of Irish farmers assessed for poor rates at £10 and above actually had the vote.

After the changes in Ireland there were 32 Irish county seats, as before, each with two seats.

There were also five extra Irish borough seats:

- one extra seat each for four major towns
- one extra seat for the University of Dublin.

Franchise

Irish counties

- £10 property owners (retaining the change made in 1829 after Catholic Emancipation)
- £10 leaseholders, providing that the lease was for at least 20 years

Irish boroughs

- £10 householders
- In some boroughs (designated 'counties of cities') £10 freeholders and leaseholders were also entitled to vote.
- Those entitled to vote before 1832 retained this right during their lifetimes.

One man in 20 could now vote.

Who benefited more from electoral reform – the aristocracy or the middle classes?

The 1832 Reform Act did not, as older textbooks sometimes suggest, simply transfer power to the urban commercial and industrial middle-classes. The situation was far more complex than that. It was still considered important that interests were represented, and here manufacturing interests were not the only ones – there were agricultural ones, too. Furthermore, the insertion of the **Chandos clause**, by extending the vote to a specific group of tenants likely to vote the same way as their Tory landlords,

Definition

Chandos clause

This was a clause inserted into the 1832 Reform Act by Lord Chandos. It gave the vote to tenants-at-will paying an annual rent of £50. Tenants-at-will could have their tenancy ended at any time by their landlord, and so they were highly likely to vote the same way as their Tory landlords.

went a long way to offsetting the loss of the mainly Tory pocket boroughs. Considerable debate has taken place over the intended and unintended consequences of reform. It is easy to make generalisations about what was desired by, and what was superficially attractive to, different social classes, in order to describe 1832 as the start of a movement towards democracy. Historians have become more cautious about such statements.

Source H

The real supporters of the Bill of 1832 were the middle class. By that measure the middle class were admitted to the franchise; they would exercise henceforth an important influence on the Lower House. The agitation of 1832 was a movement of the middle class at one with the Whig aristocracy; the idea of both was to reform the constitution, not to transform it. But the expectation of both has been falsified by the irony of history. The Bill of 1832, so far from being final, has proved to be but the first step in an irresistible process towards democracy.

From G. Lowes Dickinson, *Development of Parliament during the Nineteenth Century*, published in 1895

Source I

The Whigs in 1832 made concessions to preserve the essentials of aristocratic government. Middle-class property owners were detached from dangerous political entanglement with working-class protest; government based on property not only survived but was strengthened. The uniform £10 householder qualification was designed as a rough-and-ready means of borough enfranchisement, with inevitable anomalies deriving from variations in rental values across the country. In high-rated London, working-class voters were not uncommon; in remote Cornwall or parts of Wales even some shopkeepers failed to qualify. In northern manufacturing towns, as intended, the hurdle was stiff. Leeds, for example, had only 5,000 voters in a total population of about 125,000.

From Eric Evans, *Forging of the Modern State*, published in 2001

Source J

The standard interpretation of the Reform Act is that it was designed to incorporate the middle classes into the constitution and detach them from the workers. The Whigs clearly intended to increase the number of voters on the basis of property, but that does not make it the main intention of the Bill. The middle class was too diverse, materially and mentally, to explain much about the government's motives. £10 was an arbitrary line, which included many more occupiers in wealthy communities where rents were high than it did in poorer ones. Many working-class occupiers would creep under the net in London, whereas some middle-class citizens would fail the hurdle in remoter places.

From Boyd Hilton, *A Mad, Bad and Dangerous People: England 1783–1846*, published in 2006

SKILLS BUILDER

1 Study Sources H, I, and J. On what do they agree? On what do they disagree?

2 How do you account for these differences?

3 Now read Source K on page 33. How far are the views expressed in this source reflected in the views presented in Sources H and I?

Source K

Lay not the flattering unction to your souls that the Whig Bill of Reform will do you any good. The Bill was never intended to do you one particle of good. The object of its promoters was not to change that 'glorious constitution' which has entailed upon you so much misery, but to make it immortal. They projected the Bill, not with a view to subvert, or even re-model our aristocratic institutions, but to consolidate them by a reinforcement of sub-aristocracy from the middle classes. The Whigs have too much to lose to desire real reform. The only difference between them and the Tories is this – the Whigs would give the shadow to preserve the substance; the Tories would not give the shadow, because, stupid as they are, they know that the principle of reform once admitted, the millions will not stop at shadows, but proceed onwards to realities. Could the Tories have believed that we should be content with the Whig measure, they would have thanked their stars for it as the happiest Godsend ever given them.

From the *Poor Man's Guardian*, 27 October 1832

What was the social composition of the reformed House of Commons?

There was no sudden increase in the number of MPs from middle-class backgrounds. Successful candidates continued to be drawn from traditional social groups. After the general election of 1832 between 70 and 80 per cent of MPs represented the landed interest, and many were the sons of peers. The number of bankers, merchants and manufacturers remained roughly the same at fewer than a hundred MPs. The dominance of the aristocracy and gentry at Westminster continued well beyond the 1850s, only gradually declining towards the end of the century.

What were elections like after 1832?

It has been estimated that the number of people actually voting in 1832 increased by 500 per cent, largely because there were more contested elections. Elections were not contested when the number of candidates equalled the number of seats available. On average, only 34 per cent of potential contests had taken place at general elections between 1826 and 1831, compared to 61 per cent between 1832 and 1847.

Did electoral corruption increase after 1832?

Increased participation after 1832 did not mean that elections became wholesome and pure. The '**treating**' of voters – giving them food and alcohol – remained a vital part of electioneering, as did various underhand tricks to thwart the efforts of rival candidates. Some commentators argued that the situation was getting worse.

Definition

Treating

The practice of giving 'treats' to electors, usually in the form of meals and alcohol, in the hope of persuading them to vote for a certain candidate.

Source L

Year	Number of contests	Percentage
1826	88	36
1830	83	34
1831	75	31
1832	188	74
1835	153	60
1837	176	69
1841	138	54
1847	120	47

Contested elections 1826–47

Questions

1 Why does Parkes suggest that elections were 'injurious to shopkeepers' and 'damaging to tradesmen'?

2 What are the strengths and weaknesses of Source M as evidence of corruption after 1832?

Source M

Almost every place has a system of corruption peculiar to itself. I never heard in my life of a bribed voter at Warwick, till the election of 1831. All parties in Warwick, before the contest under the Reform Bill, lived on very amicable terms. It is scarcely credible what has subsequently been the effect of party spirit, and the consequences have also been most injurious to shopkeepers. The customers extensively transferred their custom, and the tradesmen complain that the wealthy landed proprietors and gentry in the neighbourhood have left them and gone to others. Indeed, I know that no prominent member of either party would have now any dealings with men of opposite party principles.

From the evidence of Joseph Parkes in a parliamentary report, published in 1835

Questions

1 Why does Gash suggest in Source N that the effect of reform was 'largely psychological'? Do you agree with him?

2 How does Gash justify his claim that corruption increased after 1832?

Source N

[The Reform Act] was not the subversive event it had seemed in 1831. Its importance was largely psychological: it satisfied a pent-up demand. Analysed dispassionately, the Reform Act represented no more than a clumsy but vigorous hacking at the old structure to make it a roughly more acceptable shape. Inevitably, therefore, the characteristics of the old system persisted in the new. The old franchise holders, where resident, still exercised their vote ... It is possible that with the increased party activity and greater number of contested elections after 1832 bribery and corruption actually increased. In the smaller boroughs family and personal control still sometimes decided the outcome of elections.

From Norman Gash, *Aristocracy and People*, published in 1979

Source O

[Gash] highlighted many abuses of the unreformed system that survived into Victorian England. Yet persistent flaws should not obscure the new political realities. In two-thirds of all English contests after 1832 more than 90 per cent of the electors voted a straight party ticket. Fewer than 10 per cent of all elections exhibited truly high levels of **split voting**. Some 83 per cent of the 2.9 million votes cast at elections between 1832 and 1880 were partisan, rather than non-partisan. The behaviour of tens of thousands of voters seems to us incontestable evidence of the modernising effects of Whig reforms. The most plausible explanation for the new partisan persistence after 1832 was the introduction of modern political practices, notably parliamentary parties fighting national campaigns. Reform reshaped the political landscape unintentionally, altering the relationship between elections, voters, and the parliamentary parties.

From John A. Phillips and Charles Wetherell, *The Great Reform Act of 1832 and the Political Modernization of England*, published in 1995

Computer analysis of poll books has told us a lot about voting behaviour before and after 1832, but generalised conclusions about voting behaviour may not apply across all types of borough.

Source P

Richmond (Yorkshire) and Launceston (Cornwall) were well-known-pocket boroughs. In them, between 1832 and 1885, contests were extremely rare because the dominant party always had a clear majority on the register. No contest, no poll books, no analysis. No 'runs' of poll books for consecutive elections, again no analysis, and no conclusions about partisanship. Much of Phillips and Wetherell's pioneering work derives from polling in boroughs with more than 1,000 voters. How relevant are their conclusions for boroughs with fewer than 1,000 voters, the most numerous category in England and Wales? Cornwall's small boroughs, as well as family and proprietary boroughs elsewhere illustrate how voters' preferences were the outcome of a mixture of factors, including questions of principle, electoral history, the power of patrons and local circumstance. The speed of political modernisation was slower in many smaller boroughs. Therefore firm conclusions about such modernisation between 1832 and 1868 in England should be treated with caution.

From Edwin Jaggard, *Small Boroughs and Political Modernisation, 1832–1868*, published in 1997

Definition

Split voting

Electors in a constituency with two seats had two votes. This double-vote system, which was recorded in poll books, has provided valuable evidence that has been subjected to computer analysis. The politicisation of voters can be inferred by examining whether they 'split' – by voting for candidates of opposing political views – or 'plumped' – by voting for two candidates on the same side or by throwing away their second vote if there was no suitable second candidate instead of 'splitting'.

SKILLS BUILDER

1 Study Sources O and P, and use your own knowledge. In what ways does Source P challenge Source O?

2 How far do you agree with the view that 'modernisation' was the most important feature of elections after 1832?

What were the stereotypical views of elections?

Outrageous and cynical behaviour by politicians and voters provided a rich vein of material for Victorian writers such as Charles Dickens, William Makepeace Thackeray and Anthony Trollope. The most famous fictional account of an election is given by Charles Dickens in his novel *The Pickwick Papers*. The location of the borough of 'Eatanswill' is kept deliberately vague. So too is the date of the election. The two candidates, Slumkey and Fizkin, employ unscrupulous agents who supply the voters with drink and even imprison them when necessary. Mr Pickwick and his travelling companions arrive during an election and become involved in various comic episodes.

Source Q

THE ELECTION AT EATANSWILL

Illustration by Hablot Knight Browne ('Phiz') showing the election parade at Eatanswill from *The Pickwick Papers*, published in 1836–37

Source R

Every man in Eatanswill felt himself bound to unite, heart and soul, with one of the two great parties that divided the town – the Blues and the Buffs. Everything in Eatanswill was made a party question. If the Buffs proposed a new skylight in the marketplace the Blues got up public meetings and denounced the proceedings; if the Blues proposed the erection of an additional pump in the High Street, the Buffs rose as one man and stood aghast at the enormity. There were Blue shops and Buff shops, Blue inns and Buff inns.

The Pickwickians had no sooner dismounted than they were surrounded.

'Hurrah!' shouted the mob. 'Slumkey for ever!'

'Slumkey for ever!' echoed Mr Pickwick.

'Who is Slumkey?' whispered Mr Tuckman.

'I don't know,' replied Mr Pickwick. 'Its always best on these occasions to do what the mob do.'

'But suppose there are two mobs?' suggested Mr Snodgrass.

'Shout with the largest,' replied Mr Pickwick.

From Charles Dickens, *The Pickwick* Papers, published in 1836–37

In Anthony Trollope's novel *Ralph the Heir,* there is a memorable parody of an election for the fictional borough of 'Percycross'. This was inspired by Trollope's personal experience in 1868 of standing unsuccessfully as the parliamentary candidate for Beverley in Yorkshire.

Source S

The day of the nomination at Percycross came at last, and there was a very unpleasant feeling in the town. It was not only that party was arrayed against party. That would have been a state of things not held to be undesirable, and at any rate would have been natural. But at present things were so divided that there was no saying which were the existing parties. A great proportion of the working men of Percycross were freemen of the borough, old voters who were on the register by right of their birth and family connection in the place, independent of householdership and rates, and quite accustomed to the old ways of manipulation. Not a dozen freemen of the borough would vote for Moggs. So said Mr Kirkham, Mr Westmacott's managing man. 'They'll fight for him at the hustings,' said Mr Kirkham, 'but they'll take their beer and their money, and they'll vote for us and Griffenbottom.'

From Anthony Trollope, *Ralph the Heir*, published in 1871

SKILLS BUILDER

1 Study Sources R and S.

2 Working with a partner, use your own knowledge and these sources to discuss the various views shown here. Are any rooted in fact? With which to you have most sympathy?

3 How useful are fictional sources as evidence of contemporary attitudes towards elections and party politics?

Evidence and interpretation

Contemporary attitudes towards elections in the post-reform era may be explored through different types of evidence. Historians give contrasting interpretations, and these variations stem at least in part from the differences in methodology and scope of their particular enquiries. Traditional sources such as political correspondence, debates on reform and reports from parliamentary investigations have been supplemented in recent years by an innovative analysis of poll books using computers, as you have seen. Literary sources may also be used – but with caution – to explore popular beliefs, prejudices and fears. Additionally, there were many newspapers and periodicals that both reflected and shaped contemporary opinions. People's ideas about elections and the overall impact of the Reform Act did not always come from first-hand experience. Attitudes were influenced by fictional accounts and by how electoral behaviour was reported in the newspapers.

A rural clergyman's perspective

In the aftermath of the 1852 election an obscure Shropshire clergyman, Henry Ralph Smythe, rector of Beckbury, made a personal collection of reports and cuttings about electoral corruption. This issue upset him deeply. He wrote and published a slightly peculiar 132-page pamphlet in which he cited numerous examples of corruption taken from what he had read in newspapers and official reports. Smythe bitterly denounced ignorant and grasping urban voters, exploitative capitalist factory owners and corrupt radical politicians. Smythe's specific recommendations stood very little chance of being adopted. He wanted to raise the borough franchise to £15 and reduce the county qualification for tenants from £50 to £25. Above all, he wanted parliament to pass effective laws to prevent electoral corruption.

Source T

[There] should be a feeling of universal disgust at the shameless and open corruption to which the Reform Bill of 1832 has brought the representation of the country. The evidence examined all tells the same story – that bribery is the rule, and not the exception, at the general elections in all borough towns. The best proof on this degrading subject is a sketch of a scene in a Revising Barrister's Court. Men apparently squalid, debauched and intemperate, have their names tendered to be placed on the registry. The presiding barrister hears, and is assailed by, a host of liberal attorneys in support of the claim. But when a duly qualified vote is tendered or a gentleman of education offered, the same pettifogging hostile bar – opposed to whatever is respectable in the country – stands forth to obstruct and prevent the voter being enrolled. The writer has too often witnessed such scenes. It had been the old English custom to avoid contests as much as possible; but all this is now compelled to yield to the insensate outcry of intoxicated multitudes. In the boroughs a very few solicitors have become the patrons for the sale of the greater number of the new constituencies – as the old ones of Gatton and Sarum – had been formerly sold by a few nobles and their friends.

From Henry Ralph Smythe, *Parliamentary Reform Considered*, published in 1853

Smythe's hostility to the conduct of elections in urban constituencies contrasted with his praise for the purity of the county representation. By the 1850s, though, the traditional respect for county MPs and the way they were elected was beginning to be questioned, even in such respectable places as the editorial column of *The Times* (as you can see from Source U).

Source U

Parliamentary committees and commissions have diverted so much public attention to borough elections that the state of the county franchise has not received the attention it undoubtedly deserves. The abuses of the boroughs, taking, as they generally do, the form of individual bribery and corruption, are so much more tangible and attract so much more attention than the nomination which regulates our counties. No one bribes, no one intimidates, no one cajoles, no one intoxicates a man who has nothing to give. The very abuse and degradation of the franchise proves that it is really, not nominally, possessed. The county election is, in general, accompanied by none of those disgraceful and demoralising influences. It is a select knot of large proprietors, who decide without beer, without bellowing, without tumult, who it is who shall represent them. The mass of electors have really not much to do with the matter. It is a question not of popular opinion but of territorial jurisdiction. Our county members represent great estates rather than great principles, and families rather than communities.

From *The Times*, 19 November 1853

SKILLS BUILDER

1 Study Sources T and U and use your own knowledge. You may like to work in small groups to discuss questions 1–3 before writing an answer to question 4.

   (a) How far do you agree with the claim in Source U that the Reform Act created new forms of corruption that were as bad as in the old rotten boroughs?

   (b) How justified is Smythe in blaming voter registration for electoral corruption?

2 Elsewhere in his pamphlet Smythe disapprovingly cites *The Times* article reproduced in Source U. What do you think were Smythe's objections to this newspaper editorial?

3 How far do you agree with the claim in Source V that corruption proved that borough voters possessed genuine electoral influence, whereas ordinary county voters did not?

4 How useful are Sources U and V as evidence to explain contemporary attitudes towards electoral corruption after 1832?

Question

Read Source V and use your own knowledge. How far do you agree with the view that the Reform Act 'strengthened the status quo'?

Source V

What Grey and his colleagues had done was to forge the most durable of political alliances, that between land and industry; it would stand fast for many years against the assaults of the democrats. It is no wonder that working-class leaders spoke so bitterly about their old allies, the middle-classes, after 1832. The rights of property had been given a new lease of life, largely under existing management. Britain, alone of the advanced nations of Western Europe, avoided political revolution in the 1830s and 1840s. Those revolutions depended to a significant extent upon middle-class leadership. The middle classes in Britain had been hitched to the wagon of established authority. In the short term, the Reform Act strengthened the status quo.

From Eric Evans, *The Great Reform Act of 1832*, published in 1983

Unit summary

What have you learned in this unit?

The consequences of the 1832 Reform Act were complex and interconnected. You have learned about the main changes in England, Wales, Scotland and Ireland. You have analysed both the intended and unintended consequences of reform, including its impact on local and national politics. You have considered the extent to which a two-party system existed, the differences between county and borough elections, the nature of corruption and the extent to which the Reform Act had, in fact, preserved the pre-reform system.

What skills have you used in this unit?

You have evaluated a range of different contemporary and secondary sources, including cartoons and population and election statistics. You have compared historical interpretations and considered new methodologies such as computer analysis of poll books, and you have seen how fictional sources can be used to illuminate historical analysis. You have cross-referenced and drawn inferences from these sources in order to reach judgements about key questions concerning the impact of the 1832 Reform Act on the British electoral system.

Exam tips

Below is the sort of question you will find appearing on examination papers as an (a) question.

Study Sources A, G and K. How far does the evidence of Sources A and K support the view expressed in Source G that one outcome of the 1832 Reform Act was that power had shifted to the middle classes?

Here are some tips for answering this question.

- **Don't** bring in a lot of your own knowledge. All (a) questions focus on the analysis, cross-referencing and evaluation of source material. Your own knowledge won't be credited by the examiner and you will waste valuable time writing it out.
- **Do** remember that the only knowledge you should introduce will be to put the sources into context. This means, for example, that you might explain that the Duke of Wellington was the leader of the Tories who had opposed the Reform Act, but you would not need to describe his other political or military activities or achievements.
- **Don't** describe (or even re-write) the sources. The examiner will have a copy and to do this will waste your time.
- **Do** draw inferences from the sources to show how they could be seen to imply, or not, that power had shifted as a result of the 1832 Reform Act.
- **Do** reach a supported judgement, by careful cross-referencing and evaluation, about 'How far' the sources suggest that one outcome of the 1832 Reform Act was that power had shifted to the middle classes.

RESEARCH TOPIC

Locate online or library texts from Charles Dickens' *Pickwick Papers*, Anthony Trollope's *Ralph the Heir* or William Makepeace Thackeray's *A Lucky Speculator*. Read the sections on the elections of 'Eatanswill', 'Percycross' or the letters from Fitz James de la Pluche.

Identify the comic devices and satirical targets. How far do these accounts share similar themes? What do these fictional texts reveal about contemporary attitudes towards elections?

How might twenty-first century elections be satirised by a present-day Dickens or Trollope? Write a brief outline or sketch of what you would include.

3 Aftermath: the emergence of Chartism 1837–40

What is this unit about?

This unit focuses on the rise of Chartism, a working-class movement that developed in reaction to the 1832 Reform Act and other Whig measures of the 1830s. It addresses the reasons why people joined the Chartist movement – some staying in the movement for the duration of its existence, while others dipped in and out. It considers the ways in which Chartists sought to put their ideas into action, and why and how they adopted different methods of protest. The development of the movement to its first peak of activity in 1839–40 will be followed, with a particular focus on the Chartist Convention and the Newport Rising.

Key questions

- Why did people join the Chartists?
- How serious was the challenge to the government 1837–40?

Timeline

1836	**London Working Men's Association (LWMA) founded**
	Founder members were William Lovett, Francis Place and Henry Hetherington; they aimed to appeal to skilled workers seeking reform
	National Radical Association of Scotland founded
1837	**Six points of the 'People's Charter' written**
	Produced by members of the LWMA together with six radical MPs
	First appearance of the *Northern Star*
	Chartist newspaper printed in Leeds and edited by Feargus O'Connor
1838	**Publication of the People's Charter**
	Printed in London along with a National Petition for Chartists to sign
	London Democratic Association founded
	A re-branding, by George Julian Harney, of the East London Democratic Association (formed in 1837) and intended to be the unskilled workers' alternative to the LWMA
	Mass rallies and meetings
	Held throughout the country, many to elect delegates to a National Convention
1839	**Year of action**
February	National Convention met in London
May	National Convention moved to Birmingham

June	First Chartist Petition (1.28 million signatures) presented to parliament
July	Riots at the Bull Ring in Birmingham, followed by the return of the National Convention to London
	Rejection of Chartist Petition by parliament (235 votes to 46)
	National Convention proposed strike action, known as the 'Sacred Month'
August	'Sacred Month' called off; Convention dissolved
November	Newport Rising in Monmouthshire
1840	**The end of Chartism?**
January	Attempted risings in Sheffield and Bradford
	Many Chartists, including the leaders, arrested, tried and imprisoned

Source A

The Six Points
OF THE
PEOPLE'S
CHARTER.

1. A VOTE for every man twenty-one years of age, of sound mind, and not undergoing punishment for crime.

2. THE BALLOT.—To protect the elector in the exercise of his vote.

3. NO PROPERTY QUALIFICATION for Members of Parliament —thus enabling the constituencies to return the man of their choice, be he rich or poor.

4. PAYMENT OF MEMBERS, thus enabling an honest tradesman, working man, or other person, to serve a constituency, when taken from his business to attend to the interests of the country.

5. EQUAL CONSTITUENCIES, securing the same amount of representation for the same number of electors, instead of allowing small constituencies to swamp the votes of large ones.

6. ANNUAL PARLIAMENTS, thus presenting the most effectual check to bribery and intimidation, since though a constituency might be bought once in seven years (even with the ballot), no purse could buy a constituency (under a system of universal suffrage) in each ensuing twelvemonth; and since members, when elected for a year only, would not be able to defy and betray their constituents as now.

The six points of the People's Charter 1838

Chartism takes its name from the People's Charter that was published in 1838 (see Source A). There was nothing new about the Charter's six points: they had all been part of political agitation since the 1760s. What was new, however, was the emergence of Chartism as a national movement in the 1830s and 1840s, and we have to ask not only why Chartism emerged, but also why it emerged at that point in time.

Beginnings: working men's associations and the Charter

Many working people were angered by what they saw as a series of betrayals by Lord John Russell's Whig government, which at one time had seemed to promise so much in the way of parliamentary reform. (For more information about Russell, see page 17.)

- In June 1836, Francis Place, a London tailor who had organised a political union to press for parliamentary reform, joined up with William Lovett (see page 67), a cabinet maker, to form the London Working Men's Association (LWMA). With William Lovett as its secretary and **Henry Hetherington** as treasurer, they set about holding discussion groups and public meetings. It was William Lovett who drew up the People's Charter, which became their political programme pressing for further reform. They hoped that by using persuasion the government would accept the moral force of their arguments. 'Before an educated people,' Lovett declared, 'a government must bow.' Two years later, in 1838 and encouraged by six radical MPs, the People's Charter was printed in London and widely circulated, along with a National Petition for people to sign, urging parliament to accept the Charter's six points. The appeal of the LWMA was mainly to skilled workers, those who had much to lose by open rebellion and much to gain by peaceful change.

- The East London Democratic Association, founded in 1837 by the Chartist George Julian Harney, and a year later re-named the London Democratic Association (LDA), aimed to attract the unskilled workers and those who favoured a more confrontational approach to the government. Many saw it as being in opposition to the LWMA, but in fact the LDA supported all six points of the People's Charter. The two

Biography

Henry Hetherington (1792–1849)

Hetherington was a radical journalist and publisher whose *Poor Man's Guardian* (1831–35) played an important role in the 'war of the unstamped' press. In 1819 the government had imposed a harsh stamp duty in order to make radical newspapers economically unviable. From 1830 Hetherington published newspapers illegally (i.e. 'unstamped') and was jailed three times. Eventually, the government gave way by reducing the stamp duty by 75 per cent to just 1d in 1835. Hetherington later participated in various Chartist organisations.

organisations simply disagreed over the ways in which they believed the six points could be achieved.

It wasn't only in London that associations were formed to support the People's Charter. The National Radical Association of Scotland was formed in August 1836, and the following year saw a number of radical associations formed in the textile districts of Lancashire and Yorkshire.

Why did people become Chartists in the 1830s and 1840s?

Three important factors led to the sense of disappointment, anger, resentment and despair felt by thousands of people across the country. In fact, it was this despair, anger and resentment that led them to support the Charter and to demand representation in parliament. It was only through this representation, Chartists believed, that the sometimes desperate situation of working-class people could be improved. Although these factors have been separated below for the sake of clarity, they were all inter-linked.

Factor 1: the 'betrayal' of the Reform Act of 1832

The immediate impetus behind the emergence of Chartism can be seen in the changes made to the franchise in 1832. Radical demands for universal male suffrage had been deemed unacceptable by moderate reformers. The uniform £10 franchise in the boroughs excluded the vast majority of urban working-class men. Indeed, previously, under the unreformed system there had been some boroughs with a more inclusive franchise. Although these traditional rights were allowed to continue for the lifetime of individual voters, it was clear that the Reform Act was ultimately designed to exclude working-class men from participating in the government of their country. There were, too, considerable regional variations. For example, the £10 franchise gave the vote to many better-off workers in London, but excluded many in Leeds and excluded nearly all of them in Merthyr Tydfil (Wales). Those excluded from the franchise felt betrayed. Their hopes for a new parliament that would truly represent them, and that could be trusted to pass laws in the interests of the whole nation and not just the property-owning classes, had been dashed.

Source B

The [Reform] Act was never intended to do you one particle of good. They projected the Bill, not with a view to subvert, or even re-model our aristocratic institutions, but to consolidate them. The Whigs have too much to lose to desire real reform. They knew that the old system could not last, and desiring to establish another as like it as possible, and also to keep their places, they framed the Bill, in the hope of drawing to the feudal aristocrats and yeomanry of counties a large reinforcement of the middle class. The Bill was, in effect, an invitation to the shopocrats of the enfranchised towns to join the Whiggocrats of the country, and make common cause with them in keeping down the people, and thereby to quell the rising spirit of democracy in England.

From the *Poor Man's Guardian*, a radical newspaper produced by Henry Hetherington, 27 October 1832

Source C

THE LYING WHIG REFORM BILL

The following tables exhibit the monstrous delusion that the reform bill destroyed the rotten borough system

1. Contested Elections, 1837, and subsequently, at which the votes polled for a successful candidate were less than 200.

Borough or county	Returns	Polled	Constituents from whom formed	Population
1 Ashburton	1	98	101 nom. Freem & 342 h.	4,165
2 Arundel	1	176	380 £10 h.	2,803
3 Banbury	1	185	old cor. Of 18 & 365 h.	5,906
4 Bandon (Ireland)	1	133	13 f. and 279 h.	9,820
5 Breeon	1	151	350 h.	5,026
6 Caithnesshire	1	198	...	34,000
7 Carlow (Ireland)	1	167	23 f. and 403 h.	9,012
8 Cockermouth	2	117	burgage holders & 235 h.	6,022
9 Colerain (Ireland)	1	120	52 f. and 240 h.	5,752
10 Devizes	2	109	cor. And 409 h.	6,367
11 Downpatrick (I.)	1	190	...	4,779
12 Eversham	2	168	130 h.	3,991
13 Frome	1	125	450 h.	12,240
14 Harwich	1	75	cor. and 202 h.	4,297
15 Helston	1	160	cor. and 225 h.	3,293
16 Horsham	1	147	burghage tenants & 385 h.	5,105
17 Kidderminster	1	198	500 h.	20,165
18 Kinsale	1	102	301 h.	6,897
19 Knaresborough	2	172	burghage tenants & 369 h.	6,252
20 Liskeard	1	113	cor. and 315 h.	4,042
21 Ludlow	2	194	b. and 314 h.	5,252
22 Lyme Regis	1	121	f. and 300 h.	3,345
23 Lymington	2	161	cor. and 189 h.	5,472
24 Petersfield	1	125	freeh. And 305 h.	4,922
25 Sligo (Ireland)	1	178	13 f, and 354 h	12,762
26 Totness	2	158	f. and 316 h.	3,442
27 Tralee (Ireland)	1	75	13 f. and 354 h.	9,562
28 Wallingford	1	159	cor. and 278 h.	2,467
29 Wareham	1	170	s. and c. and 54 h.	2,566
30 Woodstock	1	126	f. and 373 h.	7,655
31 Youghal (Ireland)	1	158	f. and 479 h.	9,600

2. Contested Elections, and voters polled under 300.

Borough or county	Returns	Polled	Constituents from whom formed	Population
1 Armagh	1	235	13 f. and 520 h.	9,189
2 Ashton-under-Lyne	1	234	610 h.	14,673
3 Banffshire	1	292	...	48,000
4 Bodmin	1	290	c. and 311 h.	5,298
5 Bridport	2	283	s. and l., and 342 h.	4,242
6 Buckingham	2	235	c. and 225 h.	3,610
7 Bury	1	248	765 h.	15,986
8 Bury St. Edmunds	2	289	719	11,436
9 Clonmell (Ireland)	1	284	94 f. and 752 h.	12,256
10 Gateshead	1	266	750 h.	15,177
11 Guildford	2	252	f. and 431 h.	3,916
12 Haddingshire	1	299	...	36,100
13 Ditto Districts	1	268	214 h.	...
14 Haverfordwest do.	1	247	s. and l., and 584 h.	10,832
15 Honiton	2	294	s. and ., and 318 h.	3,509
16 Hythe	1	243	f. and 537 h.	6,903
17 Inverness-shire	1	254	...	94,800
18 Kirkaldy Burghs	1	216	...	...
19 Londonderry (I.)	1	214	F, and 785 h.	14,020
20 Newport (I. of W.)	2	264	f. and 445 h.	6,786
21 Peebleshire	1	251	...	16,600
22 Poole	2	272	f. and 298 h.	6,959
23 Scarborough	2	225	c. and 508 h.	8,760
24 Selkirkshire	1	230	...	6,800
25 Shaftesbury	1	221	s. and l., and 145 h.	8,518
26 St. Albans	2	252	s. and l., and 286 h.	5,771
27 St. Andrews	1	290	452 h.	...
28 Tewkesbury	2	219	f. and 262 h.	5,780
29 Teignmouth	1	259	1,150 h.	23,206
30 Warrington	1	278	973 h.	18, 184
31 Weymouth	2	289	c. and 490 h.	8,095
32 Wigan	2	268	h. and 568 h.	20,774
33 Winchester	2	259	h. and 807 h.	9,212

NOTE. – C., corporation; s. and l. scot and lot voters; f., freemen; h., occupants of house at an annual rental of £10 and upwards

'The Lying Whig Reform Bill', published in a Chartist newspaper in 1839

SKILLS BUILDER

1 Study Source C. What evidence does its compiler produce to justify calling the 1832 Reform Act 'lying' and a 'monstrous delusion'?

2 How far does Source C support the view of the 1832 Reform Act given in Source B?

3 In what ways would Source C provide propaganda in support of the aims of Sources A and B?

It was not simply that the radical vision of universal suffrage had been thwarted by the Whigs, but also that the legislation of the ensuing period was seen by those who supported the Charter to have negative consequences for working people. Chartists were suspicious of almost everything the Whigs did. It was remembered that the Whigs had suppressed the rural labourer-led 'Swing' Riots before the Reform Act, and the punishment of the **Tolpuddle Martyrs** was seen as another Whig 'crime'. Furthermore, the Whigs passed a weak and ineffective Factory Act in 1833, which limited the hours children could work in textile mills. That said, by appointing only four inspectors, mill owners could easily get round the Act's provisions, and they opposed the campaign to limit the working day for adult males to 10 hours. However, by far the most resented item of Whig legislation after 1832 was the Poor Law Amendment Act of 1834.

Factor 2: the 'humiliation' of the Poor Law Amendment Act of 1834

Often called the New Poor Law, this piece of legislation was an attempt to centralise and impose some kind of order on the patchwork system of **poor relief** that had existed in the past. Key to this was the division of the poor into **'deserving'** and **'undeserving'**, and establishing a network of workhouses, where people were to be admitted in order to receive relief.

Although the implementation of the New Poor Law varied from place to place, and **'outdoor' relief** continued to be the most usual way of helping the poor, there was no escaping the intention of the government to replace 'outdoor' relief with **'indoor' relief**. It seemed, and not without reason, like a conspiracy between the government and the middle classes in order to reward the middle classes for their support for parliamentary reform but at the same time to separate them from the working class. It was also argued by many that middle-class ratepayers had been enfranchised in 1832, and were now being kept on the side of the government by a cost-cutting New Poor Law. This seemed plausible because one of the aims of the New Poor Law was to reduce the burden on the rates of poor relief; but these changes also spread fear and humiliation among working people. Chartism therefore gained strength both from continuing campaigns for effective factory reform and opposition, at times violent, to the hated New Poor Law. This was particularly the case between 1837 and 1839, when authorities that attempted to introduce the New Poor Law into the industrial North exposed the inadequacies of the Act to deal with cyclical unemployment and were met with violent opposition.

Source D

The New Poor Law Act was passed in order to place the whole of the labouring classes at the utter mercy and disposal of the moneyed or property owning classes.

Written by James Bronterre O'Brien in the *Northern Star*, a Chartist newspaper, 24 February 1848 (O'Brien was to become a leading Chartist)

Definitions

Tolpuddle Martyrs

In 1834 six agricultural labourers from the Dorset village of Tolpuddle were sentenced to seven years' transportation for using 'unlawful oaths' to establish a trade union.

Poor relief

Help given by the parish to people who did not have enough money to feed and clothe themselves. People who received poor relief were called paupers.

'Deserving' and 'undeserving' poor

The deserving poor were those who were poor through no fault of their own – e.g. widows and orphans, the sick and the old. The undeserving poor were the able-bodied poor who, though fit enough, were unwilling or unable to work or find work.

'Outdoor' and 'Indoor' relief

'Outdoor' relief was help given to the poor in their own homes. 'Indoor' relief was help given to the poor inside a workhouse.

SKILLS BUILDER

Read Sources D and E. How far does Source D support what Source E says about the New Poor Law?

Source E

The passing of the New Poor Law Amendment Act did more to sour the hearts of the labouring population than did all the poverty of the land. The labourers of England believed that the New Poor Law was a law to punish poverty, and that the effects of that belief were, to sap the loyalty of working men, to make them dislike the country of their birth, to brood over their wrongs, to cherish feelings of revenge, and to hate the rich of the land.

Written by Samuel Kydd, who was a young shoemaker in the 1830s; quoted in D. Thompson, *The Chartists: Popular Politics in the Industrial Revolution*, published in 1984

Source F

The local Chartist agitation grew out of the almost unrelieved commercial depression that followed the collapse of the boom of 1836. Fifty thousand workers in the Manchester area alone were unemployed or on short time by June 1837.

From D. Read, *Chartism in Manchester*, published in 1959

As a result, thousands of working people supported the Chartists because they believed that the government was not acting in their best interests and neither would it be likely ever to do so. The only way forward, they believed, was to have their own representatives in the House of Commons

Factor 3: the impact of economic depression

The vulnerability of working-class people was highlighted by the economic crises that hit Britain in the 1830s and early 1840s. Although reliable detailed statistics about economic performance are difficult to compile, it is clear that the years 1837–42 were the most difficult in the whole century for working people. The severe and prolonged trade depression of the mid-1830s, for example, hit hard. In the new industrial towns of the Midlands

Questions

1 Read Sources F and G. How far do they agree that Chartism resulted from economic distress?

2 You have been given three main factors that led to people becoming Chartists. Which, in your view, was the most important?

Source G

The principle of the Resolution [to support the People's Charter] which he had risen to speak to, was a principle which every man which breathed God's free air and trod God's free earth, to have his home and hearth, and his wife and his children as securely guaranteed to him as of any other man. The question of Universal Suffrage was a knife and fork question after all; this question was a bread and cheese question, notwithstanding all that had been said against it; and if any man ask him what he meant by Universal Suffrage, he would answer, that every man in the land had a right to have a good coat to his back, a comfortable abode in which to shelter himself and his family, a good dinner upon his table, and no more work than was necessary for keeping him in health, and as much wages for that work as would keep him in plenty, and afford him the enjoyment of all the blessings of life which a reasonable man could desire.

From a speech by the Reverend Joseph Rayner Stephens at a meeting on Kersal Moor (outside Manchester), 24 September 1838 to elect delegates to the Chartist Convention, reported in the *Northern* Star, 29 September 1838

and North, this meant short-term unemployment, reduced hours and wage cuts. Bread prices, stable since 1815, began to rise alarmingly and in 1839 wheat reached the unheard of peak price of 81 shillings a quarter, with a corresponding knock-on effect on the price of bread. For many, Chartism offered the only hope out of a desperate situation.

People who became Chartists, therefore, were craftsmen such as printers, tailors and cabinet makers, factory workers like the cotton spinners of Bolton and the wool combers of Bradford, and domestic **outworkers** such as handloom weavers, framework knitters and nail makers. Men and women in towns and villages throughout England, Wales and Scotland supported Chartism at different times and for different reasons. Some men and women turned to Chartism when times were bad. When trade was poor, wages fell and unemployment was high, they looked to Chartism to solve their problems. Some difficulties were entirely local. Manchester cotton operatives were thrown out of work for several months at a time if the American cotton crop failed. Many turned to Chartism as a result. Yet this particular problem would not affect, for example, the framework knitters of Leicester. They had their own problems, which led many of them into the Chartist movement, if only for short periods of time. There were, of course, thousands of men and women who were Chartists in good times as well as bad. Whatever the reasons for people becoming Chartists, they all believed that to get working men into the House of Commons as MPs would be the only long-term solution to their problems. Somehow parliament must be persuaded to accept the six points of the People's Charter.

Definition

Outworker

A person who works at home and is supplied with the raw materials by a manufacturer.

Source H

None of the Chartists' 'Six Points' was new. Most had been widely debated by radical politicians for at least half a century. They were all political. If Chartism was merely a reaction to bad times for working people, why were all the six points political? The Chartist Petitions to parliament did not call for a minimum wage, for additional rights for trade unionists or for the abolition of the hated New Poor Law.

From Eric Evans, 'Chartism Revisited', in *History Review Journal*, published, 1999

SKILLS BUILDER

1 How far does the historian Eric Evans (Source H) challenge the views of Joseph Rayner Stephens (Source G) as to whether Chartism was an economic or economic movement?

2 Use the information in this section to explain whether you think Chartism was a political or an economic movement. You may like to discuss this in your group.

Strategy and tactics: how did the Chartists hope to achieve their aims?

It was one thing to agree over the Charter, but quite another to agree over how the six points would be achieved. What should happen? Marches and large-scale demonstrations? A Chartist press? Associations? District meetings? Petition parliament? Above all, was the government to be persuaded by moral force or threatened by physical force?

The Northern Star

The establishment of the *Northern Star* in November 1837 was of huge importance. This newspaper was closely associated with Feargus O'Connor (see page 66), who became a figure of national importance, not only because of his participation in meetings, but because of the reporting of his speeches and ideas in the *Northern Star*. At its peak in 1839, the *Northern Star* was selling 36,000 copies a week nationally and its audience was many times greater because copies would be read out loud or passed from hand to hand (see Source I).

Source I

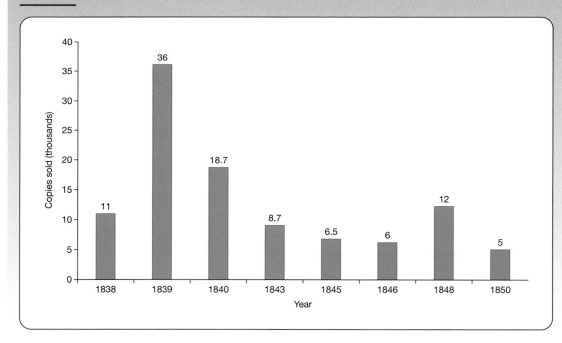

Weekly sales of the *Northern Star* 1838–50, from H. Martin, *Britain in the Nineteenth Century*, published in 1996

SKILLS BUILDER

Study Source I. What can you learn from this source about the popularity of the Chartist movement? How useful is this sort of data to a historian?

Chartist meetings

Public meetings were crucial to the growth of Chartism. These took various forms, ranging from small indoor gatherings to massive outdoor events. On 6 August 1838, all of the Chartist groups gathered together at a great rally held at Holloway Head in Birmingham. The rally accepted the six points of the People's Charter and agreed that Chartists would collect signatures for a National Petition in support of the Charter to be presented to parliament. If parliament rejected the Charter then there would be a general strike – called a 'sacred month'. The rally agreed, too, that there would be a national Chartist Convention. Members would be chosen by the various Chartist groups around the country, and would meet to prepare for the presentation of the Petition to parliament. The huge open-air meetings during September 1838 at Kersal Moor in Manchester, for example (look back to Source G), are a good example of one such Chartist meeting. Signatures were collected for the Petition and arrangements were made for the collection of a 'National Rent' to raise funds without breaking earlier laws against radical associations. But there were warnings of trouble ahead.

Source J

I stand before you as a delegate to the National Convention. Ah! Well may the Whig and Tory tyrants tremble at this meeting. The tyrants may affect to hold us in contempt but in their hearts they tremble. (Cheers). I have today seen the Shopocracy of Derby affecting to sneer at our procession. I tell these big-bellied, purse-proud, ignorant Shopocrats, to look to their tills – to stick to their counters – to fawn, and crawl, and creep to their aristocratic patrons but not to sneer at us. Or, if they do, let them take the consequences – the day of retribution may arrive sooner than they look for. My friends, we demand universal suffrage, not only because it is our right, but because we believe it will bring freedom to our country and give us bread, and beef, and beer. The Whigs charge us with being physical-force men; I fling the charge back in the teeth of these canting Liberals. Let them call to mind their own words and deeds during the humbug Reform agitation; let them remember Derby in a state of anarchy, Nottingham and Bristol in flames. We are for peace, but we must have justice – we must have our rights speedily; peaceably if we can – forcibly if we must. (Loud cheers.)

From a speech by George Julian Harney at a Chartist meeting in Derby, reported in the *Northern Star*, 9 February 1839

Source K

Meetings took place in practically every important manufacturing town between Glasgow, London and Bristol, and the election of delegates proceeded rapidly. In October meetings were held for the purpose of collecting funds destined for the support of the Convention. But the joy experienced at this rapid progress was clouded by apprehension, for which a terrifying change in the character of the northern meetings was responsible. In October meetings began to be held at night in the murky glare of hundreds of torches, in various parts of Lancashire and Yorkshire, on the pretext that the factory owners objected to meetings during working hours. The psychological effects of large crowds and excited speakers were emphasised by the eerie surroundings; it was but a short step from torchlight meetings to factory burning. The authorities were pardonably anxious and tried to put a stop to these meetings. But their action only increased the temperature of the speeches, which became inflammatory beyond words. Such meetings were held at Bolton, Bradford, Oldham, Rochdale and Bury during October, November and December.

From Mark Hovell, *The Chartist Movement*, published in 1918 (Hovell, a young scholar based at Manchester University, wrote the first history of the Chartist movement; he was killed in the trenches on 12 August 1916, aged 28)

Source L

On Whit Monday 1839, a great meeting was held at Peep Green, which I attended along with Samuel Jackson, a neighbour; we joined the procession in Halifax which was a very large one headed by a band of music, and marched by Godley Lane and Hipperholme, at which place the Queensbury procession joined us; on reaching the top of the hill above Bailiffe bridge we met the Bradford procession, headed by Peter Bussey on horseback and wearing a green sash. On our arrival at the place of the meeting some thousands of people had already assembled, and for almost an hour we witnessed the continuous arrival of processions from different directions, with bands playing and flags and banners flying, a great many of them far superior to any I have seen in our late demonstrations. The proceedings opened with prayers by Mr William Thornton, at the close of which Mr Fergus O'Connor put his hands on his shoulders and said, 'Well done, Thornton, when we get the Charter I will see that you are made Archbishop of York.'

From Benjamin Wilson, *The Struggles of an Old Chartist*, published in 1887

Question

What would the authorities have found worrying about the meetings described in Sources J and L?

SKILLS BUILDER

1 Read Sources J and K. How far does Source J support what Hovell writes in Source K about the ways in which some Chartist meetings were developing?

2 Now read Source L. How far does this source challenge Source K about the nature of Chartist meetings?

Definition

Ulterior measures

These were the actions the Chartists suggested could be undertaken if their Petition was rejected by parliament. These included withdrawing all their money from the banks at the same time, converting their paper money to gold or silver all at the same time, holding a general strike (called a 'sacred month') and supporting only pro-Chartist candidates at the next general election.

The Chartist Convention

The Chartist leadership was aware it was controversial to assemble a body of elected representatives. They were afraid it could be seen by the government as a potential threat to the authority of parliament. Moderate Chartist leaders, too, took care to avoid referring to this as a 'National Convention' because this phrase had uncomfortable echoes of the French Revolution. They wished to confine business to organising the Petition and dispatching speakers, known as 'missionaries', to promote Chartist ideas throughout the country and gather signatures. On the other hand, more radical Chartists did envisage the Convention as a 'People's Parliament' and a direct rival to the House of Commons. They began to go beyond discussing the Petition itself in order to plan for **ulterior measures** in case of its rejection by parliament.

Source M

A contemporary print showing members of the General Convention, which met at the British Hotel, Cockspur Street, London, in 1839

Source N

The 50 or so members of the Convention met in London in February 1839, some representing several 'constituencies'. A quarter of the delegates were from the capital itself, with 20 from the industrial north, eight from Scotland, five from Birmingham, three from the East Midlands and two from Wales. About half were working men, the others being mainly radical gentry and small employers.

From D.G. Wright, *Popular Radicalism*, published in 1988

SKILLS BUILDER

1 Study Sources M and N.

   (a) What impression of Chartism is conveyed by Source M?

   (b) How far does Source N support this impression?

2 How far do Sources M and N challenge Sources J and K about the nature of Chartism?

It was this discussion of 'ulterior measures' that alarmed William Lovett and the moderate 'Moral Force' Chartists, and they walked out of the Convention. The remaining members moved away from London, a city they considered to be too 'lukewarm', and transferred the Convention to Birmingham, where the 35 surviving delegates reconvened on 13 May 1839. Here the Convention drew up a list of 'ulterior measures' Chartists would consider should the Petition be rejected by parliament. The meeting then adjourned in order to test out feeling in the country. Mass meetings, demonstrations and many arrests followed, and the more moderate Chartists became increasingly concerned as to the wisdom of the course of action being advocated by those favouring physical force. The Convention re-convened in Birmingham on 1 July, resolving to return to London within a week. Events, however, were to overtake them and rioting broke out on 4 July (see Source O on page 55). The Convention passed resolutions condemning the actions of the authorities, and William Lovett was arrested as a consequence. Further arrests followed, and the Convention swiftly moved itself back to London.

The First Petition

Disagreements among Chartists did not, however, significantly impede the growth of the Petition. It was enormous, being three miles long and containing 1,280,000 signatures. On 12 July two MPs, John Fielden and Thomas Attwood, both of whom were sympathetic towards the Chartists and the six points of the Charter, formally asked the House of Commons to consider the Petition. Interestingly, Benjamin Disraeli (see page 91), later to be both a Tory Prime Minister and also a strong supporter of the 1867 Reform Act, spoke in favour. However, his fellow MPs were not interested. They voted 235 to 46 against even considering the Chartists' Petition, and it was thrown out.

Ulterior measures

When the Petition was rejected by parliament in July, Chartists were presented with a choice: whether to accept this tamely, or to proceed to what they called 'ulterior measures'. A range of actions had been discussed:

- withdrawing savings from banks in the hope of creating a financial crisis
- boycotting heavily taxed goods or even refusing to pay taxes in order to threaten government revenue
- refusing to pay rent
- calling a general strike, to be known as a 'National Holiday' in a 'sacred month' to create widespread economic disruption
- arming for defence against government repression.

All of these tactics were in some ways problematic, either on practical or moral grounds.

The only action that came close to being authorised by the Convention was the 'sacred month'. By a narrow vote this was initially approved, though it

Questions

1 Rank the 'ulterior measures' from moderate to extreme on a scale of 1 to 10, where 1 = mild and 10=extreme.

2 What practical and moral objections to these proposals can you identify ?

was soon abandoned partly on the grounds of insufficient preparation but mainly because of fears that it would be ineffective in a trade depression.

Even Feargus O'Connor was against it: 'The baker will not bake, the butcher will not kill, and the brewer will not brew; then what becomes of the millions of starving human beings?'

The government had called the Chartists' bluff. The 'sacred month' was cancelled by the Convention, which dissolved itself on 6 September 1839. The possibility of organised protest and pressure for change seemed to have been lost.

How far were the Chartists a real threat to the government?

Trouble seemed to be brewing in the Midlands and North as shown in Sources J and K. It was here that violent opposition to the implementation of the New Poor Law had met with some success (see page 47) and where the Chartists, led by Feargus O'Connor, might also reasonably have hoped for some success. Indeed, the government seemed to be thoroughly alarmed, not only by the talk in the Convention but also by rumours that Chartists were arming themselves with sticks, cudgels and guns. In April 1839, the government appointed Major-General Sir Charles Napier to command 6,000 troops in the Northern District (northern England) and gave him responsibility for keeping law and order there. The government was determined that no revolution of the French kind would happen in Britain. But were they over-reacting? (Keep this question in mind as you work through Sources O, P and Q.)

Source O

The borough magistrates, however, who had for some days been in constant communication with the Home Office, had by this time asked for 60 policemen from London. The railway train delivered them at Birmingham that evening, and without even waiting for the co-operation of the military, they proceeded immediately to the scene of confusion. They began by directing the people to disperse, but when this order was seen to take no effect, the police filed off four abreast and made for the monument of Lord Nelson which stood in the centre of the Bull-ring, set around with the flags of the Convention. These they succeeded in capturing, but the mob, who had been at first disconcerted by the impetuosity of the charge, when they beheld their flags in the hands of enemy, made a desperate return, recovered the banners, broke the poles up into short sticks, and after a fierce and indiscriminate combat in which several of the policeman, who were only armed with staves, were seriously hurt, and more than one man stabbed, the Chartists began at length to obtain the advantage.

Fortunately, however, at this juncture, the 4th Dragoons arrived on the spot. Riding up every avenue that led to the place, they completely enclosed the Bull-ring. The appearance of the military was the signal for the people to disperse, and by midnight the streets were comparatively quiet, and the military, leaving a guard in the great square, retired to their barracks.

From the *Annual Register* 1839, reporting on the Birmingham riots that occurred 4–6 July 1839 (the *Annual Register* is a reference work, published annually, which records and analyses the year's major events; it began in 1758 and has been published every year since)

Source P

At Manchester on Monday at an early hour the Chartists proceeded to carry into execution their measures for enforcing the National Holiday by stopping the factories. They commenced by organising their forces, dividing them into four distinct bodies in order to visit the mills in the districts allotted to them, simultaneously at the hour of starting work. Before their progress was arrested by the police, they succeeded in their object at nearly twenty places. One of the groups walked in procession headed by a band of music.

From the *Observer* newspaper, 18 August 1839

Source Q

These extracts are taken from the diary of Major-General Sir Charles Napier.

1 *6.8.1839*

Poor people! They will suffer. They have set all England against them and their physical force: Fools! We have the physical force, not they. They talk of their hundred thousands of men. Who is to move them when I am dancing round them with cavalry, and pelting them with cannon-shot? What would their 100,000 men do with my 100 rockets wriggling their fiery tails among them, roaring, scorching, tearing, smashing all they came near?

2 *1.12.1839*

An anonymous letter came, with a Chartist plan. Poor creatures. Their threats of attack are miserable. With half a cartridge and half a pike, with no money, no discipline, no skilful leaders, they would attack men with leaders, money and discipline, well-armed and having sixty rounds a man. Poor men!

3 *12.1.1840*

Patrolled all last night. Saw the Chartist sentinels in the streets; we knew they were armed with pistols, but I advised the magistrates not to meddle with them. Seizing these men could do no good; it would not stop Chartism if they were all hanged, and if they offered no violence; why starve their wretched families and worry them with a long imprisonment?

From Charles Napier, *Life of General Sir Charles Napier*, published in 1857

SKILLS BUILDER

1 Read Sources O, P and Q. What can you learn from these three sources about:

    (a) the activities of the Chartists

    (b) the strength of the authorities?

2 Now read Source Q again.

    (a) Is Napier sympathetic or unsympathetic towards the Chartists?

    (b) How reliable a source of evidence is Source Q?

Question

After having read this section, do you think the authorities over-reacted to the Chartists?

The Newport Rising 1839

Once parliament had rejected the Petition, various local Chartist groups took matters into their own hands. Suspicion and rumour were everywhere. Some of the rumours were started by government agents; others by the Chartists themselves. In some towns, buildings and troops were stoned; in others, hand-to-hand fighting broke out between Chartists and troops or police. Some incidents, however, were more serious. The authorities paid particular attention to rumours that there was a plan to capture key towns in South Wales and establish a republic there.

What happened at Newport in November 1839?

On the night of 3 November 1839 a violent rebellion took place at Newport in South Wales. It was led by **John Frost**, who had been Newport's delegate at the Chartist Convention. Seven thousand coalminers and iron workers assembled at various points on the outskirts of the town, planning to march into the town and attack the Westgate Inn, where the mayor and magistrates were holding captive some fellow workers. Despite this widespread mobilisation, the 'Newport Rising' was poorly managed and disrupted by bad weather. People arrived at different times and some groups failed to arrive at all. The attack on the Westgate Inn took place in the early morning of 4 November. A small body of soldiers conducted a successful defence in a skirmish that only lasted about half an hour but which resulted in over 20 civilian deaths. By the end of the day, John Frost had been arrested and the authorities had little difficulty in regaining control.

Biography

John Frost (1784–1877)

John Frost was born in Newport but had also lived in Cardiff, Bristol and London, where he became increasingly involved in radical politics. Rising from an apprenticeship, he was a successful draper by the time he returned to Newport in 1806. As a reforming local politician, Frost served as councillor, magistrate and eventually mayor (1836–37). He was elected to the Chartist Convention in 1839 and the government therefore forced his removal from the magistracy. This turned Frost into a Chartist hero of national significance. At first he advocated peaceful protest but soon changed his views for reasons that are not entirely clear. After leading the abortive Newport Rising, Frost was swiftly arrested and tried for treason in December 1839. The resulting death sentence was commuted to transportation for life. Pardoned in 1854, Frost was later allowed to return to Britain, where he lived quietly until his death.

Source R

The attack of the Chartists on the Westgate Hotel, Newport, Nov. 4th 1839

A painting by James Flewitt Mullock entitled 'The Attack of the Chartists on the Westgate Hotel Newport', printed in 1840

SKILLS BUILDER

1 Study Source R. Mullock was a successful local artist. Can you suggest why he would want to paint this particular incident?

2 Does Source R have a message? Support your answer with evidence from the print.

3 What factors would affect the reliability and usefulness of Source R as evidence of the nature of, and motives for, the Newport Rising?

What really happened at Newport?

Source S–V all give slightly different versions of the Newport Rising. Read them carefully, then answer the questions relating to them.

Source S

Sunday last (3 November) the Mayor of Newport had intimation given him that the Chartists in great numbers were come to Newport that night. Up to six o'clock in the morning, ten or a dozen men were taken before the magistrates: pistols, cutlasses, pikes, and other weapons were found on them. Some little information was drawn from them as to the proceedings and intentions of the Chartists. About six o'clock in the morning the constables met a post chaise from Newport and further information was gained from the driver. Twenty or thirty of the soldiers were sent to the Westgate Inn, where the magistrates were sitting. About nine o'clock the Chartists came down Stow Hill, six or seven deep, with their pikes and different shaped irons fixed on sticks. At the right and left of these men were those that carried fire arms; when they arrived before the Westgate Inn, a signal was given to fire, which was immediately obeyed. The soldiers, who were stationed in the large room, now began to play their part, and in about twenty minutes the work of destruction was finished, the soldiers had done their duty, and the Chartists were running in all directions. Many were wounded severely and have since died, making as far as can be ascertained, twenty killed, and fifty wounded! The scene was horrible to look at. The whole of the front of the Westgate was smashed in. The lower rooms are perforated in many places by bullets, and in the stables were the bloody corpses of the unhappy rioters.

From *Dreadful Riot and Loss of Life at Newport*, a single-sheet broadside published locally, 12 November 1839

Source T

The parcel of people I saw were armed; they had guns, sticks, etc.; the sticks had iron points, I did not see many with guns. I saw of this body two hundred or three hundred men. I was a little bit alarmed, but not particularly so, but I wished to see what they would say or do. I did not know what they came to do. I never saw anything done to the windows of the Westgate. The body of the mob stood for a space, and asked for the prisoners who were taken before daylight. The first moment or two they asked for the prisoner Smith; then a rush was made. Then I heard firing, and took to my heels. I was distanced from the door of the Westgate twenty-five yards. I could not say where the firing began. No man could judge. You nor I could not tell. It is likely enough the firing began from the Westgate Inn.

Evidence given by Edward Patton, a local carpenter, at the trial of John Frost in December 1839

SKILLS BUILDER

1 Study Sources S and T. How far does the evidence of Edward Patton (Source T) support what was said in the broadside (Source S)?
2 What was the attitude of the writer of Source S towards the authorities and the rioters? How do you know?
3 Use evidence from Source T to show whether this would be more useful for the prosecution or defence of Frost.
4 What are the main problems of evidence and interpretation that can arise when analysing riots and popular protests?

What was the significance, for the Chartist Movement, of the Newport Rising?

Some historians believe the Newport Rising was supposed to spark off a general armed rising of Chartists against the government; others, that it was a spontaneous local action, intended to release a fellow Chartist from gaol. Either way, the Newport Rising was a massive Chartist failure and shed serious doubt on the effectiveness of the use of physical force.

Source U

There is no evidence that the Newport Rising was to be a signal for a general rising. Nor is there much sense in believing that the Chartists intended to 'seize' Newport. Their purpose was a mass demonstration; as a plan to capture the town it is patently absurd. Equally absurd is the theory that their purpose was to liberate **[Henry] Vincent**. There had been much talk of doing this. But Vincent was imprisoned in Monmouth; if the Chartists thought to liberate him they would not have brought the Pontypool men down to Newport, then making them almost retrace their steps before proceeding an equal distance in the opposite direction to Monmouth. The only reasonable explanation of the Newport riot is that it was intended as a monster demonstration.

From David Williams, *Chartism in Wales*, published in 1959

Biography

Henry Vincent (1813–78)

A member of the LWMA, Vincent was arrested in London in May 1839 on a warrant issued by Newport magistrates. His recent lecturing tour in Wales had allegedly resulted in 'riotous assemblage', for which he was sentenced to 12 months' imprisonment in Monmouth gaol. Although Vincent was not among the prisoners in Newport, his release may have been an ulterior objective of the rioters. Vincent was released in 1841 and was thereafter associated with moderate reform and teetotal Chartism.

Source V

The immediate aim of the insurgents was the release of Henry Vincent from Newport gaol; yet there is evidence to suggest that they were also bent on launching a massive uprising and creating a people's republic in the Welsh valleys, which hopefully might spread across Britain. The Newport Rising emerged from a rapidly expanding industrial society, strictly demarcated on class lines. The vast mining workforce not only revealed a remarkable capacity for self-help and self-reliance but also a sophisticated political ideology. The Newport Rising was a product of this radical political culture, rather than being simply a spontaneous protest of the hungry and downtrodden.

From D.G. Wright, *Popular Radicalism: the Working-Class Experience 1780–1880*, published in 1988

SKILLS BUILDER

Study Sources U and V. In what ways do these sources differ in their views about the Newport Rising? With which view do you agree, and why?

Why did widespread insurrection fail to materialise in 1839–40?

In the weeks preceding the Newport Rising, it appears that other rebellions were also planned for England. The precise details are shady and only a small group has been identified as involved in the planning: John Frost, John Taylor, William Burns, William Ashton and Peter Bussey. For reasons not entirely clear, difficulties emerged in co-ordinating a simultaneous rebellion. Requests for Frost to delay the Newport Rising were refused. The rapid failure of the Newport Rising made it less likely that unrest would break out in England. Nevertheless, there were pockets of Chartists in several South Yorkshire towns who were ready to fight. Anger was partly fed by outrage at the death sentence imposed on Frost. Plans for armed rebellion in Sheffield and nearby towns were made for the night of 11 January 1840; yet these failed to materialise because of increased vigilance by the authorities and the actions of an informer. Only a delayed and short-lived rising in Bradford actually took place. Plans had been made to seize shops, banks and the local ironworks in the hope of encouraging insurrections elsewhere. These would-be insurgents were swiftly repelled by a group of about 40 armed men on 26 January. Interpretations vary over the severity of the danger in 1839–40; but the government reaction is suggestive. Between June 1839 and July 1840 more than 500 Chartists were imprisoned, receiving sentences ranging from a few weeks to several years.

By 1840, then, the Chartist movement seemed to have collapsed. Parliament had refused even to consider the Charter. Troops and police had mopped up the rioting that had occurred, and many ordinary Chartists had seen the inside of prison for the first time. Chartist leaders, including William Lovett and Feargus O'Connor, were in prison. Others, like John Frost, had had their death sentence changed to transportation for life. There seemed no way in which working people could force the government to listen to them.

Unit summary

What have you learned in this unit?

You have learned that the rise of Chartism was a complex process. You have seen how it grew out of a reaction to the 1832 Reform Act, the 1834 Poor Law Amendment Act and various economic crises. You have appreciated that people became Chartists for a variety of reasons, some of which were economic and others, political. You have seen how 1839 was a critical year in rallying mass support for what had become a national movement, and how there was simply no agreed plan for what was to be done should parliament reject the six points of the People's Charter, which it did. You have considered the extent of the challenge to the government, and in particular the seriousness of the Newport Rising.

What skills have you used in this unit?

You have evaluated a range of different sources, including Chartist speeches, newspapers and imagery. In addition you have looked at contemporary criticisms of Chartism and the interpretations of historians. You have compared, cross-referenced and drawn inferences from these sources in order to reach judgements about the nature and impact of Chartism in the years to 1840.

Exam tips

Below is the sort of question you will find appearing on examination papers as a (b) question.

Study Source F, G and H, and use your own knowledge. How far do you agree with the view that Chartism was purely a political movement?

Here are some tips for answering these questions.

- **Do** be clear about the question focus. What is being claimed? In this case, what is being claimed is that Chartism was purely a political movement. You will need to define what you understand by this, so that the examiner can see how you use this criterion when you test it against the sources and your own knowledge.
- **Analyse** the sources to establish points that support and points that challenge the view given in the question.
- **Develop** each point by reference to your own wider knowledge, using it to reinforce and/or develop the points derived from the sources.
- **Combine** the points into arguments for and against the stated view.
- **Evaluate** the conflicting arguments.
- **Present** a judgement as to the validity of the stated view.
- And, above all, **plan** your answer.

RESEARCH TOPIC

Several people have appeared in this section as being important in various different parts of the Chartist movement. Select one from this list:

- John Frost
- George Julian Harney
- Henry Hetherington
- James Bronterre O'Brien.

Now research their life and work, focusing on the impact they had on the Chartist movement.

4 Challenges and consequences: Chartism 1841–58

What is this unit about?

This unit focuses on the revival of Chartism after the rejection of the first Petition and the failure of the Newport Rising. It examines the progress of the second Petition in 1842 and the third in 1848. Both Petitions were also rejected by parliament, although the build up to the third Petition led the government to fear revolution. This unit addresses in some depth the reasons for the failure of the Chartists to achieve their objectives, considering in particular the different and sometimes opposing strategies adopted by Chartist leaders and that leadership itself. It considers, too, the alternative activities undertaken by leading Chartists to help and empower working people and the success of these activities.

Key questions

- How close to revolution did the Chartists bring Britain in 1848?
- Why did Chartism fail to achieve its objectives?
- In what ways can Chartism be considered significant in the development of the political culture of working people?

Timeline

1840 July	**National Charter Association founded** The Chartist conference in Manchester forms the NCA and attempts to reinvigorate the movement Lovett released from prison Local groups nominate delegates to a general council
1841 April	**Second Chartist Petition launched** National Association founded by William Lovett as a rival to the more militant NCA
Aug	Feargus O'Connor released from prison
Sept	NCA agrees to present another Petition General trade depression leads to increased Chartist support
1842 April	**Presentation of second Petition to parliament** Chartist Convention meets in London
May	Second Chartist Petition rejected by parliament
Aug–Sept	Industrial unrest, including 'Plug Plot' riots supported by Chartists
October	Trials of Chartist leaders following their arrests
1843 March	**Chartist Land Plan established** O'Connor tried in Lancaster, convicted on minor charges and released
Sept	Chartist Convention agrees to support O'Connor's Land Plan to buy land on which to settle Chartists

1847	**Chartist settlement**
	First Chartists' colony (O'Connorville) opened in Hertfordshire
	O'Connor elected MP for Nottingham
1848	**Year of revolutions**
February	Revolution in France, followed by widespread revolutions across Europe
March	Riots in London, Manchester and Glasgow
April	Massive Chartist demonstration in London on Kennington Common; third Chartist Petition rejected by Parliament
May–June	Chartist riots in London and Bradford
	Chartist land colonies opened in Oxfordshire and Gloucestershire
1851	**Chartist Land Company closed down**
	Chartist Convention adopts programme of socio-democratic reform
August	National Co-operative Land Company wound up
Dec	Ernest Jones and George Julian Harney resign from the NCA
1852	**Ernest Jones and George Julian Harney in control of Chartism**
March	Last issue of the *Northern Star*
June	O'Connor declared insane
	Support drifts away as economy revives
1858	**Last Chartist Convention held**
	Agreement made to co-operate with moderates to press for further parliamentary reform

Source A

A contemporary print of the procession attending the Chartist Petition of 1842; the flags bear slogans such as 'Reform' and 'More Pigs Less Parsons', and a group of Chartists are carrying the Petition on their shoulders

SKILLS BUILDER

SKILLS BUILDER

Study Sources A and B. What can you learn from these sources, taken together, about:

(a) the revival of Chartism after what appeared to be its collapse in 1840

(b) the significance of the 1842 Petition?

Source B

A petition from the working classes throughout the kingdom ... was brought down to the House, by a procession consisting of a vast multitude. Its bulk was so great that the doors were not wide enough to admit it, and it was necessary to unroll it, to carry it into the House. When unrolled, it spread over a great part of the floor, and rose above the level of the Table.

From *Hansard*, an official record of parliamentary proceedings, 2 May 1842

Chartism was in considerable disarray following the wave of arrests and trials in 1839–40 (see page 61). However, it quickly recovered because the will and desire to persuade parliament to accept the six points of the Charter was still there.

- As early as August 1839, Henry Hetherington (see page 44) headed up a Chartist revival in Scotland with delegates meeting in Glasgow to promote Chartism, and with the publication of a weekly journal, the *Chartist Circular*.

- Next, Hetherington turned his attention to England where, in April 1840, he set up a Metropolitan Charter Union.

- Although in prison, **Feargus O'Connor** continued to write letters to the *Northern Star*, championing the Chartist cause and pointing to the way forward.

All was most certainly not lost.

Biography

Feargus O'Connor (c. 1796–1855)

O'Connor became the most important Chartist leader, especially during the 1840s. In his early career he was associated with the Irish radical Daniel O'Connell but separated from him over various issues. Associated with London radicalism, O'Connor later shifted his focus to the northern industrial areas where his charismatic and flamboyant style gained him many followers. He established the *Northern Star* newspaper in 1837, which became an important vehicle for the transmission of his views, though he did not exercise direct editorial control. His approach was very different from that of **William Lovett**. It is conventional to see O'Connor as an advocate of physical force as opposed to moral force, but this is far too simplistic. O'Connor was not a straightforward revolutionist, and to him the language and threat of violence were part of a political strategy. In 1839 he avoided involvement in the Newport Rising and the abortive insurrections in England. He was nevertheless imprisoned for 18 months during 1840–41 for seditious libel (criticising the government and monarchy). At the head of a potentially revolutionary movement in 1848, O'Connor took care to prevent clashes between Chartists and the authorities. An Irish gentleman of independent means, he was unlike the stereotypical artisan Chartist. O'Connor was twice elected to parliament as MP for Cork: first in 1832 (as an O'Connellite); and again in 1847 as MP for Nottingham (as a Chartist). It was in this latter capacity that he presented the 1848 Petition, which marked the height of his national fame but also appears with hindsight as the beginning of a decline in public reputation. His idealistic Land Plan has often been criticised as impractical and backward looking. It certainly ended in failure but this was not entirely his fault. In his last years, O'Connor suffered serious mental illness.

Biography

William Lovett (1800–77)

Lovett was strongly associated with what has become known as 'Moral Force' Chartism. Certainly, he was highly critical of violent language, let alone action. Lovett clashed with Feargus O'Connor over rhetoric and strategy, famously dismissing him as 'The Great I Am'. Lovett's radical career may be divided roughly in two. The first phase saw Lovett progress from agitation for parliamentary reform during the 1820s to bitter resentment at the alleged betrayal of 1832. In 1836 he founded the London Working Men's Association (LWMA), from which emerged the Chartist movement. A leading member of the National Convention, Lovett was arrested in 1839, following the Birmingham riots, and spent a year in prison. Thereafter, Lovett focused on educational reform and self-help, more commonly referred to as 'Knowledge Chartism', setting out his philosophy in *Chartism: A New Organization for the People* (1840). He remained an influential figure for the next few years but became increasingly marginalised from mainstream Chartism after 1842. In later life Lovett advocated various worthy causes including teetotalism, international peace and the abolition of slavery.

The National Charter Association

Beginnings

The stirrings of a Chartist revival inspired the formation of the National Charter Association (NCA) in July 1840. The NCA was to become the major national organisation for Chartism over the following decade. Local Chartist and other working men's associations were drawn into the NCA; in April 1841 the NCA claimed to have 13,000 members, which by April 1842 had grown to 50,000. This enormous increase in support, even though it was probably exaggerated, was due partly to an economic downturn but largely to the influence of O'Connor. He had influenced NCA policy while in gaol through letters and directives to leading Chartists and through his column in the *Northern Star*. Once released from prison, his dominance over the movement was clear.

Source C

At the end of August 1841, Feargus O'Connor, 'the lion of freedom', came from his den in York Castle gaol. Chartism's most dynamic leader was again free and able to breathe life into what he considered to be *his* movement. In triumph he toured the country, feeding his enormous sense of self-importance on the cheers and congratulations of his loyal subjects. At one such meeting in Birmingham in September, Peter [Murray] McDouall proposed a plan for another National Petition and Convention. The NCA took up the proposal, and plans went ahead for a Convention to meet in London in February (later deferred to April) 1842.

From Edward Royle, *Chartism*, published in 1980

Source D

The lion of freedom comes from his den,
We'll rally around him again and again,
We'll crown him with laurels our champion to be,
O'Connor, the patriot of sweet liberty.

The pride of the nation, he's noble and brave
He's the terror of tyrants, the friend of the slave,
The bright star of freedom, the noblest of men,
We'll rally around him again and again.

Though proud daring tyrants his body confined,
They never could alter his generous mind;
We'll hail our caged lion, now free from his den,
And we'll rally around him again and again.

Who strove for the patriots? Was up night and day?
And saved them from falling to tyrants a prey?
It was Feargus O'Connor was diligent then!
We'll rally around him again and again.

From the *Northern Star*, 11 September 1841

SKILLS BUILDER

1 Read Source C. To what extent is the author critical of Feargus O'Connor's leadership?

2 Now read Source D. How far does it support the view of O'Connor given in Source C?

Better organisation – but still rejection

The NCA had a formal constitution and a mass membership paying subscriptions that funded propaganda activities and the payment of officials. Members of the Convention that was to meet to plan for another Petition (see Source C) were elected by paid-up members of the NCA, and it was the NCA that organised a new Chartist Convention and the second Petition. This was all far more competently organised than the lead up to the first Petition had been, and a total of 3,317,752 signatures were collected.

Source A shows something of the enthusiasm this second Petition seems to have generated but, again, it was all to no avail. The House of Commons voted by 287 to 49 not to consider the Petition, let alone debate the six points!

What about William Lovett?

William Lovett had written the six points of the People's Charter and played an active part in the movement although he had always favoured peaceful, persuasive methods. He, like many other Chartists, had been arrested, tried and imprisoned in 1839. While in Warwick gaol he and John Collins, another Chartist, wrote *Chartism: A New Organization for the People*. In it, they proposed a national system of education, funded by a penny tax on all those who signed the Chartist Petition. Lovett remained convinced that it was essential to educate the working classes, making them worthy of the vote (and convincing the middle classes that they were) and able to use it intelligently.

Released from gaol in July 1840, Lovett began to implement his scheme for a 'National Association for the Moral, Social and Political Improvement of the People'. O'Connor was furious. He denounced Lovett's scheme in the *Northern Star*, criticising it as destroying Chartist unity. He used his position within the National Charter Association to stir up opposition to Lovett and the National Association – and he succeeded. In the northern industrial towns, for example, Lovett and Collins' work was roundly condemned as deflecting Chartism from its main objective. From 1841 onwards, Lovett was increasingly to devote himself to the educational side of Chartism, leaving O'Connor to steam ahead with his aggression and his National Charter Association.

> **Question**
>
> Would the obvious split between O'Connor and Lovett be likely to strengthen or weaken the Chartist movement?

1842: a summer of discontent

After the failure of the May 1842 Petition, Chartists were left to re-think their strategies and tactics, and re-group their supporters. This re-thinking was carried out against a background of severe economic crises and social distress as the country was plunged into a severe industrial depression, and waves of strikes and associated rioting swept through the industrial areas of the Midlands and North.

What were the 'Plug Plot' riots?

The catalyst to industrial unrest began with wage cutting by mine owners in Staffordshire. Trouble quickly spread to the textile industry, when the mill owners of Ashton-under-Lyne and Stalybridge decided to reduce wages in the face of a trade downturn. Two mill owners changed their minds in the face of fierce opposition from their weavers; the others did not and so the workers went out on strike.

Mass meetings and marches followed, and by 11 August most of the cotton mills, dye works and machine shops in Manchester and the surrounding area had stopped work, leaving approximately 50,000 workmen idle. A conference of delegates from all the trades involved met in Manchester, appealed for law and order, and, importantly, endorsed the Charter. Unrest quickly spread across the Pennines to Yorkshire, where one of the techniques used by strikers was to draw the plugs from boilers, thus putting out the furnaces. Without steam, factories and mills couldn't work. This technique was extremely effective because it prevented employers from bringing in strike-breaking workers.

The strikes continued into September 1842 but had been largely suppressed by October, with around 1,500 arrests and a tightening of control by the police and military.

Source E

The number of men and women who marched up to Mr Akroyd's mill [near Halifax] could not be less than 10,000. Two of their number demanded an interview with Mr Akroyd, at which they insisted that the plugs should be drawn out of the boilers. Mr Akroyd not only agreed to this modest request, but also permitted one of his workmen to assist. They then not only requested, but insisted, that the reservoir should be let off. On this point they were met, on the part of Mr Akroyd, with a decided negative for by turning off the reservoir, the works would have been stopped for several weeks. A £5 note was tendered to the men to induce them to go quietly about their usual work. This temptation not having the desired effect, the military were hastily sent for. The soldiers secured six young men for riotous conduct.

From the *Leeds Mercury*, 20 August 1842 (Akroyd had reduced wages paid to his workers by 20 per cent)

Source F

From the *Illustrated London News* showing the Preston riot of 13 August 1842

Source G

The mob then proceeded down Lune-street [in Preston], followed by the military, and when near the Corn exchange halted. The Riot Act was then read, and Chief-constable Woodford, and Mr Banister, superintendent of police, endeavoured to persuade the mob to retire. One of the rioters aimed a stone so surely at Captain Woodford that it felled him to the ground, and while there he had the brutality to kick him. Immense bodies of stones were now thrown at the police and soldiers. Under these circumstances, orders were given to fire; the military immediately obeyed. It is scarcely known how many have been wounded, but it is supposed 12 to 15, some of them mortally.

From *The Times*, 5 August 1842

SKILLS BUILDER

1 Read Source E. What were the strengths and weaknesses of the method of protest described?

2 Study Sources F and G, which describe the same riot. In what ways do they reveal the intentions of those publishing them and the ways in which they would appeal to their readers?

3 Now look back over all three sources, E–G, each of which is from a newspaper or journal. Using them as examples, explain the strengths and weaknesses of using this sort of media as evidence.

Source H

That while the Chartist body did not originate the present cessation from labour, this conference of delegates strongly approve the extension and continuance of their present struggle till the People's Charter becomes legislative enactment and pledge ourselves, on our return to our respective localities, to give proper direction to the people's efforts.

From a speech by a leading Chartist, Peter Murray McDouall, to the NCA executive conference, 17 August 1842

What was the connection between the 'Plug Plot' riots and the Chartists?

It would seem, from the available evidence, that the Chartists did not initiate the strikes and associated violence; in fact, in many ways the 'Plug Plot' riots took them by surprise. Nevertheless, they were quick to take advantage of the unrest, particularly as many strikers were Chartists. The situation was further complicated by the fact that, as the delegates representing the striking workers were meeting in Manchester, so was the Executive of the National Charter Association. They were there to unveil a statue of the radical Henry Hunt on the anniversary of Peterloo (see pages 10 and 11). Although they met immediately to discuss the situation created by the 'Plug Plot' riots, not all of them supported Peter Murray McDouall's motion that the NCA give official support to the strike, although the majority agreed with O'Connor that they had been presented with a marvellous opportunity to show Chartist solidarity with the trades delegates.

Source I

Our columns have been filled with particulars of the strangest and wildest Holiday-Insurrection that has ever been attempted; an Insurrection the most extensive, an Insurrection more foolish than wicked in the dupes who have caught the contagion, but we fear, much more wicked than foolish in the leaders who planned it.

If any class is so deplorably ignorant as to imagine that they are observing law and order while they are ranging the country, forcibly putting a stop to industry, crippling the first movement of every mill and every workshop, driving the workmen from their labour, and preventing the masters from making use of their own lawful property, and all this for the avowed purpose of overawing the government, and compelling it to change the Constitution; if, we say, any class is so deplorably ignorant as to think that acts like these are justifiable, are honest, are consistent with the existence of Freedom or of Peace; if they think that the Terror inspired, the Tyranny exercised, and the immense Danger incurred, may be excused because the authors of these acts do not commit wholesale destruction, rapine and bloodshed. However much we may commiserate with such ignorance, it is necessary for every friend of his country to exclaim with a voice of earnest warning and indignant reprehension, that law and order must be maintained.

From an editorial in the *Leeds Mercury*, 20 August 1842

Source J

After working in the factory for seven years, a reduction of wages began to worry me. There were some masters who always wanted to give less wages than others. Seeing this to be an evil, and knowing that all depended on the wages of the common man, I became an opponent to the reduction of wages to the bottom of my soul; and, as long as I live, I shall continue to keep up the wages of labour to the utmost of my power. For taking part in Stockport, and being the means of preventing many reductions of wages, the masters combined as one man against me and neither me nor my children could get a day's employment.

From the evidence of Richard Pilling, a power-loom worker and a Chartist, charged in 1843 with offences relating to the 'Plug Plot' riots

Source K

The Chartists did not create the grievances, nor the economic depression which caused employers to demand wage reductions, but they did organise the workers' reaction and turned local strikes into a concerted challenge to the forces of law and order and ultimately the government itself. They did so all the more effectively because they were not outside agitators with an abstract political programme but members of their own local communities. The strikes of 1842 were more than industrial actions. Local Chartist leaders provided organisation and co-ordination and directed the strikes to a political end.

From Edward Royle, *Revolutionary Britannia*, published in 2000

SKILLS BUILDER

1 Read Source I. The *Leeds Mercury* was a newspaper read widely by mill and factory owners. How far was its reporting of the 'Plug Plot' riots likely to reflect and form their views?

2 Now read Source J. How would Richard Pilling argue with the editor of the *Leeds Mercury* that he was right to strike? Set up a debate between the two men. Who will win?

3 Read Source K. Reflect on Sources H–J and on what you know about the 'Plug Plot' riots. How likely is it that Edward Royle was correct about Chartist involvement in them?

The strikes continued into September but had been largely suppressed by October, with around 1,500 arrests and a tightening of control by the police and military. The link between strike action and the Charter was significant, but this strategy had never stood much chance of overawing the government. The authorities could hold out longer than the strikers. Although Chartist leaders including O'Connor were tried in Lancaster in 1843 and found guilty, they were never called up for sentence owing to a fault in the indictment. As in 1839, the government balanced vigorous action with a degree of leniency to avoid creating a popular backlash. Moreover, the harvest of 1842–43 had been good and the economic depression had lifted. There was work to be had and strikers returned to their workplaces. There were no further serious outbreaks of unrest until 1848.

Case study

1848: why was there no British revolution?

There was a sharp economic downturn in 1847 caused by a commercial crisis and a bad harvest. In the early months of 1848 there was a revival of Chartist activity, and signatures were collected for a third national Petition. A Chartist Convention met in London and organised a mass meeting for 10 April. The plan was to assemble on Kennington Common, south of the River Thames, and march from there to present the Petition to parliament. The proceedings of the Convention were reported in detail in the newspapers and a great deal of attention was given to the inflammatory language of some Chartists. Tension was heightened by recent events in Europe: a series of revolutions, triggered by popular protests in capital cities, had toppled old regimes across several countries. Perhaps the Chartist demonstration would lead to the same outcome in Britain?

Source L

Glory to the Proletarians of Paris. Germany is revolutionised from end to end. Princes are flying, thrones are perishing. Everywhere the oppressors of nations yield, or are overthrown. 'Reform or Revolution' is now the order of the day. How long, Men of Great Britain and Ireland, how long will you carry the damning stigma of being the only people in Europe who dare not will their freedom?

From an editorial by George Julian Harney in the *Northern Star*, 25 March 1848

Source M

CHARTIST
DEMONSTRATION!!
"PEACE and ORDER" is our MOTTO!

TO THE WORKING MEN OF LONDON.

Fellow Men, —The Press having misrepresented and vilified us and our intentions, the Demonstration Committee therefore consider it to be their duty to state that the grievances of us (the Working Classes) are deep and our demands just. We and our families are pining in misery, want, and starvation! We demand a fair day's wages for a fair day's work! We are the slaves of capital—we demand protection to our labour. We are political serfs,—we demand to be free. We therefore invite all well disposed to join in our peaceful procession on

MONDAY NEXT, April 10,

As it is for the good of all that we seek to remove the evils under which we groan.

The following are the places of Meeting of THE CHARTISTS, THE TRADES, THE IRISH CONFEDERATE & REPEAL BODIES:
East Division on Stepney Green at 8 o'clock; City and Finsbury Division on Clerkenwell Green at 9 o'clock; West Division in Russell Square at 9 o'clock; and the South Division in Peckham Fields at 9 o'clock, and proceed from thence to Kennington Common.

Signed on behalf of the Committee, JOHN ARNOTT, *Sec.*

A Chartist poster advertising the meeting on Kennington Common on 10 April 1848

Source N

The present question is, 'Shall an organised mob be allowed to approach the vitals of the metropolis?' We answer plainly, No. There may be only a row, and a few heads deservedly broken, but even that had better be avoided. There may be something worse than a row. Within these six weeks everything unexpected has come to pass. Half the royal and imperial cities of Europe have fallen into the hands of mobs: Paris, Vienna, Berlin, Rome, Naples, Palermo, Turin, Milan, Venice, Munich. Wherever the army and police have been beaten in the streets, it was for want of a timely and energetic resistance. This is not the time to play with public safety and tamper with sedition.

From *The Times* newspaper, 6 April 1848

Source O

A PHYSICAL FORCE CHARTIST ARMING FOR THE FIGHT.

A cartoon from *Punch* magazine, published in the run-up to the Chartist meeting on Kennington Common on 10 April 1848

SKILLS BUILDER

1 Study Sources L and M. How far does Source M support George Harney's rallying cry, published in the *Northern Star* on 25 March 1848 (Source L)?

2 Now read Source N. How justified was *The Times* in its fears?

3 Look carefully at Source O. What point is the cartoonist making? Does this mean that the proposed Kennington Common rally wasn't a threat to the government at all?

Did the government really take the threat of revolution seriously? They certainly seemed to. The Queen was moved to the safety of Osborne on the Isle of Wight, although the Foreign Secretary Lord Palmerston worried that the defences of the island were inadequate, and the Duke of Wellington was put in charge of the defence of London. Eight thousand soldiers were called up, along with 1,500 Chelsea Pensioners (who were all ex-soldiers) and some 150,000 special constables enrolled. Property owners in the capital seemed excessively nervous and feared that this was the start of an English revolution.

Source P

It is intended that no opposition shall be offered to the assembling of persons on the Common, provided they do not appear armed and their conduct and demeanour is peaceable and orderly. The police authorities will give them notice the petition will be allowed to proceed, but that orders have been given not to permit such procession to pass over any of the bridges. If an attempt shall be made to force a passage, it is confidently anticipated that the police will be able successfully to resist. In order, however, to be prepared, a military force composed of both cavalry and Infantry will be posted in the immediate neighbourhood. If the conduct of the persons whose progress shall have been stopped shall be peaceable and orderly, they may be allowed, on the expiration of an hour after the petition has gone forward, to pass in small numbers at a time. Parties of police and special constables will patrol the streets and prevent the assemblage of any number of persons and any obstruction to the thoroughfares.

From a memorandum by the Home Secretary Sir George Grey, dated 9 April 1848

Source Q

The measures of the government, devised and perfectly worked out by the Duke of Wellington, were on a large and complete scale, though so arranged as not to obtrude themselves needlessly on the view. The Thames' bridges were the main points of concentration; bodies of foot and horse police, and assistant masses of special constables, being posted at their approaches on either side. In the immediate neighbourhood of each of them within call, a strong force of military was kept ready for instant movement. At other places, also, bodies of troops were posted, out of sight, but within sudden command. The public offices at the West End, at Somerset House and in the City, were profusely furnished with arms; and such places as the Bank of England were packed with troops and artillery, and strengthened with sandbag parapets on their walls, and timber barricading of their windows, each pierced with loopholes for the fire of defensive musketry. In addition to the regular civil and military force, it is credibly estimated that at least 120,000 special constables were sworn and organised throughout the metropolis, for the stationary defence of their own districts, or as movable bodies to cooperate with soldiery and police.

From the *Annual Register*, published in 1848

Question

What impression do Sources P and Q give of the government's preparations for the defence of London?

The police, fearing the worst, asked Feargus O'Connor to deliver the Petition to parliament by himself and not at the head of a large – and possibly threatening – procession of Chartists. O'Connor, perhaps afraid that he could not control vast hordes of Chartists if they became violent, agreed. When the day came, crowds of Chartists assembled on Kennington Common to listen to O'Connor address the virtues of the Charter. Numbers in the crowd vary between O'Connor (500,000), Gammage (170,000–150,000) and Lord John Russell, the Prime Minister (12,000–15,000). Half a million people could not fit onto the Common, and it is likely that Russell under-estimated the figure. So the number of Chartists and Chartist supporters actually on the Common (and, according to many, preparing to overthrow the government) would probably be around 20,000 people in all. There was no violence, and the crowd, having listened to O'Connor, peacefully dispersed. The Petition was taken to the House of Commons in three cabs, and Feargus O'Connor left in another cab to assure Sir George Grey, the Home Secretary, that all was well.

Source R

Yesterday was a glorious day, the Waterloo of peace and order. Men of all classes and ranks were blended together in defence of law and property. The Chartists made a poor figure and did not muster more than fifteen thousand on the Common. Feargus was frightened out of his wits and was made the happiest man in England at being told that the procession could not pass the bridges.

From a letter by the Foreign Secretary, Lord Palmerston to a fellow Whig, Lord Normanby, dated 11 April 1848

Source S

The Kennington Common Meeting has proved a complete failure. About 12,000 or 15,000 persons met in good order. Feargus O'Connor, upon arriving on the ground, was ordered by Mr Mayne [the Commissioner of Police] to come and speak to him. He immediately came, looking pale and frightened. Upon being told that the meeting would not be prevented, but that no procession would be allowed to pass the bridges, he expressed the utmost thanks, and begged to shake Mr Mayne by the hand. He then addressed the crowd, advising them to disperse, and after rebuking them for their folly he went off in a cab to the Home Office, where he repeated to Sir George Grey his thanks, his fears and his assurances that the crowd should disperse quietly. Sir George Grey said that he had done very rightly.

The last account gave the numbers as 5,000 rapidly dispersing.

The mob was in good humour, and any mischief that now takes place will be the act of individuals; but it is to be hoped the preparations made will daunt those wicked but not brave men.

The accounts from the country are good. Scotland is quiet. At Manchester, however, the Chartists are armed and have bad designs.

A quiet termination of the present ferment will greatly raise us in foreign countries.

Lord John Russell trusts your Majesty has profited by the sea air.

From a report sent by the Prime Minister, Lord John Russell, to Queen Victoria, on the afternoon of 10 April 1848

SKILLS BUILDER

Read Sources R–T and use your own knowledge. How credible do you find these explanations of the ending of the 'revolution' on Kennington Common?

Source T

The government, I believe, knew better than the press or its propertied readers what would happen, but ultimately found it convenient to behave as if it shared its illusions. There was a substantial political dividend to be earned by slaying a paper tiger, which so many thought was real. Russell and Grey kept their heads for the good reason that they were amply informed and anyone with sense could see there was nothing to fear in the way of violence. Russell, however, was eventually persuaded to let the Duke have his way and post soldiers since it dawned on him that credit was to be got by appearing to be 'firm and vigorous' as all the 'be up and at 'em' brigade from the Duke downwards were demanding. It would raise British prestige abroad enormously and wipe out the impression of feebleness that the government had given earlier in the year by its mishandling of financial questions.

From David Large, *London in the Year of Revolutions*, published in 1977

What happened to the Petition?

This time, government officials did read the Petition. The signatures were counted and inspected. It was found that, far from the 6 millions that Feargus O'Connor had claimed, there were slightly fewer than 2 millions, and many were discounted because the signatures were clearly fictitious: 'Victoria Rex', the 'Duke of Wellington' and 'Punch', for example. Others were all written in the same hand and so were also discounted. Yet this isn't quite fair. It was common, at that time, to sign with names that were clearly fictitious for fear of retribution from the authorities. Additionally, many people could not write, not even their own name, and, again, it was usual to get others who could write to sign for them. Even so, the Petition had nowhere near the millions of signatures claimed for it, and the government was easily able to turn it, and the Chartists, into a laughing stock.

There were no more mass meetings and no more petitions. Chartism, or so it seemed, was over. It is appropriate, perhaps, to let that veteran Chartist, Robert Gammage and the historian Edward Royle have the final words about Kennington Common.

Source U

O'Connor was wrong, not in abandoning the procession, but in having encouraged so long the empty braggarts, and enthusiastic but mistaken men of the Convention, and in inducing them, almost to the last moment, to believe that he would head the procession to the House of Commons. The boasting which took place on this subject, and the miserable result, inflicted a wound on Chartism from which it has never recovered.

From Robert Gammage, *History of the Chartist Movement,* published in 1854

Source V

The sense of anti-climax after 10 April is more a measure of the fear (feigned or real) of the government, and of the very real scare which its supporters had experienced, than of the degree of Chartist failure. The subsequent attempt to portray the meeting and the petition as fiascos is as much ideological as historical. Chartism was made to look ridiculous, Chartists were made to feel ridiculous; their self-confidence was gradually undermined by the (largely retrospective) scorn of the propertied classes.

From Edward Royle, *Chartism*, published in 1980

SKILLS BUILDER

1 Read Sources U and V. Who, or what, do Gammage and Royle blame for the failure of the Kennington Common rally to bring about revolution?

2 Use any sources in this case study, along with your own knowledge, to explain which author you agree with.

Why did the Chartists fail to achieve the six points of the People's Charter?

In analysing the reasons why the Chartists failed to achieve the six points of their Charter, historians and contemporaries have focused on Chartist leadership and Chartist tactics. Both, of course, are tightly linked: different leadership styles generated different tactics and different supporters. Leadership was vitally important to the Chartists and to their movement. Most supporters were poorly educated and many struggled with desperate economic distress, leaving no time for quiet reflection. They relied on their leaders to show them the way forward through inspiring speeches, rallies and by example.

Leadership

It was clear that William Lovett's leadership style focused less on confrontation and more on persuasion (see Unit 3). Following his imprisonment in 1839, Lovett moved out of mainstream leadership, and the 'voice' of Chartism became that of Feargus O'Connor. Indeed O'Connor never forgave Lovett for founding the National Association for the Moral, Social and Political Improvement of the People (see pages 68–69). It is therefore to O'Connor's leadership skills and style that we must now turn.

Feargus O'Connor's leadership

O'Connor's leadership has been criticised as indecisive and cowardly. Contemporary critics such as William Lovett and Robert Gammage disliked O'Connor's leadership style and disapproved of his blustering language. They also believed that he had fatal character flaws – a desire for domination and an inflated sense of his own importance. In part this was nothing but 'sour grapes'. Lovett's less flamboyant style and his focus on moral improvement failed to catch the imagination of a mass movement. Nevertheless, the charge that O'Connor 'failed' the movement has some substance.

In 1839 O'Connor initially approved of the idea of a general strike, but later persuaded the Chartist Convention to abandon it. During the 'Plug Plots' in 1842, O'Connor was overtaken by events, only belatedly and half-heartedly giving support. He originally thought that the strikes were part of a middle-class plot, and continued to harbour doubts, believing that strikes would be insufficient to force the authorities to back down. In 1848 O'Connor was ridiculed for his decision to hold the mass meeting on Kennington Common, while at the same time tamely accepting the government ban on the planned procession to parliament.

O'Connor, in fact, showed decisive leadership in 1839, consulting with local associations and recognising that the 'sacred month' was impractical. He therefore acted decisively to reverse an ill-judged policy. A similar defence can be made over the 'Plug Plots'. He was probably right to have doubts about Chartists assuming national leadership over a series of diverse economic protests that had not been coherently planned. O'Connor did manage to regain a measure of influence over the strike movement, but was tried for seditious conspiracy as a result.

Was O'Connor to blame for the 1848 'failure'?

O'Connor was convinced of the moral principles behind Chartism and that the injustice of government repression would be revealed by Chartist protests. The threat of physical confrontation was a necessary strategy, but O'Connor was not prepared to 'sacrifice' his supporters simply to create propaganda. It made sense, therefore, to avoid violence on 10 April 1848. The Chartists could not hope to win against impossible odds, and the location of the meeting – on the wrong side of the River Thames – indicated that a revolutionary clash was never intended. Many Chartists had actually marched peacefully across the river earlier in the day. This would have made no sense if the plan had been to seize key locations in Whitehall and Westminster. Nevertheless, O'Connor's actions were a gift to the authorities, which immediately began propagating the myth of 1848 as a 'fiasco' caused by the 'cowardice' of O'Connor.

Tactics

There is no escaping the weight of evidence that a perceived division existed within Chartism between proponents of moral and physical force. This featured in contemporary speeches and newspapers, and became an important theme in early histories of Chartism. More recently, however, historians have challenged the idea that there was a simple and sharp division. The terms 'moral' and 'physical' force tend to obscure what was held in common by Chartists, and fails to reflect the range of views that existed. The alleged split into two camps – on the one hand peaceful protesters; and on the other violent revolutionaries – was used by early historians to explain why Chartism failed. Moral force was generally treated sympathetically and associated with William Lovett, while blame was heaped on those who used the language of physical force, especially O'Connor.

One of the main problems with a traditional interpretation that splits Chartism into neat categories of 'Moral' and 'Physical' force is that it tends to take too literal a view of the language of Chartism. Certainly there were differences of emphasis, and some Chartists were far more inclined to encourage direct action than were others. Yet it is important to realise that the use of inflammatory language should not be confused with actual violence. In many cases, the language of physical force was a device rather than a call to arms.

Source W

I regard Fergus O'Connor as the chief **marplot** of our movement. He began his career by ridiculing our 'moral force **humbuggery**!' By trickery and deceit, he got the aid of the working classes to establish an instrument, the *Northern Star*, for destroying everything intellectual and moral in our movement. By his constant appeals to the selfishness, vanity, and mere animal propensities of man, he succeeded in calling up a spirit of hate, intolerance and brute feeling. I will have nothing to do with such a man, knowing him to be politically and morally dishonest.

From the *Life and Struggles of William Lovett*, an autobiography written from the 1840s onwards but not published until 1876

Source X

Quarrelling was almost inevitable when not one man but many men desire to become dictators. It was almost equally inevitable when such a man as Feargus O'Connor, who had few of the qualities of a powerful leader save extraordinary force of character, had acquired absolute dominion. The common notion of O'Connor outside the ranks of his personal followers was that he was a **charlatan** and a humbug. A more correct notion would have been that he was a victim of his own delusions.

From W.E. Adams, *Memoirs of a Social Atom*, published in 1903; Adams (1832–1906) was a radical journalist and former supporter of Chartism

Definitions

Marplot

A person who spoils something by meddling or interfering.

Humbuggery

A hoax, fraud or sham meant to deceive or cheat.

Charlatan

Someone who falsely claims a special skill or expertise.

Household suffrage

Giving the vote to the male head of a household.

Source Y

O'Connor has often been severely criticised for having exerted an undemocratic 'dictatorial' control over the Chartist movement. The central problem of national Chartist leadership was the maintenance of radical working-class unity. The magnitude of this task should not be forgotten. With remarkable forbearance, energy and enthusiasm O'Connor battled to overcome the divisions within the working class movement. Both from outside and within the Chartist ranks the movement was faced with a series of 'rival' or alternative agitations. In the spring of 1841, O'Connor published his famous condemnation of 'Church Chartism, Teetotal Chartism, Knowledge Chartism and **Household Suffrage** Chartism'. His opposition was based upon his fears that these various tendencies might become splinter groups, dissipating the movement's strength.

From James Epstein, *The Lion of Freedom: Feargus O'Connor and the Chartist Movement*, published in 1982

SKILLS BUILDER

Read Sources W–Y. How far does Source Y challenge the views of Feargus O'Connor given in Sources W and X?

The power of the state

Major General Charles Napier wrote in his diary (see Source Q, page 56): 'Fools! We have the physical force, not they.' This was exactly the point. Whatever powers of persuasion, either by force or argument, or both, the Chartists possessed, it was nothing compared to the power of the state. You read (on pages 57–59) about the ways in which the Newport Rising was put down in 1839 and (on page 73) about the ways in which the government avoided direct confrontation during and after the Kennington Common meeting in 1848. Throughout this unit and Unit 3 you have seen how local outbreaks of violence were always contained and ended by the forces of authority. How had this been possible?

- By the late 1830s and 1840s, the government had built up a wealth of experience in dealing with riots and violent demonstrations. They knew, for example, not to create martyrs and they achieved this by their technique of imprisoning Chartists for short periods of time. You have seen how this was done at critical times such as 1839–40, 1842 and in 1848. Chartist leaders, both local and national, were under constant threat of imprisonment.

- Legislation was in place for the creation of new, professional police forces. This applied to London in 1829 and to the counties from 1839. Recruitment was steady, and the new police forces were increasingly used by the authorities to contain and control demonstrations – some of which could, and did, turn violent.

- The 1830s and 1840s were periods of great railway building: by 1840, 1,500 miles of track linked most of Britain's major towns and cities and this had risen to almost 6,000 miles by 1848. The government made full use of the rail network to move troops (for example, Napier and his men) quickly to any trouble spots.

- The government could command huge numbers of men to control any Chartist outbreak – far more than any Chartist demonstration or rally could raise. Look back at the numbers deployed to control the Kennington Common meeting (page 75). Of particular significance were the special constables. Most of them came from the middle classes, enrolled for specific events and dedicated to support the government in maintaining law and order and to protect property.

- The Whig strategy, in engineering the 1832 Reform Act (see Units 1 and 2), had been to separate the middle classes from what had seemed like a dangerous alliance with the working classes. In this, they had largely been successful. The post-1832 government felt far more confident in repressing working-class movements, secure in the knowledge that the newly enfranchised middle classes would support them.

Source Z

The political interpretation is attractive because it offers a subtler reason for the movement's decline than a simple improvement in living standards. For if Chartism was rooted in the belief that the state was corrupt, all that politicians had to do was to prove that it was not so. Hence – so the argument goes – it was the 'political' aspects of the government's economic reforms that did the trick. By taxing the upper-middle class incomes in 1842, by clamping down on financial speculation with the Bank Charter Act of 1844, and above all by removing the landlords' corn monopoly in 1846, Peel effected the moral rehabilitation of the state, and thereby undermined Chartism more effectively than any mere repression could have done.

From Boyd Hilton, *A Mad, Bad and Dangerous People*, published in 2006

- Not all state activity was repressive. One of the main planks in the Chartists' argument was that only by getting working-class people (probably men) into parliament would legislation be enacted to improve their lot. This argument was partially undermined by the policies of Robert Peel's Tory government (1841–46) and by the Whig administration of Lord John Russell (1846–52). The Factory Acts of 1844 and 1847, for example, and the Mines Act of 1842, together with the repeal of the Corn Laws in 1846 would seem to indicate that the government was moving towards ruling in the interests of the whole nation and not just the propertied classes.

What did the Chartists achieve?

It is clear that the Chartists failed to achieve the six points of the People's Charter. They had failed, even, to persuade parliament to debate them. However, these obvious failures have tended to overshadow what was achieved. This is partly because failure was dramatic, well-documented and clearly explained. Success was far less tangible but even the more significant for that.

Working-class consciousness

Chartism was the first genuinely working-class movement in Britain. Meeting in church halls, public houses and back kitchens, talking about their concerns and then meeting up with other like-minded people in mass meetings, gave working people an enormous sense of purpose. There was tremendous satisfaction in feeling that others cared about their situation – which, in days before television and radio, many had felt were unique to their trade or town. Perhaps above all was the feeling that, united, working people could make a difference.

Questions

1 What, in your judgement, was the most effective element exercised by the state in controlling the Chartists? You could draw a spider diagram to show how they were all linked – and this would help show which, or which combination, was the most effective.

2 Read Source Z. How convincing do you find the author's opinions about the reasons for the decline of Chartism?

Working-class solidarity and focus

Emerging from this sense of purpose was a shared focus of hostility towards a state that appeared to be operating in the interests of the propertied classes. This found expression in Chartist opposition not just to the Reform Act of 1832 but to the Poor Law Amendment Act of 1834 and in pressure for further factory reforms as well as, of course, for the Charter.

Working-class organisation of protest

Chartism had provided many working people with their first experience of the language and vehicles of protest. The *Northern Star* was 'their' publication and gave them a public voice. On a smaller scale, the writing and printing of posters, handbills and banners was an invaluable preparation for later involvement in, for example, the trade union movement. Equally important was the organisation of Chartist outings, tea parties and soup kitchens, giving to many experiences of being part of, and having to provide for, a larger number of people than found in their own street, courtyard or square.

Chartists and education

You have seen already the importance that William Lovett placed on education, and his mantra 'Before an educated people a government must bow' was one taken up by many hundreds of Chartists. Existing schools did not always embrace Chartist ideals and where such schools were considered unsatisfactory or were non-existent, enthusiastic Chartists took over. Because they were working people, they were involved more in setting up and running evening and Sunday schools than day schools, although there were some successful day schools. At Stalybridge, for example, Chartists set up a Sunday school and a day school in the People's Institute; Chartist halls in Oldham, Keighley and Hanley all ran schools; Thomas Cooper, in Leicester, established an extensive system of Sunday schools and adult evening classes, and in Mottram some 500 children were taught reading and writing. Although many of these only lasted for a short time, they were nonetheless important to those involved.

Chartists and Christianity

Only a handful of Chartists rejected Christianity altogether and, while many might disagree with the structure of the institutional Church, most believed that Chartism was consistent with Christianity. William Hill wrote in a pamphlet: 'A man may be devout as a Christian, faithful as a friend, but if as a citizen he claims rights for himself he refuses to confer upon others, he fails to fulfil the teachings of Christ.' Many Chartists agreed with him. They flooded into churches as part of their 1839 agitation, which must have alarmed the middle class congregations in many places. Other churches – for example, that of the Reverend Hook of Leeds – worked well with their Chartist churchwardens. The early 1840s saw a number of Chartist churches being founded, where emphasis was placed on the teachings of Christ, rather than on the authority of the Church.

Chartists and landownership

Feargus O'Connor gave Chartists their first experience of landownership. He believed that industrial society had created an artificial imbalance in the labour market. His remedy was to encourage some working people to return to the land as smallholders. This would, he argued, have the effect of reducing the over-supply of labour, thereby forcing up the wages of industrial workers. It would also provide another focus for collective activity, during a period when it looked unlikely that the Charter would be granted. It represented one of the most important Chartist initiatives in the period between the ending of the strikes in 1842 and the revival of Chartist activity in relation to the Charter in 1847.

The Chartist Land Company was enormously popular, especially with handloom weavers and similar craft workers, who were facing harsh conditions as they competed with factory-produced goods. More than £100,000 was collected from some 70,000 subscribers, hopeful of being able to acquire land. The lucky subscribers were given land through a lottery system; they then paid rent of £5 a year to provide funds for further purchases of land, so that ultimately all subscribers would be settled. At least, that was the idea! The Chartist Land Company succeeded in creating about 250 settlements before it was wound up in 1851. On a practical level, many of the settlers found it difficult to make a living. They sometimes avoided paying rent or alternatively resented the fact that they could not become outright owners. Furthermore, O'Connor encountered numerous legal complications, which the government showed little interest in solving.

Parliamentary investigation resulted in a decision that the Land Company was neither a friendly society nor a joint-stock company but simply a lottery. Continuation of the Land Plan would be illegal and O'Connor's attempts to find an alternative framework were rejected by the courts. Therefore, O'Connor had no choice but to secure a private Act of Parliament to settle its debts. The houses and plots were sold off. The Land Plan was certainly idealistic and O'Connor failed to find a way of making it work. However, he was not entirely to blame: the hostility of the authorities should not be underestimated.

Source AA

Despite a sense of failure and disappointment, there was surprisingly little bitterness and regret shown in the aftermath off the movement, but rather a nostalgic pleasure in having played some part in an honourable campaign which had probably not been fought in vain.

How far the agitation was responsible for any improvement in the mental and physical welfare of the British people is beyond exact assessment. The movement provided a vehicle for the expression of their pent-up grievances, and was the means of training considerable numbers of working class families to adopt a high sense of social obligation. The process of political education of the people was speeded up on a remarkably widespread scale by the Chartists.

From Alex Wilson, 'Chartism', in J.T. Ward (editor) *Popular Movements c. 1830–1850*, published in 1970

Question

What evidence can you find to back up the claims made by Alex Wilson in Source AA?

Unit summary

What have you learned in this unit?

You have learned about the revitalising of the Chartist movement after the release of Feargus O'Connor from gaol, and about his founding of the National Charter Association. You have seen how, despite better organisation and management, the 1841 Petition was rejected by the House of Commons. You have considered the 'Plug Plot' riots of 1842 and the ways in which Chartists were involved and made use of them. The leadership styles of William Lovett and Feargus O'Connor have been addressed, along with their different approaches to strategy and tactics in attempting to achieve the six points of the People's Charter. You have considered the significance of 1848 – the year of revolutions in Europe – and have analysed the reasons why no such revolution occurred in Britain, despite it being the year the Chartists presented their third Petition to parliament. You have, throughout, addressed the power of the state in combating and controlling Chartist activities, and finally you have reflected upon what it was that the Chartists achieved in the face of their failure to persuade parliament to consider their People's Charter.

What skills have you used in this unit?

You have worked with a range of contemporary and secondary sources, cross-referencing, where necessary, to enhance your understanding of the dynamics of the Chartist movement. You have conducted an extended source enquiry into the significance of 1848 and, through the evaluation of different types of source material, developed your understanding of the ways in which the power of the state worked against the Chartist movement as well as your ability to use evidence in context.

Exam tips

Below is the sort of question you will find appearing on examination papers as a (b) question.

Study sources W, Y and Z, and use your own knowledge. How far do you agree with the view that Chartism failed to obtain the six points of the People's Charter because of poor leadership?

You tackled a (b) question at the end of Unit 3. Look back at the exam tips you were given on page 61 before developing and building on them here. Then look at these tips.

- Write the given 'view' in the middle of a spider diagram.
- Read Sources W, Y and Z carefully. Establish points that support and points that challenge the given view regarding poor leadership, using knowledge to reinforce and challenge.
- Cross-reference between the different 'legs' for similarities and differences.

You are now ready to write your answer. Remember to:

- combine the different points into answers for and against the stated view
- evaluate the conflicting arguments by reference to the quality of the evidence used
- reach a supported judgement.

RESEARCH TOPIC

The Chartist slogan for 'universal suffrage' was misleading in one notable respect: few Chartists anticipated it would include women. Research the role of women in the Chartist movement. You may find it useful to begin by looking at a website called Chartist Ancestors.

UNIT 5 The triumph of democracy?

What is this unit about?

This unit focuses on the Parliamentary Reform Act of 1867. It addresses the question of why further reform was considered necessary, 35 years after the 'Great' Reform Act of 1832. Consideration is given to the changed national social and economic context and to pressures outside parliament that led to reform being considered appropriate at this time. The situation at Westminster is addressed in some detail, because, unlike the situation in 1832, the main pressures for change came from parliament, not from extra-parliamentary factions. There, the political manoeuvrings between parties and politicians are explored, and particular attention is paid to the political expediency and self-interest that led to the somewhat surprising outcome of reforming legislation being brought in by a Conservative, not a Liberal, government. Finally, the unit considers the reasons why the 1867 Act was not sufficient and why further legislation was considered necessary in the years to 1885.

Note: It was during this period that the Whigs emerged as the Liberal Party and the Tories as the Conservative Party. This is more fully explained in Units 6 and 7. For the sake of clarity, in this and following units Whigs will usually be referred to as Liberals and Tories usually as Conservatives.

Key questions

- Why was there pressure for further parliamentary reform?
- What were Disraeli's motives in supporting parliamentary reform in 1867?
- How democratic was Britain by 1885?

Timeline

1852 — **Reform Bill brought in by Lord John Russell's government (Liberal)**
Proposed to extend the vote to men living in property in boroughs worth £5 a year and in the counties, £10
Radicals opposed the Bill because it didn't go far enough; others opposed it because it went too far, and so Russell withdrew the Bill

1853 — **Reform Bill brought in by Lord John Russell's government (Liberal)**
Proposed to extend the vote to £10 county and £6 borough householders
Bill fell on the outbreak of the Crimean War

1859 — **Reform Bill brought in by the Earl of Derby's government (Conservative)**
Proposed to extend the vote to £10 householders in boroughs and counties, and no redistribution of seats
Minority government, and Bill defeated in the House of Commons by 39 votes

1864 — **Formation of National Reform Union**
A mainly middle-class organisation, pledged to fight for household suffrage and redistribution of seats

1865	**Death of Palmerston (Liberal)** Palmerston had been a leading opponent, within the Liberal Party, of further reform **Bad harvest** Widespread distress **Formation of Reform League** A mainly working-class organisation pledged to fight for universal manhood suffrage
1866	**Financial crisis** Speculation leads to the collapse of Overend and Gurney, a leading London financial house **Reform Bill brought in by Lord John Russell's government (Liberal)** Introduced in Commons by Gladstone Proposed to extend the vote to £14 county and £7 borough householders, lodgers paying £10 a year rent, men with £50 savings and to redistribute some seats Bill defeated by a combination of Conservatives and some Liberals Government falls
1866–67	**Cholera epidemic** 14,000 people die
1867	**Reform Bill brought in by the Earl of Derby (Conservative)** Introduced in Commons by Disraeli, who accepts a range of radical amendments Bill accepted by parliament and becomes law
1872	**Ballot Act** Voting in general elections and by elections becomes secret
1883	**The Corrupt and Illegal Practices Prevention Act** Wipes out the more severe forms of bribery and coercion
1884	**The Representation of the People Act 1884 (the Franchise Act)** The counties are given householder representation
1885	**The Redistribution of Seats Act** Seats are redistributed more sensibly to reflect the population distribution

SKILLS BUILDER

Look at Source A, which was published in the same month in 1867 that the Parliamentary Reform Bill became law. What conclusions can you draw from this cartoon?

Source A

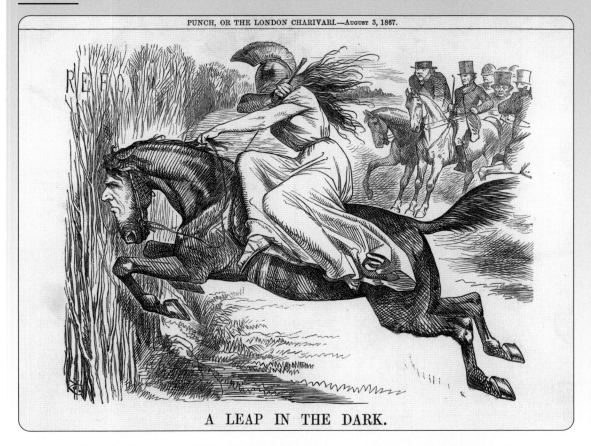

PUNCH, OR THE LONDON CHARIVARI.—August 3, 1867.

A LEAP IN THE DARK.

A cartoon by John Tenniel, published in *Punch* magazine on 3 August 1867; the horse is shown with Disraeli's face; the woman on his back is Britannia (who represents Great Britain); the two other horse riders in the background are John Bright and William Gladstone.

'Finality Jack' – or was he?

It seemed to many that the 1832 Reform Act (see Units 1 and 2) was the permanent settlement that the Whigs had intended it to be. Indeed, Lord John Russell, who had piloted the bill through the Commons, was nicknamed 'Finality Jack'. No further parliamentary reform was now deemed necessary. The government had successfully resisted the Chartist demands to enfranchise the working class (see Units 3 and 4) and had not even seen the need to debate the six points of their People's Charter. Chartism itself had died out in the 1850s; those originally committed to the Chartist cause had turned their attentions away from parliamentary reform and focused on bringing pressure to bear on the government to introduce reforms that would improve working and living conditions for the working classes. However, you can see from the timeline for this unit (pages 87–88) that 'Finality Jack' himself had tried three times to get Reform Bills through parliament, which is in itself evidence that he had changed his mind about the finality of the 1832 Act. Why had he changed his mind? Where did the pressure for parliamentary reform come from?

A country ripe for change: the 1850s

Unlike the situation in 1832, there was no intense, strong and determined pressure from outside parliament demanding reform. Rather, by the 1850s, there had been subtle changes in the country beyond Westminster that meant attitudes were shifting. A 'modernising' population, becoming more aware of changes in the world around them, and a parliament that reflected more eighteenth-century concerns about interest and property rather than nineteenth-century ones about democracy, were getting out of step with each other.

Source B

The 1832 Act was essentially an eighteenth-century measure passed to deal with an eighteenth-century problem, but by the 1850s times had changed considerably.

The nineteenth century had already seen rapid and breathtaking achievements in technology and industry. In this brave new world of the claims of what were termed Capital and Labour to play their part in determining the future of the country could hardly be dismissed or ignored.

These were the years of what was known as the 'Condition of England' question: heart searching over horrifying official reports into cholera or sewerage, fuelled by the pen of novelists like Mrs Gaskell. Closely linked to this was a growing sense of anger at the culture of amateurism and inefficiency in official circles, which produced this misery. Above all, the Crimean War revealed to an appalled Victorian public the depths of muddle and incompetence to which the hierarchy of the armed forces and the War Office could sink in times of crisis.

In the context of the 1850s, therefore, it did not take a particularly radical outlook to recognise that a largely agricultural and rural parliament, still heavily influenced by patronage and the interest groups of the previous century, and overseeing the fortunes of the world's foremost industrial nation, was more of an anomaly with every passing year.

From Sean Lang, *Parliamentary Reform 1785–1928*, published in 1999

Source C

The Whigs who passed the Great Reform Act of 1832 argued to the opponents of that highly controversial measure that it would settle a festering sore for good and all. It rapidly became clear that it did nothing of the kind. Virtually all in parliament could unite to oppose the wild extravagances of universal manhood suffrage, as advocated by the Chartists, but many MPs could see nothing wrong with increasing the electorate to embrace those solid, educated working men who did not occupy property worth more than £10 a year or more, but who could certainly be trusted to vote wisely if given the chance.

The reduction of social tension and the long period of boom also helped create a climate of optimism rather than fear.

The impact of gentle inflation and substantially improved electoral organisation had already combined to increase the number of voters under the old rules. There were about 400,000 more voters on the electoral registers in 1866 than there had been in the year after the Great Reform Act became law.

From Eric Evans, *The Birth of Modern Britain 1780–1914*, published in 1997

SKILLS BUILDER

Read Sources B and C. How far do the two sources agree on the ways in which Britain in the 1850s was ready for further parliamentary reform?

Pressure points: the 1860s

It was one thing to feel that the time had (probably) come for further parliamentary reform, but quite another for events to push people into action. Several events and interests came to the fore in the early 1860s that had the effect of kick-starting parliament on the path to reform.

Organisations

- The National Reform Union, formed in 1864, was led by wealthy Manchester merchants, industrialists and radical MPs, and was mainly supported by middle-class Liberals. Respectable and attractive to the intellectual elite of the Liberal Party, its aims were to persuade the government to extend the franchise to that of a household suffrage, distribute seats more evenly and bring in secret voting. By 1867, some 150 branches had been established throughout Britain, mainly in industrial towns.

- The Reform League, established in 1865, pressed for complete manhood suffrage. Meeting in pubs and working men's clubs, it attracted trade unionists and ex-Chartists, and was a predominantly working-class organisation. Supported by various left-wing organisations, it had 400 branches by 1867.

The Union had the money and the League, the membership. By the beginning of 1867, they were working together to urge the government to bring in parliamentary reform.

People and politics

- In many ways, the death of **Lord Palmerston** in 1865 was liberating for the more radical wing of the Liberal Party. Palmerston had conducted an enormously popular foreign policy, which gave him the prestige to block measures he did not like. His ministries had brought in important reforms in health, education, law and poor relief, but he was never in favour of reform for its own sake. He saw no overwhelming reason, in the 1860s, to support parliamentary reform, commenting that democracy would 'bring the scum to the top' and so set his face and his influence against it. Within weeks of his death, Lord John Russell who had become an earl in 1861, had taken over as Liberal Prime Minister, and brought forward a parliamentary Reform Bill.

- **William Gladstone**, who, in the 1860s, had worked as Chancellor of the Exchequer in the Liberal administrations of Palmerston and Russell, was a slow, but finally committed, convert to the need for parliamentary reform. He had visited the Lancashire cotton mills during the 'cotton famine' of the early 1860s, caused by the interruption of cotton supplies because of the American Civil War, and declared himself impressed by the steadfast, respectful and sensible qualities of the working-class people he met. Encouraged by the radical MP **John Bright**, he reinvented himself as a popular politician, 'the People's William', and was ready to support extending the franchise to the 'respectable' working class. The conversion to reform of a man who was likely, at some point, to lead his party had considerable significance.

- **Benjamin Disraeli** worked as Chancellor of the Exchequer in the Earl of Derby's administration (June 1866 to February 1868). He was desperate to end the Liberal's dominance of politics and would take every opportunity offered to him of exploiting any divisions in their ranks. To achieve parliamentary reform where the Liberals, traditionally the party of reform, had failed, would be a huge triumph both personally and for his party.

Biography

William Ewart Gladstone (1809–98)

The son of a Liverpool merchant, educated at Eton and Oxford, he entered parliament as Conservative MP for Grantham in 1832. He served as Chancellor of the Exchequer in the Whig/Peelite administration of Aberdeen (1852–55), and in the Liberal administrations of Palmerston (1855–58, 1859–65) and Russell (1865–66), becoming Liberal Prime Minister in 1868–74, 1880–85, 1886 and 1892–94. His first ministry concentrated on overdue reforms in the Army, education, the legal system, elections and Ireland. His second ministry passed the third Reform Act but failed to solve the 'Irish problem', which caused his third administration to crash following his conversion to Home Rule. His fourth ministry, although dominated by his obsession with Ireland, failed to pass a Home Rule Bill. He didn't work well with colleagues, especially in later life when he tended to make unilateral decisions and tell his Cabinet colleagues about them afterwards. Queen Victoria disliked him, complaining that he addressed her as if she was a public meeting. His political rivalry with Disraeli enlivened parliamentary debates, interesting the general public more than previously in the goings-on at Westminster. Gladstone's use of speech-making and political meetings to bring great issues to the notice of the public was innovative and helped create political awareness among the general public after 1867. One of his favourite forms of exercise was cutting down trees, and special trains were run so that people could see him at work with his axe.

Biography

John Bright (1811–89)

The son of a carpet manufacturer from Rochdale, a Quaker and supporter of **temperance**, Bright was elected Liberal MP for Durham (1843), then for Manchester (1847–57) and then for Birmingham. His pacifism made it difficult for him to give much support to Palmerston's somewhat belligerent foreign policy and he refused the offer of the Secretaryship of State for India in 1868 because of its military responsibilities. A leading spokesman for the un-enfranchised working class in the 1866–67 debates on parliamentary reform, he nevertheless opposed legislation limiting the hours of adult factory workers. He supported land reform in Ireland but opposed Gladstone's Home Rule proposals in 1886. He worked in Liberal Cabinets as President of the Board of Trade (1868–70) and Chancellor of the Duchy of Lancaster (1873–74 and 1880–82). He has been described as one of the greatest orators of the nineteenth century.

Biography

Benjamin Disraeli (1804–81)

The son of a Jewish author who had converted to Christianity, Disraeli entered parliament as MP for Maidstone in 1837. A Tory radical, he supported the 'Young England' movement, which wanted to bridge the gulf between rich and poor, opposed Peel over **Free Trade** in 1846 and led the **Protectionists** in the Commons for 22 years. His novels *Sybil* and *Coningsby* reflected his political views, which were those of a reforming Tory. He worked as Chancellor of the Exchequer in 1852, 1858–59 and 1867, as Prime Minister for ten months in 1868, and then again 1874–80 during which time he was often referred to by the nickname 'Dizzy'. He pursued a vigorous foreign policy and promoted the concept of 'Empire at home' as well as undertaking various domestic reforms to improve, for example, housing conditions and public health. His loathing of Gladstone was notorious and it is sometimes difficult to determine how many of his policies were determined by his desire to outsmart his Liberal rival. Queen Victoria liked him and was particularly enchanted when, in 1876, he made her 'Empress of India'. The previous year, on his own initiative, he secretly purchased 40 per cent of the Suez Canal shares, demonstrating his belief in the Suez Canal venture, which, when built, enabled faster journeys to be made to India.

Definitions

Temperance

Not drinking any alcohol whatsoever.

Free Trade

International trade not limited by interference from government, regulations or tariffs intended to restrict foreign imports. It is the exact opposite of protectionism.

Protectionism

Protectionism consisted of policies to defend national economic interests. This was to be achieved by imposing duties on foreign imports in order to safeguard domestic production. Protectionism was attractive to some politicians because it provided revenue and appeared patriotic. It also appealed to those domestic producers who were guaranteed artificially inflated prices.

Politics were at the stage of being dominated by rivalry between Gladstone and Disraeli who, quite simply, loathed each other. Gladstone believed that Disraeli lacked principle, while Disraeli regarded Gladstone as a pompous humbug.

Question

Re-read the section 'Pressure points: the 1860s', starting on page 91. Prioritise these pressure points. Which, in your view, was necessary before parliament was prepared to discuss reform? Discuss your views in small groups. (Remember, it's important not just to know why reform happened, but also why it happened at that point in time, and not earlier or later.)

International events

British interest in movements in Italy for unification and in the American Civil War were interpreted (not necessarily correctly) as popular struggles for freedom, and these helped to fuel demands for reform at home.

Economic matters

- The harvest of 1865 was bad, forcing hundreds of people unexpectedly to claim poor relief.

- Cholera again stalked the land, claiming 14,000 lives in the 1866–67 epidemic.

- Unwise speculation as a result of the 1862 Limited Liability Act ended with the collapse, in 1866, of one of the great London financial houses, Overend and Gurney, alarming investors and sending shockwaves through the City.

Source D

Every man who is not presumably incapacitated by some consideration of personal unfitness, or of political danger, is morally entitled to come within the pale [boundary] of the constitution. Of course, in giving utterance to such a proposition, I do not recede from the protest I have previously made against sudden, or violent, or intoxicating change. Hearts should be bound together by a reasonable extension, at fitting time and among select portions of people, of every benefit and every privilege that can justly be conferred on them.

From a speech by William Gladstone in the House of Commons, May 1864

Source E

If you establish a democracy, you must in due season reap the fruits of a democracy. You will in due season have great impatience of the government bodies combined in due season with great increase of the public expenditure. You will in due season reap the fruits of such united influence. You will in due season have wars entered into from passion, and not from reason; and you will in due season submit to peace ignominiously sought and ignominiously obtained, which will diminish your authority and perhaps endanger your independence. You will, in due season, with a democracy find that your property is less valuable and that your freedom is less complete.

From a speech by Benjamin Disraeli in the House of Commons during the debate on the 1859 Reform Bill

SKILLS BUILDER

1 Carefully read Source D. Which people does Gladstone want to enfranchise? How does he want to do it?

2 Now read Source E. What, in your own words, are the problems Disraeli finds with democracy?

3 Taking both sources together, which parliamentary leader, Gladstone or Disraeli, would you expect to be the more supportive of parliamentary reform?

The Representation of the People Bill 1866

Debates and disloyalty in the Commons

Sensing the time was right, William Gladstone introduced the Representation of the People Bill into the House of Commons on 12 March 1866. The Bill proposed extending the franchise in the boroughs to householders paying more than £7 in rent and, in the counties, to householders with or without land who paid more than £10 a year in rent. This would have the effect of increasing the electorate by about 400,000. The Liberals had done their homework. Working through the poll books (remember the ballot was not yet secret) they had established that those of the working class who already had the vote were, in the main, casting it for Liberal candidates. The Liberals told themselves that not much of a risk would be taken by adding a relatively small number of skilled working-class voters to the electoral roll. The unskilled who were, so the argument went, likely to be in receipt of poor relief, or irresponsible or criminal, would still be excluded.

The bill was not well received. There were some who thought it did not go far enough, and others who believed it went too far. Dangerously, the bill split the Liberal Party. **Robert Lowe**, a right-wing Liberal, was horrified (see Source G on page 96). Indeed, he led a section of equally appalled Liberals in opposition to their own party's bill. Despite Gladstone's response that the working classes he wanted to enfranchise were 'our fellow subjects, our fellow Christians, our own flesh and blood' and John Bright's derisive comment that the Liberal rebels had 'retired to a Cave of Adullam' (a biblical reference to a cave where the discontented gathered), Lowe and his colleagues were neither silenced nor appeased.

Source F

The wages of a man occupying such a house [paying £7 a year rent] would be a little under 26 shillings a week. That sum is undoubtedly unattainable by the peasantry, but is generally attainable by artisans and skilled labourers. To give the vote to £6 householders would be to transfer the balance of political power in the boroughs to the working classes, and we cannot consent to this. We believe, however, that these persons whom we ask you to enfranchise ought to be welcomed as if they were recruits to your army.

From Gladstone's speech in the House of Commons, introducing the Representation of the People Bill, March 1866

Biography

Robert Lowe (1811–82)

The son of a rich clergyman, Lowe was educated at Winchester and Oxford. He emigrated to New South Wales in 1842 where he made his name on the legislative council and a fortune from his legal practice and property transactions. He also formed firm opinions there about the undesirability of legislatures elected on a wide franchise. Returning to Britain in 1850, he was elected Liberal MP for Kidderminster and later for the small borough of Calne (1859–67). Responsible for education in Russell's Liberal administration, he introduced the 'Revised Code' in 1862 which linked government education grants to results in basic subjects. Leading the revolt against Russell's Reform Bill of 1866, he was later wrong-footed when Disraeli introduced what quickly became a far more radical measure, which became law. He worked in Gladstone's administration of 1868–73 first as Home Secretary and then as Chancellor of the Exchequer. He was made Viscount Sherbrook in 1882.

Source G

Is it not certain that causes are at work which will have a tendency to multiply the franchise? There is no doubt an immense power in expansion and therefore it is certain that, sooner or later, we shall see the working classes in the majority in the constituencies. Look at what that implies. If you want venality [corruption], if you want ignorance, if you want drunkenness and facility for being intimidated; or if, on the other hand, you want impulsive, unreflecting and violent people, where do you look for them in the constituencies? Do you go to the top or the bottom? We know what those people are who live in small houses – we have had experience of them under the name of 'freemen' – and no better law could have been passed than that which disenfranchised them. The first stage, I have no doubt, will be an increase of corruption, intimidation and disorder. The second, is that the working men of England, finding themselves in a full majority of the whole constituency, will awake to a full sense of their power.

From Robert Lowe's speech to the House of Commons, March 1866

Question

Did Robert Lowe make a serious political error? Use Sources F and G and your own knowledge in your answer.

All Disraeli and the Conservatives had to do was watch and wait as the debates raged. Out of office for most of the 1850s and 1860s, the Conservatives were looking for any opportunity to exploit Liberal weaknesses, and here was a golden opportunity. They allied with Robert Lowe and more than 40 discontented Liberals to defeat the Bill. Russell resigned almost immediately, leaving the Queen with no alternative but to ask the Earl of Derby to form a Conservative administration, which was exactly what Disraeli had wanted. What Lowe and his discontented Liberals had not considered was that the Conservatives in general, and Disraeli in particular, were hungry for a high profile success. Parliamentary reform would give them this.

Reaction on the street

The parliamentary debates in the years 1831–32 were accompanied by demonstrations and riots in the country (see pages 20–21) as the tendency to accept or reject reform seemed more or less likely. No such excitement accompanied the 1866–67 debates.

However, the Reform League and Reform Union had not been idle, and neither had John Bright and other radical MPs. Beginning in the early months of 1866 they, jointly and separately, organised a series of rallies in support of reform. On 23 July, a League rally in Hyde Park, London, got out of hand and a mob tore down some railings. Violence continued for a couple of days before it was contained and controlled by police and troops. This was no more violent than some demonstrations that normally accompanied elections, and at no point were the Hyde Park riots indicative of a country teetering on the brink of revolution. Indeed, the Earl of Derby's son, Edward Stanley, wrote in his diary: 'The political excitement among the upper classes is greater than it has been for the past seven or eight years. I do not believe it is shared to any considerable extent by the people.' He wasn't wrong. The Hyde Park riots were the final straw that convinced Derby and Disraeli to take up the cause of reform. A Conservative government would have a better chance of getting such a Bill through the House of Lords, and would have the added political delight of beating the Liberals at their own game in the Commons.

The Representation of the People Bill 1867

Disraeli was taking a considerable risk in introducing a parliamentary Reform Bill. Derby's administration was a minority one, which meant that it didn't have an overall majority in the House of Commons. Not only would Disraeli have to convince his own backbenchers of the sense of such a reform, but also he would have to find supporters on the Liberal benches. And he had just spearheaded the defeat of the Liberals' own Reform Bill. The question facing Disraeli was whether the Conservative bill should be more moderate than the Liberal one (and so attract the support of backbench Conservatives and the Liberal **Adullamites**), or more radical (and attract the support of Robert Lowe and his Liberal supporters, at the risk of upsetting his own backbenchers). It turned out that the bill began life as one and ended as the other. First, though, there was a bill that hardly got started before it was withdrawn.

The main difficulty facing Derby and Disraeli was getting any sort of parliamentary reform past the right wing of the Conservative Party. Their instinct was to be bold and to propose household suffrage in the boroughs, made more palatable to the Conservative right wing by giving certain groups of people more than one vote. However, faced with threats of resignation, the Hyde Park riots and the anxiety of the Queen, an emergency bill – called the 'Ten Minute' Bill – was hurriedly put together. It proposed, simply, to extend the franchise to include £6 ratepayers in the boroughs and £20 ratepayers in the counties. No one liked it much. A majority of Conservatives preferred a bolder approach and the government withdrew the bill. Lord Cranborne, who in 1881 was to become the leader of the Conservative Party, resigned from the government, and a new, much more carefully thought-out, bill was put before the Commons in March 1867.

What did the Representation of the People Bill propose?

The bill Disraeli introduced in March 1867 was a more moderate bundle of clauses than that introduced by the Liberals the previous year.

- In the boroughs there was to be a household suffrage, provided the (male) householder had lived in the property for two years and paid rates separately from rent. These men were deemed to be more respectable than those who paid rates through their landlords (called **compounders**).

> **Definition**
>
> **Adullamite**
>
> Those MPs who had opposed the 1866 Liberal Reform Bill.
>
> **Compounder**
>
> A person who paid rent and rates together, to his landlord.

- University graduates, members of the professions and those with savings of more than £50 were to be given extra votes. Many Conservatives liked this 'plural voting' clause as it was called, believing it would help to balance out the increase in working-class electors. On the other hand, John Bright and radical Liberals attacked it as being a 'fancy franchise'.

- In the counties, the occupancy franchise was to be reduced from £50 rent to £15.

- Fifteen seats were to be redistributed.

A 'Leap in the Dark'

Disraeli handled the passage of the bill through the Commons with daring, skill, and (some would say) political deception and a considerable amount of hypocrisy.

Gladstone unleashed a deadly onslaught, pointing out a range of anomalies and criticising, for example, Disraeli's statistics, his 'class legislation' of plural voting and the treatment of 'compounders'. Yet despite this attack unnerving Conservative waverers, it actually caused them to rally behind Disraeli. Even Gladstone's Liberals worried, fearing that the ferocity of his attack would bring down the government, landing them back in the 1866 situation and no Reform Bill at all. What was to be done? The best course of action was unclear to many Conservatives and Liberals.

The debates that followed were lively and passionate, but Disraeli out-witted and out-manoeuvred all his opponents. In 1866 he had allied with the Liberal Adullamites to defeat reform and bring down the government; he now chose to abandon them and ally with the left-wing, radical element of the Liberal Party. He was willing to accept amendment after amendment from Liberal radicals, to ensure the bill was not lost. What emerged was a bill that was far more radical than the one he had opposed the previous year. For example, lodgers in unfurnished premises worth more than £10 a year were enfranchised; the 'fancy-franchises' were dropped and an amendment to enfranchise 'compounders' was accepted.

It was this amendment, proposed by the radical Liberal MP Grosvenor Hodgkinson that caused the greatest consternation. Moderate Liberals stoutly maintained that 'compounders' should not be given the vote, believing them to be generally poorer, less well-established and more likely to 'flit' when in debt than those who paid their rates personally. Disraeli first stated his firm opposition to extending the franchise to 'compounders' (see Sources H and I), then decided that giving them the vote should be the subject of separate legislation (Source J). Finally, realising this would delay his Reform Bill, he accepted extending the franchise to 'compounders' (Source K).

The acceptance, by Disraeli, of this amendment marked the end of the road for the Liberals, as a key element of their opposition had been dealt with. No wonder Robert Lowe complained angrily that the Constitution was being auctioned to the highest bidder as it became clear to him and the Adullamites that they would have been wiser to have backed Russell's 1866 bill.

Source H

The question arises, ought a compound-householder have a vote? Well, Sir, in our opinion, assuming that the House is of the same opinion that the foundation of the franchise should be rating and a payment of rates, and that that is adopted by the House, not as a check, as some would say, but, on the contrary, as a qualification. Because it is the best evidence of the trustworthiness of the individual, we have no hesitation in saying ourselves that we do not think that the compound-householder ought to have a vote.

From Disraeli's speech on 18 March 1867, when he introduced the Conservative Reform Bill in the House of Commons

Source I

As far as the borough franchise is concerned, I must repeat, at the risk of wearying the House, what I have said from the first, that the franchise in our plan is founded upon principles from which we cannot swerve. And the House has always in its discussions accepted that. Nor is it a novelty when we say that personal payment of rate and residence are the only conditions upon which we consent to this arrangement of the borough franchise.

From Disraeli's speech in the House of Commons, 12 April 1867

Source J

Her Majesty's government can have no opposition whatsoever to the [Hodgkinson's] amendment. It is the policy of their own measure – a policy which, if they had been masters of the situation they would have recommended long ago for the adoption of the House. But I do not think myself, as far as I can form an opinion on the subject – and it is one to which I have given long and painful thought – that it would be desirable or possible to deal with this question by a clause in the Reform Bill. My opinion is that separate legislation would be the better course. You will, otherwise, cause great delay, impede the progress of the Reform Bill and not so efficiently deal with the question.

From Disraeli's speech in the House of Commons, Friday 17 May 1867

Source K

We have given that subject [Hodgkinson's amendment] consideration; and it is our opinion that the policy can be brought about by clauses in the Bill before the House, and if it can be so accomplished, it shall be.

From Disraeli's speech to the House of Commons, Monday 20 May 1867

Question

Read Sources H–K. How do you account for Disraeli's change of mind over Hodgkinson's amendment?

Not only had Disraeli completely out-witted Gladstone and the more moderate Liberals but also, by focusing on the franchise, he had managed to conceal the fact that his modest proposals for the redistribution of seats served to consolidate, rather than destroy, the landed interest in the counties. It was clever stuff indeed, as by sheer opportunism Disraeli had seized the chance to strengthen the Conservative Party at Westminster and boost his own career at the same time. He had taken an enormous gamble – and won. The bill met few problems in the House of Lords and became law on 15 August 1867.

Source L

THE DERBY, 1867. DIZZY WINS WITH "REFORM BILL."

Mr. Punch. "DON'T BE TOO SURE; WAIT TILL HE'S *WEIGHED*."

A cartoon by John Tenniel, published in the magazine *Punch* 25 May 1867. Jockeys have to be a certain weight in order to be allowed to ride in specific races; once a horse race is over, the winning jockey has to be weighed in order to find out whether or not he has cheated; riding behind Disraeli and looking furious, is Gladstone

SKILLS BUILDER

Look carefully at Source L, and in particular at the caption and at what 'Mr Punch' is saying. What point is the cartoonist making? Use your own knowledge to explain whether or not you agree with him.

What changes were made by the Reform Act of 1867?

The new legislation brought in changes to both the franchise and the distribution of seats.

- Franchise extended in the boroughs to men:
  - owning or occupying houses provided they paid rates and had lived there for at least a year
  - living as lodgers in property worth at least £10 a year, provided they had been living there for at least a year.
- Franchise extended in the counties to men:
  - owning, or leasing, land worth at least £5 a year
  - occupying land with a rateable value of at least £12 a year, providing they had paid the relevant rates.
- Distribution of seats:
  - 45 seats were removed from boroughs with under 100,000 inhabitants
  - 25 seats were given to the counties
  - 20 seats were given to new boroughs
  - 6 boroughs were given an extra seat.

Similar Acts were passed for Scotland and Ireland in 1868. The redistribution of seats were made in part by Disraeli in an attempt to protect the influence of the mainly Conservative-voting counties from the increase in voter numbers in the boroughs. Furthermore, the extension of borough boundaries in some areas made the counties there much more securely Tory.

What about the women?

You will have noticed that all the changes made by the Act have affected men and that there does not appear, at least on the part of Disraeli, to have been any thought given to the enfranchisement of women. But MPs had not been silent on the subject. On 20 May 1867, John Stuart Mill proposed an amendment that the word 'person' should be substituted for the word 'man' in the Bill, In this way, suitably qualified women (women householders, for example) would be entitled to vote on the same terms as men. The amendment was defeated by 196 votes to 73, but nevertheless the subject of female enfranchisement had been debated.

What was the impact of the 1867 Act?

Impact on the electorate

One very clear result of the 1867 Act was that the electorate was considerably enlarged. In 1866, approximately 1,400,000 men could vote. The Act gave the vote to a further 1,120,000 and thus the electorate almost doubled – from one man in five having the right to vote, to one man in three. The most striking difference came in the boroughs. Here, about 830,000 voters were added to the electoral registers. Birmingham's voters, for example, rose from 8,000 to 43,000. Overall, the working classes, for the first time, dominated the borough electorate.

It was different in the counties. Here, the electorate increased by about 45 per cent, meaning that the county constituencies remained largely middle class and, before the secret ballot, some were still influenced by the political persuasion of the local aristocrat or landowner.

Impact on elections

Whether or not the doubling of the electorate had any actual impact on the outcome of general elections was in many ways dependent on the distribution of seats. Disraeli's minimal redistribution tended to soften the impact of an electorate where the working classes were for the first time in the majority. Rural areas were still over-represented, as were the south and south-west. For example, the south-west returned 45 members of parliament, whereas the north-east, with three times the population, returned only 32.

Impact on party politics

Disraeli had gambled on the grateful working classes in the boroughs voting Conservative but it didn't quite work out like that. The Liberals won the 1868 general election, but the Conservatives won that of 1874. Here, they gained their first clear majority in the Commons since 1841. This may have been due, in part, to the development of efficient party machines designed to locate and persuade potential voters: the National Union of Conservative Associations was formed in 1867 and the National Liberal Federation in 1877. This will be addressed in greater detail in the next two units.

Impact on education

Many politicians viewed with alarm the enfranchisement of thousands of working-class men, regarding them as being illiterate, brutish and without any sense of what was politically appropriate. They would have agreed with Robert Lowe's comment: 'We must educate our masters to compel our future masters to learn their letters.' And so there is a direct link between the 1867 Reform Act and the 1870 Elementary Education Act, which created a system of school boards to provide basic state education to fill gaps left by the voluntary system. These schools were for children aged between 5 and 13, and aimed to provide basic literacy and numeracy for their pupils. However, it was not until 1880 that education was made compulsory and 1891 that it was provided free. This government move towards providing education for all the children of the working class applied, of course, to the children of non-voters as well as the children of voters, and made further extension of the franchise almost inevitable.

What were Disraeli's motives in bringing about reform?

Much has been written about the role of Disraeli in the years 1866–67. Was he a skilful politician? An opportunist? Was he seeking to rebuild the Conservative Party or further his own career? Was he motivated to support reform because of his hatred of Gladstone? Was he a lover of democracy, or hypocritically supporting reform because of what success could bring? Was he, perhaps, a mixture of all these elements?

Source M

MR CHILDERS: [I] could not help drawing the conclusion that Her Majesty's government entirely approved of the proposal of his Honourable Friend Mr Hodgkinson. Yet in neither of the Reform Bills they had brought forward during the present session had that principle been embodied. This, then, was the third change of policy on the part of Her Majesty's government in reference to the reform question, though it was one with which he would not quarrel.

From a speech by Hugh Childers, a Liberal MP, in the debate on the 1867 Reform Bill, reported in *Hansard*, May 1867

Source N

VISCOUNT CRANBORNE: [Disraeli] has announced a change of startling magnitude, a change which involves a *certain*, instead of an *uncertain*, admission of some 500,000 people to the franchise. Of this policy I express no opinion; but I say it is entirely a denial of all the principles of his party.

From a speech by Viscount Cranborne, a Conservative MP, in the debate on the 1867 Reform Bill, reported in *Hansard*, May 1867 (Cranborne became Lord Salisbury on the death of his father, and led the Conservative Party from the House of Lords 1881–1902)

SKILLS BUILDER

Read Sources M and N. To what extent are Childers and Cranborne criticising Disraeli for the same reasons? Whose criticism, in your view, was the more serious?

Source O

In the end, Disraeli needed to pass the 1867 Reform Act more than Gladstone needed to defeat or influence it. The Conservatives had presented the Liberals with a lacklustre opposition since the Corn Law crisis of 1846; it had taken twenty years to put together a credible front bench, and in 1866 they were still in a minority. Inevitably, the Liberal benches were full of men with long years of ministerial experience behind them, not least Gladstone himself who had ten years' experience as Chancellor of the Exchequer alone.

In many ways parliamentary reform presented the Conservatives, and Disraeli himself, with a make-or-break opportunity: it was their one chance to pass a really weighty piece of legislation, and a complex one at that, which would establish them again as major players in the political field, and their leaders as statesmen. In this sense it is certainly accurate to accuse Disraeli of opportunism, as long as it is understood that this does not of itself diminish his achievement in either political or tactical terms.

From Sean Lang, *Parliamentary Reform 1785–1928*, published in 1999

Source P

Disraeli's guiding principle, insofar as this most unprincipled of politicians had one, was to prise his party from the clammy grip of permanent minority status. The perfect boost for Tory morale would be a reform mission accomplished by a Conservative minority government, where a Liberal majority had failed. For Disraeli personally, it would be the perfect riposte to the insufferably superior Gladstone. In politics – even in Victorian politics – great issues frequently turn less on principle than on personal rivalry.

Tory backbenchers were bounced by Disraeli into a Reform Act. Few supported it on its merits, but they could reflect that their party had brought off a tactical coup of the first magnitude. It was a triumph of expediency over principle.

Disraeli was never a democrat. His success in 1867 rested on the two talents for which he was pre-eminent: parliamentary management and the ability to think more quickly on his feet than his opponents.

From Eric Evans, *Forging of the Modern State*, published in 2001

SKILLS BUILDER

1 Read Sources O and P. How far do they disagree on Disraeli's motives for introducing parliamentary reform in 1867?

2 Now look back to Source A. The horse has the face of Disraeli. Use your own knowledge to explain to what extent Disraeli really was taking a 'Leap in the Dark'.

Towards democracy: ending corruption and intimidation?

One of the main arguments against reform, back in 1832, had been that parliament was not meant to represent the people, but was there to represent various interests – the landed interest and the manufacturing interest, for example. The doubling of the electorate and the dominance of the working classes in the borough electorate made the representation of 'interest' virtually unworkable as well as unsupportable as an argument. People and not 'interest' were henceforth to be represented and, if this was to happen effectively, intimidation and corruption at elections had to stop.

The Ballot Act 1872

A secret ballot had been one of the Chartists' demands (see page 43) and, indeed, had figured in most radical demands since the end of the eighteenth century. Why was this thought to be so important?

Reformers believed that a truly representative system of government would only be possible if electors were able to vote for their candidate of choice, free from fear of intimidation. There was also an element of self-interest here: radicals believed that people were much more likely to vote for them if they could vote in secret without their employers knowing where their political sympathies lay. In the years before 1872, electors had their vote recorded in a poll book and sometimes, because of difficulties involved in getting to the poll for some voters, an election could last for several days.

Those opposing a secret ballot, and this included most peers and many Conservative MPs, maintained that it was somehow non-English and furtive to vote in secret, believing that people should have the courage of their own convictions and vote openly. There was an element of self-interest here, too. They were unsure as to what outcome secret ballots would have, and preferred a system where employers and landowners had more control over voting behaviour.

Why did matters come to a head in the early 1870s?

There were two main reasons why changes were proposed in the early 1870s.

1   A Liberal administration was elected in 1868, the first general election to be held after the Reform Act of 1867. Gladstone, still smarting from having been outwitted by Disraeli over the question of reform, and determined to show that the Liberal Party was really the reforming party, had included the veteran radical John Bright in his government. Bright, always an advocate of the secret ballot, was pushing hard to get this onto the statute books and Gladstone needed a seemingly small reform to boost the Liberals' image in the eyes of the electorate.

2   The report about the way in which the general election of 1868 was conducted in Blackburn was published in 1870 (see Source Q) Most contested elections were pretty violent affairs but this one was worst than most and an official enquiry was held, with John Bright being one of the members of the committee of enquiry. Unsurprisingly, the report recommended the introduction of a secret ballot.

Source Q

With regard to Parliamentary Elections in boroughs, your Committee have examined many witnesses, but the evidence does no more than confirm what has frequently been established before. In former and in the last Elections, various corrupt practices occurred, of which bribery and treating were the chief, to such an extent as to invalidate many Elections. It has been proved that in some instances rioting and violence to persons and property have occurred, so as to interfere with the freedom of the Election, while in a much larger number of cases Elections are accompanied by drunkenness and disorder.

County elections have been, in the main, free from bribery. It is, however, alleged that intimidation and undue influence are very largely practised. Evidence from Wales and Scotland has been brought before us, showing that tenants have actually been turned out of their farms on account of their votes. It is certain that an influence, greater than that legitimate influence which a popular and respected landlord must always exercise in his neighbourhood, is often brought to bear on tenant farmers, and other voters in agricultural districts.

From the *Report of the Committee of Enquiry on the 1868 Election*, published in 1870

The Act and its impact

Despite criticism in the House of Lords, Gladstone's Bill became law in 1872. From that point onwards, all general and local government elections, as well as by-elections, would be conducted by secret ballot. Electors would vote by making a cross beside their candidate of choice, and their ballot paper would then be put in a sealed box. The ballot papers were counted in front of the candidates or their agents. Voters who could not read or write, or who were blind, could ask the electoral official to mark their voting paper for them.

The first by-election to use a secret ballot was held in the same year the Act was passed, and the first general election in 1874. It did limit rowdiness at elections, but because the ballot was now secret, it is difficult to see immediately what impact the Act had. Certainly, in the short term there was fear among agricultural workers that, somehow, their landlord would get to know how they had voted and, in any case, the rural habit of deference seemed to last until the First World War. Many factory workers felt the same. However, once working-class voters had confidence in the secrecy of the system, the long-term effect was profound because it did significantly reduce the power that could be exerted by over-bearing masters and enabled the growth of political pressure groups. In Ireland, for example, it enabled electors to vote against their landlords and greatly helped support for, and the development of, **Irish Home Rule** movements.

The Corrupt and Illegal Practices Prevention Act 1883

All politicians were aware that the Secret Ballot Act meant they could not rely any more on bribery to return their candidate of choice. An elector might well accept a bribe from one candidate – and accept a bribe, too, from the opposing candidate. The secret ballot meant that no one would ever know which way an elector voted and which bribe had been effective. So how were the candidates to get round this? They got round it by employing local people on a temporary basis (in order to get their votes) and by ostentatiously buying local goods in order to display their commitment to the constituency. This meant that election expenses soared. Politicians didn't like this, but there seemed to be no way out of this form of corruption.

Definition

Irish Home Rule

Self-government for Ireland.

Source R

1 The practice has become almost universal for candidates to lavish immense sums of money upon purposes not in themselves corrupt, but quite useless for the attainment of any legitimate object. The true aim of such expenditure was to distribute money among the greatest possible number of electors, and a candidate who refused to conform to this universal custom had, or was believed to have, no chance of being returned. Every article purchased, every service rendered, was paid for at more than double its market value. Both sides employed an army of messengers to deliver their communications to the electors.

2 It is noteworthy that our chief expense was due to our agents having, according to the custom of the day, engaged every conveyance [vehicle] in the area for the day of the poll. This was in order to ensure reaching the limited number of polling places and the creation of a corresponding difficulty for our opponents.

Two politicians writing about their involvement in elections, quoted in Robert Pearce and Roger Stearn, *Government and Reform 1815–1918*, published in 1994

The Liberal government's dilemma

Gladstone decided to act against this sort of electoral corruption, but it could have caused problems for his own party. Conservatives tended to be wealthier than Liberals, and so a reduction in electoral expenses would hit them less hard than the Liberals; on the other hand, because they tended to be wealthier their opportunities for influencing elections would be reduced. In any event, the Conservatives decided to support the Liberal bill.

The Act and its impact

The Corrupt and Illegal Practices Prevention Act was passed in 1883 with very little opposition. The Act laid down the maximum sum of money that could be paid out in election expenses, calculated according to the size of the constituency and the number of voters, and outlawed the practice of one party booking up in advance all available means of transport to the polls. Fines and/or imprisonment would result if a politician or his agents were found guilty of corrupt practices, and the MP so elected would forfeit his seat.

In the first general election (1885) following the passing of the Act, electoral expenses fell by three-quarters. Of course, there are always ways round various laws, and this one was no exception. The Act only applied when a general election had been called; there was nothing to stop prospective MPs ingratiating themselves with the electorate in between elections. But even so, this Act was a huge step towards enabling electors to make up their own minds about whom they would want to represent them, based on policies and not on which candidate paid out the biggest bribe.

The Ballot Act (1872) and the Corrupt and Illegal Practices Prevention Act (1883), taken together, had a profound effect on politicians and the electorate. Bribing and treating before a general election were no longer possible and so, in the long run, relatively poorer men could afford to

Questions

1 Read Source R. How did the two politicians hope to influence the outcome of the elections in which they were involved?

2 How far do you think the politicians approved of what was happening?

Question

In your view, which was the more important Act in moving Britain towards a democratic system: the Secret Ballot Act or the Corrupt and Illegal Practices Prevention Act? You could debate this in your group.

stand as parliamentary candidates. Of course, this was provided they had sufficient private income to support themselves while working as an MP because MPs were not yet salaried. More immediately, voluntary work in the run-up to elections was vital if a particular party's candidate was to be elected, and this in turn emphasised the importance of party membership and organisation. Secret ballots meant that political parties had to be clearer in their policies as they worked to gain the support of different sections of the electorate. This, in turn, increased the importance of local party organisation in getting appropriate party propaganda out to the electorate. The electorate, too, became gradually more willing and able to question candidates' policies and affiliations, and led to candidates and party leaders achieving a higher profile in the constituencies.

The Third Reform Act: achieving democracy?

The Third Reform Act was not really one Act, but two separate ones – the Franchise Act of 1884 and the Redistribution Act of 1885 – linked together by confrontation and compromise and hence frequently regarded as one Act.

The issue

The issue was one of two parts, and concerned both the franchise and the distribution of seats.

- Town householders in the boroughs had been enfranchised in 1867, and by the early 1880s it seemed reasonable to enfranchise householders in rural areas, too. The old argument that agricultural labourers were less literate than town factory workers was no longer valid as the 1870 Education Act had ensured the spread of literacy and numeracy to rural areas.

- The redistribution clauses in the 1867 Act were very mild and still left a preponderance of seats in the South and West as opposed to the manufacturing areas of the Midlands and North.

The pressure for reform was far less specific than that for the reforms of 1832 or 1867; it emerged, rather, as part of a growing democratisation of British society in the 1870s and the realisation by people of all political persuasions that anomalies in the franchise and the distribution of seats could no longer be defended. However, the realisation that change was necessary sometimes conflicted with party interest. In short, would the Conservatives or Liberals gain from any reform?

From confrontation to compromise

Gladstone introduced a Liberal Reform Bill into the Commons in February 1884 that was very straightforward. He simply wanted to extend the principles of the 1867 Act to the counties: every male householder was to be entitled to vote. He made his position clear: 'I take my stand upon the broad principle that the enfranchisement of capable citizens, be they few or be they many, is an addition to the strength of the state.' Debates were swift and practical, and Gladstone quickly dispensed with any amendments; the one in favour of female suffrage, for example, was rejected by 271 to 135 votes. The Liberal majority in the Commons ensured that the Bill was approved and it was sent to the Lords.

Confrontation

In the House of Lords it was a different matter. The Conservative Party, led by **Lord Salisbury**, was in the majority, and Salisbury had set his face against reform. He believed, probably correctly, that to extend the franchise would lead to a considerable electoral advantage for the Liberal Party because the newly enfranchised agricultural labourers would be more likely to vote Liberal than Conservative. Salisbury, using his in-built Conservative majority in the Lords, therefore refused to support Gladstone's Reform Bill unless and until it was accompanied by a redistribution of seats. This was a high risk strategy and echoed, at least in its thinking, that followed by Disraeli in 1867. It was high risk because:

- it hinted at blackmail, which could stiffen Gladstone's resolve to get the Franchise Bill through parliament and so risk a Lords/Commons confrontation
- it played into Joseph Chamberlain's hands; a radical Liberal MP, he had been pressing for parliamentary reform for some time and would have relished a clash with the Lords over something as basic as democratic rights

Biography

Robert Gascoyne-Cecil, 3rd Marquess of Salisbury (Lord Salisbury) (1830–1903)

Born in February 1830, he was the second son of the 2nd Marquess of Salisbury, and educated at Eton and Oxford. In the years to 1865 he was known simply as Lord Robert Cecil, accepting the courtesy title of Viscount Cranborne until 1868, when he inherited his father's title. His marriage to Georgina Alderson, though opposed by his family because she was of a much lower social standing than he, was long and happy, producing eight children. Before being elected to the Commons he contributed hundreds of articles to various journals.

Elected to the House of Commons in 1854 as MP for Stamford in Lincolnshire, he worked in Derby's government as Secretary of State for India (1866–67) until he resigned over Disraeli's 1867 parliamentary Reform Bill. He worked again as Secretary of State for India in Disraeli's 1874 administration and then as Foreign Secretary in 1878. After Disraeli's death in 1881, Salisbury emerged as leader of the Conservative Party in the House of Lords with Sir Stafford Northcote leading the party in the Commons. He negotiated with Gladstone over the Franchise Bill (1884) and the Redistribution Bill (1885). An excellent negotiator and a maker of alliances when it suited him and his party, he was a highly intellectual, highly principled man. An anti-democrat, easily provoked to anger, in many ways he was a difficult colleague. Nevertheless, he out-manoeuvred potential rivals and served as Prime Minister 1885–86, 1886–92 and 1895–1902, being the first Prime Minister in the twentieth century and the last one to lead a government from the House of Lords.

- by delaying a reform that most people regarded as non-controversial, he could upset moderate opinion in parliament and in the country, and lose support for the Conservatives.

Salisbury argued that, if franchise reform went ahead without some form of redistribution, the Liberals could gain as many as 47 seats. If he held out for redistribution as well as franchise reform, the Liberal Party might well tear itself apart, as it had in the past, while the redistribution detail was being worked out. It was already in difficulties, with the radicals led by Chamberlain urging more and more reform and the old guard, headed up by Gladstone, resisting change. On the other hand there could always be a general election, which the Liberals might win. So Salisbury took the risk, and on 8 July 1867 the Lords announced that they would block the Franchise Bill unless a Redistribution Bill was put in place at the same time.

Compromise

Neither Conservatives nor Liberals wanted to mobilise the electorate; both wanted a quiet and agreeable compromise, reached by negotiation. And so the unprecedented happened. Urged and supported by Queen Victoria, secret meetings took place between Salisbury and Gladstone, together with leading politicians from both sides (including Chamberlain), in order to hammer out a solution. Salisbury held out for radical redistribution, whereby double-member constituencies were replaced by smaller, single-member ones. He had calculated that this would create a substantial number of middle-class constituencies that could be relied on to return Conservative MPs. By re-drawing constituency boundaries on more or less class lines, Salisbury hoped for minority representation in cities like Birmingham. Like Disraeli, he counted on redistribution correcting the perceived imbalance in favour of the Liberals that would be created by extending the franchise. Finally, the politicians arrived at the '**Arlington Street compact'**, whereby Salisbury got the redistribution he wanted and Gladstone got his extension of the franchise.

Definition

Arlington Street Compact 1884

The agreement between Salisbury (Conservative) and Gladstone (Liberal), whereby Salisbury got the redistribution he sought and Gladstone the extension of the franchise he wanted.

The Representation of the People Act 1884 (The Franchise Act)

The Act applied to the whole of Great Britain and gave the vote to all male householders in the counties and to male lodgers, provided they had occupied their houses or lodgings for at least twelve months. This meant that some two million agricultural workers were added to the electorate, which would now number around five million. Two in three men were now entitled to vote – but who was left out? Soldiers in barracks, for example, did not qualify under the householder franchise, and neither did domestic servants. And women, whether or not they were householders, still could not vote in general elections.

The Redistribution of Seats Act 1885

This Act also applied to the whole of Great Britain where all counties and most boroughs became single member constituencies, with an average population of 50,000. In order to achieve this, small boroughs with fewer than 15,000 people lost both members and boroughs with populations of between 15,000 and 50,000 lost one of their members. The 142 seats thus freed up were distributed to more fairly represent the UK population distribution. For example:

- London's constituencies were increased from 22 to 55
- Cornwall was represented by seven MPs instead of the original 44
- Lancashire gained 15 new seats
- The West Riding of Yorkshire gained 13 seats.

Only 24 boroughs remained as two-member seats, largely out of deference to traditionalists like Gladstone.

What was the long-term significance of these two acts?

The long-term significance was profound, although it was not necessarily recognised at the time.

- The stranglehold of the landowners, and the political power and influence of the aristocracy, was gone forever. There were only about a dozen county constituencies where influence was exercised by powerful patrons.
- The number of aristocratic ministers and MPs declined.
- The end of the old constituencies meant that emphasis was placed in elections on national, rather than local, issues.
- MPs began to argue that the only basis of political legitimacy lay in direct election by all the people rather than by selected groups.
- The position of the middle classes received an enormous boost: after the 1885 general election, manufacturers and commercial men outnumbered landowners in the House of Commons for the first time ever.
- The influence of the party as a political force and the party system of government became more prominent, and so party organisation became even more important.

Question

To what extent had democracy been achieved by 1885?

Unit summary

What have you learned in this unit?

You have learned that, in the 1850s and 1860s, there was a groundswell of feeling in the country at large and within parliament, and that the time was right for further parliamentary reform. Attitudes were changing, and a country that was the world's leading industrial nation needed representation that was not so closely tied to interest and property. You have seen that there was pressure for change outside parliament with the formation of the middle-class National Reform Union in 1864 and the working-class Reform League the following year, and that this was accompanied by economic distress caused by the collapse of the financial house of Overend and Gurney in 1866 and the bad harvest of 1865. However, parliamentary reform at this point in time came far more as a result of parliamentary manoeuvrings than by anything external to Westminster.

You have seen how the death of Lord Palmerston in 1865 enabled his Liberal Party to pursue reform with some expectation of success, and present a Representation of the People Bill to parliament in 1866. This moderate proposal was defeated by an alliance of Disraeli and the right-wing Liberals, scared of further reforms. The defeat of the bill brought down the government and the minority Conservative government that replaced it introduced a parliamentary Reform Bill of their own. Here, Disraeli, desperate for parliamentary success to ensure the stability of the Conservative Party and his own place within it, accepted amendment after amendment, and the final bill that became law was far more radical than the Liberal one of 1866, which Disraeli had been instrumental in defeating. Whereas before 1867 one man in five had the vote, after 1867 one man in three could vote in general elections.

You have seen how this reform wasn't enough. Corruption needed to be wiped out, and a significant way of doing this was by making the ballot secret. The logical development of the household suffrage granted to boroughs in 1867 was to extend it to the counties. This was done in 1885 as a result of clever manoeuvring by Salisbury, who ensured that any impact the extension of the franchise would have on the fortunes of the Conservative party would be nullified by redistribution. By the end of the period, only one man in three *couldn't* vote and, of course, no women yet had this privilege.

The introduction of the secret ballot and the ending of bribery at general election time emphasised the importance of party membership and organisation, and enabled the voters to have a free choice when electing their MP. This, in turn, meant that the political parties had to tailor their policies to the needs of the electorate and politicians developed a higher profile in the constituencies.

What skills have you used in this unit?

You have worked with a range of primary and secondary source material to enable you to deepen your understanding of the context of the 1867 Reform Act, and the reasons why further reform was needed. You have used your skills of comprehension, inference-making, cross-referencing and analysis in order to understand the dynamics of the political situation as it developed in Westminster in connection with the 1867 reforms and those that happened between 1872 and 1885. You have analysed the ideas of modern historians, specifically enabling you to gain an insight into different interpretations of the role played by Benjamin Disraeli.

Exam tips

Below is the sort of question you will find appearing on examination papers as a (b) question.

Study Sources N, O and P, and use your own knowledge. How far do you agree with the view that Disraeli was a politician without principles?

You tackled (b) questions at the end of Units 3 and 4. Look back at the tips you were given then. Different types of plan were suggested, and so you must choose the one that suits you best. It doesn't matter which you choose, but you must be sure to plan!

RESEARCH TOPIC

Return to the research topic you undertook at the end of Unit 1. (If you didn't do it, do it now!) Go back to your nineteen-century constituency and find out what impact the changes made in 1867 would have had. You could display your findings on a large-scale nineteenth-century map of the area. Where were men living who had the vote in 1830, 1833 and 1868?

6 Parliament, party and people 1832–67

What is this unit about?

This unit focuses on one of the important consequences of the 1832 Reform Act: the development and organisation of political parties in response to the enlarged electorate and redistribution of seats. The passage of the Reform Bill sharpened the divide between the parties, giving the Whigs the appearance of being a pro-reform party and the Tories being against reform and in favour of the status quo. Prior to 1832, MPs constantly grouped and re-grouped, depending on the issue under discussion; after 1832, individual allegiances to a particular party tended to become more or less fixed. Politicians now paid closer attention to the relationship between policies and electoral success as they came to terms with a new electoral landscape of redistributed seats and a larger electorate. This meant that political organisation came to be a key element in electoral success and extended from the parliamentary centre in Westminster into the constituencies to a greater degree than previously.

Key questions

- How far had the Tory/Conservative Party and Whig/Liberal Party developed distinctive and separate identities by the 1860s?
- To what extent had politics inside and outside of parliament become organised along party lines?

Timeline

1832	**Reform Act**
	Franchise enlarged and some seat redistribution
	General election
	Whigs/Liberals in control of Commons
	Founding of Tory/Conservative Carlton Club in London to encourage voter registration and dissemination of Tory propaganda
1834	**Tamworth Manifesto**
	Sets out Robert Peel's vision for the future Conservative Party
	Peel becomes Prime Minister in December
1835	**General election**
	Peel leads a Conservative minority administration
	Lichfield House Compact
	Combination of Whig, Irish and radical MPs bring down Peel's government

1835 **Municipal Corporations Act**
Borough corporations, the body of people responsible for running the boroughs, to be elected annually
Establishment of local political clubs and associations

1836 **Founding of Reform Club**
Formed by Whigs and middle-class radicals to encourage voter registration and dissemination of Whig/Liberal propaganda

1837 **Accession of Queen Victoria**
General election: combination of Whig and Irish MPs control the Commons

1839 **Bedchamber Crisis**
Melbourne offers resignation of Whig ministry
Queen Victoria refuses to swap some of her Whig-leaning ladies of the bedchamber for Conservative-inclined ones; Peel refuses to form a ministry and Melbourne's Whigs carry on

1841 **General election**
Peel and the Conservatives have a Commons majority of about 80 seats

1846 **Repeal of the Corn Laws**
Peel's Conservative Party splits between Peelites, who favoured repeal, and the majority, who did not

1850 **Death of Peel**
Peelites absorbed into the emerging Liberal Party under, first, Lord Aberdeen (himself a Peelite) and then Lord Palmerston

Ministries 1832–67

Date	Party allegiance	Prime Minister
1830–34	Whig	Earl Grey
1834 (July–Nov)	Whig	Lord Melbourne
1834 (Nov–Dec)	Tory	Duke of Wellington
1834–35	Conservative	Sir Robert Peel
1835–41	Whig	Lord Melbourne
1841–46	Conservative	Sir Robert Peel
1846–52	Whig	Lord John Russell
1852 (Feb–Dec)	Conservative	Earl of Derby
1852–55	Liberal/Peelite coalition	Earl of Aberdeen
1855–58	Liberal	Viscount Palmerston
1858–59	Conservative	Earl of Derby
1859–65	Liberal	Viscount Palmerston
1865–66	Liberal	Earl Russell
1866–68	Conservative	Earl of Derby

Source A

I consider the Reform Bill a final irrevocable settlement of a great Constitutional question – a settlement which no friend to the peace and welfare of this country would attempt to disturb, either by direct or by insidious means.

Then, as to the spirit of the Reform Bill, and the willingness to adopt and enforce it as a rule of government: if, by adopting the spirit of the Reform Bill, it be meant that we are to live in a perpetual vortex of agitation; that public men can only support themselves in public estimation by adopting every popular impression of the day, by promising the instant redress of anything which anybody may call an abuse, by abandoning altogether that great aid of government –more powerful than either law or reason – the respect for ancient rights, and the deference to prescriptive authority; if this be the spirit of the Reform Bill, I will not undertake to adopt it.

But if the spirit of the Reform Bill implies merely a careful review of institutions, civil and ecclesiastical, undertaken in a friendly temper, combining, with the firm maintenance of established rights, the correction of proved abuses and the redress of real grievances, in that case, I can for myself and colleagues undertake to act in such a spirit and with such intentions. Such declarations of general principle are, I am aware, necessarily vague, but I will endeavour to apply them practically to some of those questions which have of late attracted the greater share of public interest and attention.

From Robert Peel's address, *To the Electors of the Borough of Tamworth*, published 18 December 1834, just before the general election of 1835 (Peel was standing for election as MP for the borough of Tamworth); it became known as the Tamworth Manifesto

SKILLS BUILDER

1   Read Source A. What assurances is Peel giving to his electors?

2   Peel was, at this time, the leader of the Conservative Party in the House of Commons. What does this election manifesto tell us about the central ideas of his type of conservatism and so the direction in which he was likely to lead the Conservative Party?

What was the importance of the Tamworth Manifesto?

In the crisis over the Reform Act (look back to Unit 1) you saw that politicians moved relatively easily between political parties, depending on the various issues under discussion. It had been like this throughout the eighteenth century, with MPs grouping and re-grouping depending upon interest, inclination and persuasion.

Matters firmed up, somewhat, during the election of 1832, held after the passage of the Reform Act. The election of 1832 was not really fought between a Whig and Tory Party. Rather, it was fought between those who supported reform and those who had opposed it. Those who supported reform were a mixed bunch. They included:

- those who wanted reform 'in order to preserve', and who supported the Church of England and the monarchy

- radicals who favoured free trade, the abolition of the monarchy and the **disestablishment of the Church of England**, and who saw parliamentary reform as the first step to getting what they wanted.

This proved to be a difficult body of MPs to keep together as a political party and even as a government, and splits over Irish affairs led to the resignation in 1834 of Earl Grey, the Whig Prime Minister. At the same time Lord Althorp, the Whig Leader of the House of Commons, inherited his father's title and so moved to the Lords. Two important Whigs now needed replacing in the Commons.

William IV tried to engineer a coalition between the Whig Lord Melbourne and the Tory Robert Peel. When this failed, the King, unable to agree with Melbourne's choice of leader (Lord John Russell) in the Commons, dismissed the Whig government even though it had a secure majority. Invited by the King to form a government, Peel hurried back from Italy where he had been on holiday, and formed a ministry which, interestingly, included William Gladstone. Having no majority in the Commons, Peel decided to fight an election at once, which was when he issued the Tamworth election manifesto.

In the Tamworth Manifesto, part of which forms Source A, Peel is appealing directly to his electors in the borough of Tamworth: he is setting out his political position. There was nothing new in a politician doing this; what *was* new was a politician appealing to electors – an action that would have appalled Lord Liverpool for its sheer vulgarity. Gentlemen may explain their position to fellow MPs, but to go beyond Westminster was unheard of. Peel went even further than this; his manifesto was released to the press and published in the newspapers (he never actually went to Tamworth to read it out) and so it reached a far wider audience than his own constituents. In doing this he was quite clearly setting out his view of conservatism and his vision of what the principles of a new Conservative Party should be.

What was the result of the 1835 general election?

The Conservatives did well and gained around 80 seats. However, this was not enough and Peel was once again left leading a minority government. If the opposition could reunite, he would be brought down. This is exactly what happened. As a result of the **Lichfield House Compact**, a combination of Whigs, Irish and radicals, Peel's government was defeated over the question of Irish Church revenues, and he resigned.

In many ways, the confused and complicated political situation in the years between 1832 and 1835 can be seen as a watershed in British politics.

- William IV had been within his constitutional rights in dismissing Melbourne and appointing Peel to a minority ministry. However, this would be the last time a monarch dismissed a ministry that had the support of the House of Commons.

Definitions

Disestablishment of the Church of England

The ending of official and legal links between the Church of England and the state.

Lichfield House Compact

An unwritten agreement made at Lichfield House in February 1835 between the Whigs, led by Lord John Russell, and a group of Irish MPs, led by Daniel O'Connell, whereby the Whigs could depend on Irish support in the Commons in return for promising to consider some reforming legislation for Ireland.

- Pre-1832, the King's minister who fought a general election could be certain of returning to the Commons with a majority because of the vast amount of influence and patronage wielded by the monarch. The 80 or so seats, which were all Peel could pick up when campaigning as the King's minister, sent him back to the Commons at the head of a minority government, and demonstrates the impact the 1832 Reform Act had had on the power of the monarchy.

- Because of the dramatic lessening of royal influence, general elections, and particularly political parties, assumed a greater importance than ever before.

- By appealing directly to the electorate, the Tamworth Manifesto represented a completely new attitude and approach on the part of a leading politician with regard to elections, the electorate and party.

- The Tamworth Manifesto set out Peel's vision for the new Conservative Party: it was his mission statement.

Source B

The Conservative Party is not identical with the Tory Party. It includes, indeed, the Tories but it is a more comprehensive term and the basis is a wider one. The Conservative Party may be said to consist of all that part of the community who are attached to the Constitution in Church and State, and who believes that it is threatened with subversion by the encroachments of democracy. This does not necessarily suppose an abstract horror of all innovation, or an illiberal and narrow view of politics. On the contrary, the opinions and feelings of the great body of the Conservatives in this country are liberal, candid and generous. They consider that the march of democracy, with its eternal warfare against all that exists, is a retrograde one.

From Sir J.B. Walsh, MP, *Chapters of Contemporary History*, published in 1836

Source C

[The Tamworth Manifesto] was a turning point, not just in Tory fortunes, but also in the nature of the Tory Party. Peel for the first time committed his party to accepting the irreversibility of the Reform Act and also a programme of moderate reform for the correction of 'proved abuses'.

Peel's primary target in his manifesto was not the 'Ultras' [i.e. far right-wing Tories].

For the moment they had nowhere else to go. He looked beyond the shires and the small boroughs in search of voters who would see in the Tory Party both a guardian of the constitution and a vehicle for cautious, measured reform. The Tories even adopted a new name, which increasingly implied the rejection of mere reaction. Though the word 'Conservative' was, apparently, first used to describe the party in 1830, it came increasingly to be applied to the fusion of the old Tory interest with moderate reformers.

In the election of 1835, the Conservatives made a net gain of about 80 seats. Virtually all these gains came at the expense of the Whigs rather than the radical elements. Those who were anti-radical and firmly attached to the constitution in Church and State were beginning to see Conservatism as a better guarantor of what they held dear than the Whigs.

From Eric Evans, *Political Parties in Britain 1783–1867*, published in 1985

SKILLS BUILDER

1 Study Sources A and B. How far does Sir J.B. Walsh (Source B) support Peel's vision of conservatism expressed in Source A?

2 Read Sources A, B and C. How far do Sources A and B support the views given by Eric Evans in Source C?

Question

In what ways did the Tamworth Manifesto signal a new beginning in British politics?

Discussion point

Robert Peel was re-elected MP for Tamworth in 1835. He was the only candidate and so was re-elected unopposed. Why, then, did he bother to write the Tamworth Manifesto?

From the Lichfield House Compact to the 1841 election: Whigs in decline?

The Lichfield House Compact achieved its objective, and Lord Melbourne and the Whigs were returned to government. Were they going to mirror the Conservatives and form themselves into a distinctive political party? Ironically, it was the very nature of the Lichfield House Compact that prevented this happening and which finally tore them apart. A combination of MPs comprising moderate Whigs, left-wing radicals and Irish was never going to hold together successfully for very long.

The significance of the general election of 1837

The death of William IV and the accession of the 18-year-old Victoria caused a general election to be held. The result – the Conservatives won 313 seats – left Melbourne and the Whigs dependent on Irish MPs for their overall majority in the Commons. This was viewed with suspicion by a predominantly English electorate who were by now (post-1832) overwhelmingly middle-class and property-owning. The Whigs had found it – and would increasingly find it – difficult to win seats in the counties, where the number of seats had been increased from 80 to 144, and where the Conservatives were increasingly being seen as the 'English' party. The Whigs' strength lay in the borough vote, and specifically in the newly enfranchised boroughs of the Midlands and North. The Whigs desperately needed to re-invent themselves. Hampered by their reliance upon the support of Irish MPs in the Commons, Melbourne's ministry lacked the will and the vision to do this. However, it was during this time that the Whigs passed some significant legislation that was to become the bedrock of their later emergence as the party of reform.

Source D

The Tories left the country in such a state [in 1830] that it was no wonder that now they wanted to give up the name 'Tory' and to assume some title that would not be so much associated with their former acts. (*Cheers.*) Yet now the country was called upon to pay to the successors of those Tories all possible respect under their newly assumed name of Conservatives (*cheers and laughter*) which, after all, was only an alias for the name of Tory. If they chose to abolish the old names of Tory and Whig, he had no objection to be distinguished from the new name of Conservative, and to be called a Reformer. (*Cheers.*) He was ready to be called a reformer – to see the country advance in all that was good, and generous and enlightened. (*Cheers.*) He was unwilling to see the country go back, or stand still, in [its] great institutions. He was an advocate for reform in the truest sense of the word, and he would do all in his power to promote those measures of reform of which he was already an avowed advocate. If other measures of reform were proposed, he was ready to discuss them, and if they could be shown to be good, in God's name let us have them (*cheers*); but let them not be deterred by any bugbear from boldly and fearlessly arguing for them in the first instance, and if right from adopting them. (*Cheers.*)

From a report in *The Times*, 31 July 1837, on a speech by Lord John Russell immediately after his re-election as one of the two Whig MPs for Stroud in Gloucestershire

Source E

In recasting the representative system, that point has been reached beyond which it is impossible to proceed with safety if the rights of property are to be respected, and an aristocracy maintained.

The struggle against the progressive advance of democracy may, or may not, take a long time, and may end in unforeseen results. But my part was taken at the passing of the Reform Act. I pledged myself to resist the [secret] ballot, short parliaments, and further extension of the suffrage because of the great change we were then enabled peacefully to bring about. Reason, honour, duty, combine to restrain me from agreeing directly or indirectly to any of these measures on which the Radicals insist, and which inevitably must tend to the destruction of our mixed form of government. The resistance may be hopeless, but I am bound to make it; and it would not be so desperate if all who promised to resist were united, and in time opposed the open designs of that Radical Party which is now stronger in the House of Commons than the Whigs.

From a letter by Sir James Graham to Lord Tavistock (Lord John Russell's elder brother), dated 29 August 1838; both men were Whigs

SKILLS BUILDER

1 Read Sources A and D. How far do Peel's vision and Russell's vision differ?

2 Now read Sources D and E. Both were written by leading Whigs. How far do they disagree about the ways in which the Whig Party should develop?

3 Using Sources D and E, and your own knowledge, in what ways do these two sources illustrate the difficulties faced by the Whigs/ Liberals as they try to rebuild their party?

The Bedchamber Crisis

On the surface, the Bedchamber Crisis seems nothing more than a petty squabble between the Queen and her potential Prime Minister, Robert Peel. But beneath the surface it reveals some skilful political thinking on the part of Peel. Melbourne offered his resignation in 1839 following a narrow victory on the Government of Jamaica Bill. Peel could have formed a Conservative government, but his request that Queen Victoria replace some ladies of her bedchamber who had Whig sympathies with others who were more inclined to support the new Conservatism was angrily rejected by her. As a result, Peel refused to form his second minority government, and Melbourne carried on.

This 'storm in a teacup' was the result of clever calculation by Peel. He reckoned that Melbourne could not hope to revive his party if he was returned to office. And so he worked a situation where Melbourne was forced to continue in office. Peel gambled on Whig/Liberal fortunes falling even further and, as a result, the Conservative victory, when it came, would be even greater. And so it proved to be.

The 1841 general election

The last two years of the Whig ministry under Melbourne's ministry were particularly troublesome.

- The country was going through a severe economic depression.
- The economic depression led to severe social discontent, mass poverty and enormous pressure on the poor law, and demands for relief escalated.
- Chartism revived as a result of escalating social and economic problems.
- The **Anti-Corn Law League**, founded in Manchester in 1838, pressed for the abolition of the Corn Laws as a solution to both economic and social problems – economic, because it would encourage free trade; social, because it would reduce the price of bread.

It was a financial crisis that finally brought matters to a head. Declining revenues and a budget deficit of £6 million led, on 4 June 1841, to a Conservative motion of 'No confidence' in the government being won by a single vote. Melbourne and the Whig government resigned, and the country prepared for a general election.

The Liberals were tired and the electors saw them as politicians without solutions to the troubles facing the country.

- Some radicals, weary with the Whigs, turned to the Conservatives, but most focused on single issues, such as repeal of the Corn Laws.
- The attempted Whig manoeuvre to break this potential Radical–Tory alliance, by ending the sliding scale of duties on imported corn and replacing it with a fixed duty, did not impress.

Definition

Anti-Corn Law League

A middle-class radical movement that gained tremendous popularity. Dissatisfied with the tinkering via 'sliding scales' that had taken place since 1828, the League campaigned for total repeal. It was well funded and highly organised, employing various techniques such as public meetings, pamphlets, newspaper articles and campaigns in support of pro-repeal MPs. Beyond the specific target of repealing the Corn Laws, the League also promoted the ideology of free trade.

Source F

The Conservative Party stood for the defence not merely of the landed aristocracy but of the interests of the solid middle classes. The electoral successes in the urban constituencies which, added to the more predictable victories in the counties, provided the majority of 1841. This was a practical reward for all that Peel had worked for in the previous decade.

From Norman Gash, *Wellington and Peel*, published in 1974

- Feargus O'Connor, banking on the appeal of Tory criticism of the new Poor Law, urged Chartist supporters to vote for Conservative candidates.

And so the alignments that had brought the Whigs to power 11 years earlier now combined to bring them down. Peel and the Conservatives were returned with a majority of nearly 80 seats.

One major significance of the 1841 election was that it divided electors not so much on issues but along party lines. It revealed, too, where the strengths of the Conservative Party lay. Conservative strength lay in the counties and small boroughs. Peel's party controlled 136 out of 159 county seats in England and Wales; they won 44 seats in the larger urban areas such as Bristol and Liverpool, but made no inroads into the textile towns of the Midlands and North, which remained staunchly Liberal. The Conservatives seemed to be looking for, and gaining, support in their traditional base, thus they were consolidating their appeal, not extending it. Furthermore, only 47 per cent of seats were contested – fewer than in any general election since the passing of the Reform Act of 1832. Thus, many Conservatives held or gained their seats by nomination, not election. Historian Eric Evans claims that: 'It is clear that the Conservatives in 1841 were the better organised party; it is far from clear that they were the more popular.' It would be difficult to disagree.

Source G

Conservative gains had come from the counties and the small English boroughs with under a thousand electors. Of the English boroughs with more than two thousand electors, Conservatives secured only 15 of 58 seats. The Conservative majority, calculated at 78 overall, was therefore based mainly on their overwhelming superiority in the English counties and small boroughs. The pattern of Conservative representation suggests that Peel did not succeed, as he intended, in broadening the base of Conservative support.

From Ian Newbould, *Sir Robert Peel and the Conservative Party, 1832–41: A Study in Failure?*, published in 1983

Source H

It does seem that Peel's exhortations to the new urban middle classes, as distinct from the older professional and commercial elite, fell largely on deaf ears. It was the traditional Tory slogans – the Church in danger, the Corn Laws under threat – rather than the new spirit of the Tamworth Manifesto, which prevailed in 1841. This is a sombre reflection on Peel's efforts to educate his party in the 1830s. The Conservative Party still remained above all the party of land – a fact that was to have dramatic consequences for his party in the 1840s.

From Paul Adelman, *Peel and the Conservative Party 1830–1850*, published in 1974 (third edition 1990)

SKILLS BUILDER

1 Read Sources F and G. How far do these sources agree about the nature of Peel's success?

2 Now read Source H. Would you agree that the 1841 election results showed that Peel's party of 1841 showed little relationship with the Tamworth Manifesto?

Party or principle?

Peel's concept of government

All the policies Peel implemented were based on his concept of government and the role of party within it. Peel believed that in accepting the monarch's invitation to form a government it was his responsibility to govern with due regard for both national security and national prosperity. Everything, even party interest, had to be secondary to those two guiding principles. It was this that was to lead Peel into conflict with his backbenchers, which was to destroy both him and the party he was leading.

The problem of free trade

Peel's belief that it was his government's responsibility to promote national prosperity led him towards free trade. He maintained that free trade – that is, trade without the restriction of import tariffs – was essential if the nation was to prosper. It was this issue that revealed the fragile nature of the unity of different factions within the Conservative Party and of the lack of loyalty towards the party when it ran counter to individual interest.

However, the immediate economic problem was to reduce the deficit left by the outgoing government. Peel believed that the answer lay in the stimulation of trade through reductions in import duties. But there was a balancing act to play here. The steady reduction of import duties would inevitably lead to a reduction in government revenue. How was this to be made up? The reintroduction of income tax in 1842, the free trade budgets of 1842 and 1845, and the Bank Charter Act of 1844 were aimed to cover this revenue gap. Peel believed that the reduction of the deficit left by the outgoing government would lead ultimately to prosperity. However, he had counted without his backbenchers.

The strength of the Conservative Party after the 1841 election, as you have seen, lay in the counties and not the boroughs. Most Conservative MPs still represented land and the landed interest. These men generally were staunchly Anglican, hated Catholics and were generally opposed to reform, although they were grateful to Peel for getting them back into government. Perhaps above all, they were deeply suspicious of the new commercial class whom, or so it seemed, they were being asked to help by Peel's progressive tariff reductions. They began to turn against him.

- Ninety-five Conservative MPs voted against Peel on a Factory Act they considered to be too favourable to industrialists.
- In 1845, the government proposed, as part of a campaign to attract Irish Catholics into the Conservative fold, to increase its annual grant to the Catholic Maynooth College in Dublin from £9,000 to £26,000. Half of the Conservatives in the Commons voted against renewing the grant; a young Conservative MP, William Gladstone, resigned from the Cabinet because he felt that, in the light of a book he had written some time

earlier, people might expect him to oppose the Maynooth grant, which he didn't. His resignation speech left everyone mystified as to the exact reasons for his decision.

Interest, it would seem, took precedence over party. The internal contradictions, that finally were to break the party, were being revealed.

The repeal of the Corn Laws and the destruction of Peel's party

The Corn Laws gave considerable protection to arable farmers and, therefore, to the landed interest. Although Peel had managed to introduce a sliding scale of tariffs, protection still remained. It was the only major obstacle remaining to achieving Peel's aim of free trade and his vision for national prosperity. But as you have already seen, the strength of the Conservative Party lay in the counties and with the landed interest. Those who supported the retention of the Corn Laws did so partly for economic reasons. Their support for the Corn Laws also stemmed from the belief that land, and not commerce, was the basis of a stable society. With the right to vote still vested in land and property ownership, it was (they maintained) the agricultural, landowning interest that should have the status afforded by protection and which would emphasise their superiority over the upstart commercial classes.

Peel disagreed, believing firmly that national interest should take precedence over party interest and factional interest. Party should be subordinated to national interest, and so his decision was made. The debates surrounding repeal were fast and furious, with the Conservatives Lord George Bentinck and Benjamin Disraeli rounding on their leader and rallying Protectionists behind them. It was to no avail. The Repeal Bill passed through the Commons by 339 votes to 242. But of these 339 votes, only 112 were from Conservative MPs. The remaining 227 came from the Liberal opposition. The Liberals were far less wedded to land than were the Conservatives, and far readier to listen to the arguments of trade and commerce in their manufacturing-based constituencies in the larger boroughs, backed by the free-trade arguments of the Anti-Corn Law League. Significantly, Peel's support from his own party came mainly from those Conservative boroughs where there was a strong commercial interest. From the county representation, 86 per cent of MPs voted with Bentinck and Disraeli. In the Lords, Wellington supported Peel and, on 26 June 1846, the Corn Bill passed its third reading without any trouble. At the same time, and after an all-night debate, Liberals and Protectionists combined against Peel to defeat an Irish Coercion Bill, and the following day he resigned.

Discussion point

Should Peel have put the interests of the Conservative Party before his own principles?

Peel had stuck to the logic his principles dictated, and had ensured the repeal of the Corn Laws. In doing so he had destroyed the Conservative Party he had worked so hard to create and ensured his own downfall as Prime Minister and party leader.

Source I

A cartoon published in *Punch* magazine on 3 October 1845; Richard Cobden (featured in the cartoon) was a founder member and leader of the Anti-Corn Law League and a strong believer in free trade

Definition

Irish Famine

Between 1845 and 1851 at least a million Irish people died of starvation and disease. The famine was triggered by a fungal infection that destroyed most of the potato crop in 1845. This subsistence food had taken on an enormous significance because of exploitation of the peasantry through subdivision of landholdings. Potato blight was therefore the immediate but not the underlying cause of Irish distress. The government response was inadequate; but the crisis provided further grounds for repealing the Corn Laws in order to make it cheaper to import foreign grain.

Source J

It is difficult to contend that the Corn Laws were repealed because of League pressure. That pressure was not so strong in 1845–46 as it had been in 1843–44. The Corn Laws were repealed because Peel no longer believed in them. Protection was untenable when Britain's swollen population craved bread. The old argument that protection kept farmers producing for the home market was no longer sufficient. Additionally, Peel knew that a substantial proportion of the landed interest no longer set great store by protection. He hated extra-parliamentary pressure and coercion and he would not countenance that either could force legislative change. [The year] 1846 was timely precisely because League pressure was for the moment less strident. Peel's actions in 1846, though they were hastened by the **Irish famine**, completed the process whereby the forces of property were strengthened, not weakened.

From Eric Evans, *Forging of the Modern State*, published in 2001

SKILLS BUILDER

1 Study Source I. What point is the cartoonist making?
2 Read Source J. How far does this source challenge the view of Corn Law repeal given in Source I?

Source K

I advise that we all – whatever may be our opinions about free trade – oppose the introduction of free politics. Let men stand by the principle on which they were elected, right or wrong. I make no exception. If they be in the wrong, they must retire to private life.

It is not a legitimate trial of the principles of free trade versus the principle of protection if a parliament, the majority of whom are elected to support protection, be won over to free trade by the skill of the very individual whom they were elected to support the exact opposite. It is not fair to the people of England.

The fate of a government, whether we are to have a Liberal administration or a Conservative one, whatever may be the impact of Cabinets on parliament as an institution, (and still a popular institution in this country) is dependent, not upon the government, but on the consideration of the vast majority of the members of this House. Do not, then, because you see a great man giving us his opinions – do not cheer him on, do not give so ready a reward to political tergiversation [changing of loyalties]. Above all, maintain the line of demarcation between parties, for it is only by maintaining the independence of party that you can maintain the integrity of public men, and the power and influence of parliament itself.

From a speech by Benjamin Disraeli in the House of Commons on 22 January 1846

Source L

So far from regretting expulsion from office, I rejoice in it as the greatest relief from an intolerable burden.

To have your own way, and to be for five years the Minister of this country in the House of Commons, is quite enough for any man's strength. He is entitled to his discharge, from length of service. But to have to incur the deepest responsibility, to bear the heaviest toil, to reconcile colleagues with conflicting opinions to a common course of action, to keep together in harmony the Sovereign, the Lords and Commons; to have to do these things, and to be at the same time the tool of a party – that is to say, to adopt the opinions of men who have not access to your knowledge, and could not profit by it if they had, who spend their time in eating and drinking, and hunting, shooting, gambling, horse-racing and so forth – would be an odious servitude, to which I will never submit.

I intend to keep aloof from party combinations. So far as a man can be justified in forming such a resolution, I am determined not again to resume office.

I would be nothing but the head of a government, the real 'bona-fide' head, and to be that requires more youth, more ambition, more love of official power and official occupation, than I can pretend to.

I will take care, too, not again to burn my fingers by organising a party. There is too much truth in the saying, 'The head of a party must be directed by its tail.'

As heads see, and tails are blind, I think heads are the best judges as to the course to be taken.

From a letter by Sir Robert Peel to Sir Henry Hardinge, a senior
Conservative, dated 24 September 1846

SKILLS BUILDER

1 Read Source K.

   (a) In what ways is Disraeli criticising Peel?

   (b) What does Disraeli believe should be the proper relationship between government and parliament?

2 Read Source L. What problems did Peel find in managing the relationship between Prime Minister and Party?

3 Read Sources K and L. How far do Disraeli's and Peel's attitudes to party differ?

4 Does the fact that Peel was ready to destroy the Conservative party mean that the concept of party was not as firmly rooted in parliamentarians' minds as Disraeli in Source K appears to believe?

What was the impact of the Peelites on the party system?

The year 1846 marked the disintegration of the Conservative Party, which had been so carefully built up by Robert Peel. It also marked the formation of the Peelite faction, loyal supporters of Peel, and consisting of about one-third of the members of the 'old' Conservative Party. Led by Peel until his death in 1850, he dominated the Commons in an elder statesman role. His main aim was to ensure that any attempt to return to agricultural protection was defeated, and so he was prepared to go to any lengths to keep the Liberal government that replaced him in power, even if this meant supporting it against its own radical wing and, of course, against the Protectionist Conservatives.

Source M

By attempting to act as an independent member of the House of Commons, Peel was not only deluding himself, he also placed his followers who voted with him in favour of repeal in an impossible position. He refused to support even the most tentative attempts at Conservative reunion in 1846–47, though this was almost certainly a forlorn hope while Bentinck led the Protectionists in the Commons. But neither was he prepared to encourage any positive moves towards the Whig camp, despite his benevolent attitude towards the government. This negative attitude bewildered and irritated even his most loyal disciples, especially Gladstone, who wrote some years later of Peel's 'thoroughly false position for the last four years of his life'. Peel thus contributed decisively during this period to the confusions and uncertainties of political life, and 'kept the party system in a state of suspended animation'.

From Paul Adelman, *Peel and the Conservative Party 1830–1850*,
published in 1974 (third edition 1990)

The split in the Conservative Party had been so bitter on a personal level, with attacks on Peel by Bentinck and Disraeli, that reconciliation was impossible, even after Peel's death in 1850 and the Conservatives' abandonment of protectionism in 1852. So where were the Peelites to go? Was this the beginning of a three-party system? Peel had set his face against melding his supporters into a separate party, so almost inevitably even the strongest members drifted away. After Peel's death, the Peelite Lord Aberdeen became Prime Minister in 1852 by forming a coalition with the Whigs. After the fall of the Aberdeen government in 1855, the Peelites lost further cohesion when Gladstone, Graham and Herbert joined Palmerston's Liberal government. Reduced in numbers by the 1857 general election, the Peelites finally disappeared as a separate political faction when they combined with the Liberals, radicals and Irish MPs to bring down the Conservative government of the Earl of Derby in 1859.

Thus, Sir Robert Peel was not only the architect of a Conservative revival in the 1830s, but also became one of the founders of the new Liberal Party that was emerging under Gladstone.

Party and constituency organisation 1832–67

The years between the first Reform Act of 1832 and the second of 1867 saw the gradual emergence of two separate political parties – the Conservatives and the Liberals. This was mirrored and enhanced by a parallel development of party organisations in the provinces, spearheaded and united by party headquarters in London.

The 1832 Reform Act (see Unit 2, pages 26–28) increased the numbers of men able to vote and made some concessions towards redistribution of seats. This had an immediate impact on the constituencies: interest in politics grew as those eligible to vote gave thought to where their votes should be placed, and those party agents whose job it was to manage elections and promote candidates attempted to attract electors new and old to their side.

The impact of voter registration

The 1832 Reform Act enlarged the franchise to include all £10 householders in the boroughs, providing they had lived at the same address for over a year and had not claimed poor relief. However, there was a complication in that in order to vote, a man's name had to be on the relevant electoral register. This cost one shilling per person (which inhibited some) and inclusion on the register could be challenged. It was obviously in the interests of a particular candidate to get all his supporters onto the electoral register – and to challenge their place on the register of those supporting the rival candidate. Challenges could, and were, made on many grounds. The most common involved having moved house, not having paid the local rates that were due from them and having received poor relief. Names were frequently confused, 'evidence' was often wrong and not all challenges were upheld. Nevertheless, they served as a useful delaying tactic, particularly if an election loomed. Indeed, it took eight years for the electoral register in Leeds to be finalised because of all the challenges and counter-challenges to particular names being included. Candidates' agents were usually local solicitors, who knew the area well and the people living there. They were also well placed to argue, defending and challenging, in the local Barristers Revising Court. It was therefore not surprising that, certainly in the larger boroughs, parties began to establish organisations dedicated to raising awareness of voter eligibility, supporting their own candidates and generally disseminating party propaganda on a range of issues. This, in turn, increased the likelihood of contested elections.

Question

How far do you agree with Gladstone's view (quoted in Source M) that, after 1846, Peel 'kept the party system in a state of suspended animation'?

Source N

The Reform Bill has made a change in the position of parties and in the practical working of public affairs, which the authors of it did not anticipate. There is a perfectly new element of political power – namely, the registration of voters, a more powerful one than either the Sovereign or the House of Commons. That party is the strongest in point of fact which has the existing registration in its favour.

From a letter by Sir Robert Peel to Charles Arbuthnot, a British diplomat and Tory politician, dated 1839

Definitions

Nonconformists

Nonconformists were Protestants, of various denominations, who refused to conform to the Anglican Church. They had gained a degree of civil equality after 1828, when the Test and Corporation Acts were repealed, but still suffered discrimination. There was a longstanding tradition of Whig support for civil and religious liberty. The Municipal Corporations Act boosted the influence of Nonconformists and helped to create a strong link with the emerging Liberal Party.

Reform Club

The Reform Club was founded in 1836 by a combination of Whigs and middle-class radicals, in response to the Carlton Club. Like its rival, the Reform Club aimed to combine sociability with better political organisation, enjoying also the added attraction of a renowned French chef.

Political activity in the boroughs

It was not just the 1832 Reform Act that generated greater political activity in the boroughs. As significant was the reform of local government. The Whig government appointed a sympathetic reformer, **Joseph Parkes**, as secretary to a royal commission to investigate this issue. As expected, Parkes found that:

- small groups of property owners perpetuated their own local power
- these cliques were often dominated by Tory supporters of the Church of England.

The commission's recommendations led to the Municipal Corporations Act of 1835, which replaced 178 'closed' boroughs with new 'open' corporations that were elected annually by rate-paying householders. Each corporation would have a mayor, aldermen and councillors. This system was also extended to urban areas such as Birmingham and Manchester, which had previously lacked adequate municipal institutions. Reform of municipal corporations was popular with **Nonconformists**, who often played a key role in local elections, especially in Midland and northern towns, thereby providing a new powerbase for the Whig/Liberal Party.

This heady combination of annual municipal elections, religious and political rivalry, plus competition to register voters for general elections, amounted to something of a revolution in local political life.

Biography

Joseph Parkes (1796–1865)

A native of Warwick and a solicitor by training, Parkes was linked to middle-class radicalism in the Midlands. In the reform crisis he acted as a go-between for the Whigs with the Birmingham Political Union. From the mid-1830s onwards, he became the leading parliamentary agent for the Whig/Liberal Party. As a founder member of the **Reform Club**, Parkes was actively involved in promoting voter registration and supporting electoral candidates.

Conservative associations

As would be expected, the party in opposition was quickest to organise itself to meet the new situation. The Tories, despite their earlier ideological opposition to parliamentary reform, were quick off the mark under the new system. Professional agents were appointed for most of the large towns and dealt with challenges to the electoral roll. They also ensured that the views of 'their' candidate were publicised through meetings and handbills – the frequency and intensity of which increased as elections drew near. To combat the rising influence of Liberal nonconformity, the Conservative Party created local clubs with names such as 'The Tradesman's Conservative Association'. Conservative clubs became popular with those who disliked the 'holier than thou' attitude of some Nonconformists and their campaigns against alcohol, the 'demon drink'.

Centrally, the able and efficient **Francis Bonham** administered the Conservative **Carlton Club** in London. From there, a Conservative election committee offered advice, distributed propaganda and, on occasions, gave sums of money to support a candidate in a strategic seat.

Definition

Carlton Club

Founded in 1832 in response to the Tory defeat in the wake of reform, the Carlton Club aimed to rally support by encouraging voter registration and co-ordinating propaganda in the press.

Biography

Francis Bonham (1785–1863)

Bonham trained as a lawyer but devoted his life instead to politics – both as an MP (1830–37) and Tory whip (ensuring that MPs voted consistently), and as the party's chief electoral expert from 1832 onwards. A founder member of the Carlton Club, from where he conducted most of his work, Bonham was a superb organiser who acquired detailed understanding of candidates and constituencies. His efforts contributed significantly to the Conservative victory at the 1841 general election.

Source O

We have raised here £2,400 for Dublin City and £3,300 for Westminster. The candidates and their Committees must do the rest.

From a report by Sir Henry Hardinge, a wealthy Tory, on the money raised by the Carlton Club for candidates in the 1837 general election

Liberal organisations

In a similar way to the Conservatives, the Whigs/Liberals built up party organisations in the provinces – especially in the boroughs, where they were more likely to pick up radical and reformist voters than in the counties. Centrally, in London, the Reform Club was established in direct opposition to the Carlton Club. Managed with breathtaking efficiency by the Birmingham agent, Joseph Parkes, it attracted both Liberals and the less extreme radicals. Parkes' efficiency and hard work was epitomised in his own borough, where, without fail in all the elections held between 1832 and 1867, Birmingham returned two Liberal MPs.

The Liberal Party tended to attract a far more diverse range of supporters than the Conservatives. This meant that in a two-member borough they were able to field two contrasting candidates that would appeal to different elements in the electorate.

Source P

Our aims are to promote by all legal and constitutional means the return of truly Liberal Members for this Borough – to give the Utmost Efficiency to the provisions of the Reform Act by carefully watching the formation of the Official Lists of Voters and the proceedings of the revising Barrister's Court to maintain Freedom and Purity of Election, and to Protect the Electors from Intimidation and Oppression, and the demoralising Effects of Bribery and Corruption and to facilitate the Expression of Public Opinion on important Public Questions.

From the *Proceedings of the Bradford Reform* Society, 1835

The Municipal Corporations Act had revitalised public interest in local elections and in electing councillors who were in favour of civic improvement. Many took the opportunity to remove the old-fashioned Tory elite and replace them with Liberal councillors who were more forward-looking. This was a far more likely occurrence in the large urban boroughs than in the rural counties, where the habit of deference was still strong. Indeed, the first municipal elections held in Birmingham and Manchester in 1838, resulted in no Tory councillors being elected at all. It was in the cities and towns, too, that religion played a major part, with Liberal nonconformists being generally preferred over the Tory Anglicans. It was this local regeneration of interest in politics that both initiated and developed the rival party organisations. These organisations would then throw themselves into action during the fairly frequent local elections and remained poised for the more rare by-elections and general elections.

Source Q

Local political activity after 1835 helped to consolidate party identity and allegiance in general elections. Organisation and discipline were now at least as likely to be developed locally as imposed from the centre. Local political issues, such as water supply and civic amenities, tended to be much more vigorously and consistently debated than were national ones. Political candidates were also selected on the basis of how well they would represent local interests. Party allegiance in the constituencies remained firm in the later 1840s and 1850s, when, according to many accounts, party politics at Westminster were supposed to have been thrown into confusion by the split in the Conservative Party over the repeal of the Corn Laws.

From Eric Evans, *Political Parties in Britain 1783–1867*, published in 1985

SKILLS BUILDER

Read Sources P and Q. How far does Source P support the views expressed in Source Q about the strength of local political organisations?

Unit summary

What have you learned in this unit?

You have seen how, from the mid-1830s, the Tory Party virtually reinvented itself as the new Conservative Party, and developed a strong identity at Westminster, only to tear itself apart over the repeal of the Corn Laws, thereafter entering a long period of ineffectiveness. You have learned that the emergence of the Liberal Party from the old Whig Party was sometimes a much slower and more disjointed affair, and yet the Whigs, who by contrast appeared much less cohesive than the Conservatives, spent far longer in power. You have understood how, out in the counties and boroughs, it was the combination of the 1832 Reform Act and the 1835 Municipal Corporations Act that revitalised politics, leading to the polarisation of Whig and Tory, Liberal and Conservative with the traditional Conservatives dominating the counties and the reforming Liberals, the urban boroughs. The interplay between local and central party organisations led to MPs being returned to parliament who more firmly represented the interests of their electors and their constituencies than ever before.

What skills have you used in this unit?

You have worked with a range of primary and contemporary sources to investigate the emergence of the Conservative Party under Sir Robert Peel. You have considered the significance of the Tamworth Manifesto as a 'mission statement' of Peel's Conservative Party and have had due regard to the reactions of Tories and Whigs. You have used your empathetic skills to understand, through cross-referencing between sources and your own knowledge, why the Whigs took longer to emerge as a coherent political party, as the Liberals, than the Conservatives. You have seen how fragile Westminster party loyalties were, as evidenced by the collapse of Peel's Conservative Party after the repeal of the Corn Laws. You have looked at the ways in which the Reform Act of 1832 and the Municipal Corporations Act of 1835 impacted on political life in the provinces and in particular how they together enabled the larger boroughs to be dominated by Liberal, nonconformist politics.

Exam tips

Below is the sort of question you will find appearing on examination papers as an (a) question.

Study Sources N, O and P. How far do Sources O and P support the views given in Source N?

You tackled (a) style questions at the end of Units 1 and 2. Now let's develop what you learned there about approaches to the (a) question.

- What is the question asking you to do? It is asking **how far** Sources O and P **support** the views given in Source N.
- Consider the sources carefully and make **inferences** and **deductions** from them rather than using them as sources of information. You might put these inferences in three columns.
- **Cross-reference** points of evidence from the three sources by drawing actual links between evidence in the three columns. This will enable you to make comparisons point by point and so use the sources as a **set**.
- **Evaluate** the evidence, assessing its quality and reliability in terms of how much weight it will bear and how secure the conclusions are that can be drawn from it.
- Reach a **judgement** about how far Sources O and P can support the views given in Source N.

RESEARCH TOPIC

Investigate the Anti-Corn Law League. How much pressure did this body bring to bear on the political parties with regard to the abolition of the Corn Laws that broke the Conservative Party?

7 Landing in daylight? Party reform 1868–85

What is this unit about?

Lord Derby, in 1867, described the Reform Act as a 'great experiment' and 'taking a leap in the dark'. But as Liberals and Conservatives took this leap and tried to turn it to their own party advantage, did both parties, in fact, land in daylight? This unit explores the ways in which both the main political parties adapted their traditional policies and outlooks to try to appeal to the greatly enlarged electorate that, after 1867, included most of the 'respectable' working class. It addresses, too, the intense activity in the constituencies as they organised themselves far more sharply than they had in the years 1832–67 to ensure loyalty to party and effective turnout at the polls. However, the two spheres of activity were not separate. The ways in which party leaders appealed to the electorate had a direct link to the ways in which party affiliations in the constituencies were organised. This, in turn, raised the acute problem of whether constituency opinion or parliamentary parties were to determine policy.

Key questions

- In what ways did the Conservative Party under Disraeli and the Liberal Party under Gladstone appeal to the new electorate?
- How effective was party organisation in the constituencies?

Timeline

1867	**Parliamentary Reform Act**	Size of the electorate almost doubled to include most of the 'respectable' working class
	Conservative National Union founded	Aimed at uniting all existing Conservative Working Men's Clubs under one umbrella organisation
	Birmingham Education League founded	Founded by Joseph Chamberlain and Jesse Collings to press for universal, secular education Chamberlain begins to develop the Birmingham Caucus
1868	**General election: Liberal victory**	
1869	**National Education League founded**	Joseph Chamberlain and other radicals press for a system of national, secular education
1870	**Conservative Central Office established in London**	John Gorst employed as party manager

1870   **Education Act**
Increases grant to Anglican Church schools and establishes secular school boards to provide schools in areas where no schools previously existed

1871   **Trade Union Act**
Trade unions given legal status and the right to strike

Criminal Law Amendment Act
Severe penalties for picketing

1872   **Licensing Act**
Creates crime of being drunk in public and regulates opening times in public houses

1874   **General election: Conservative victory**

1877   **National Federation of Liberal Associations**
Founded by Joseph Chamberlain, in Birmingham, with the aim of providing an umbrella organisation and co-ordinating body for all the local Liberal organisations and pressurising government to accept their policies

1879–80   **Midlothian campaign**
Gladstone attacks Disraeli's imperial policy as being 'immoral', and takes issues directly to his electors

1880   **General election: Liberal victory**

1883   **Primrose League founded**
Admitted men and women in an hierarchical membership scheme and aimed to promote Conservatism and Conservative candidates

Source A

I often think its comical
How nature always doth contrive
That ev'ry boy and ev'ry gal
That's born alive
Is either a little Liberal
Or else a little Conservative!

When in that House MP's divide
If they've a brain and cerebellum too,
They've got to leave that brain outside,
And vote just as their leaders tell 'em to.
But then the prospect of a lot of dull MPs
In close proximity
All thinking for themselves,
Is what no man can face with equanimity.

The sentry's song from the light opera *Iolanthe*, written by W.S. Gilbert, first performed in 1882; the sentry is standing guard outside the Houses of Parliament reflecting on political parties and the electorate

SKILLS BUILDER

Read Source A. What is the sentry's attitude to political parties and the electorate? How likely is it that this song reflects public attitudes in 1882? Remember that this particular Gilbert and Sullivan opera was a political **satire**. Gilbert had spotted a trend and had exaggerated it. But, importantly, his audience would have understood exactly what he meant.

Definition

Satire

The use of humour, sarcasm and ridicule to attack institutions and individuals.

What were the characteristics of the Liberal and Conservative Parties at this time?

The Reform Act of 1867 (as you saw in Unit 6), almost doubled the size of the electorate by the addition of around one million, mainly working class and all male, voters. In this changed political landscape, both Liberals and Conservatives realised they had to adapt policies, attitudes and structures if they were to attract the working class voter and therefore achieve electoral success in general elections. At the same time, though, they had to ensure that their traditional voters remained loyal. The months immediately after the passage of the Reform Act saw the resignation of Lord John Russell and the succession to the leadership of the Liberal Party of William Ewart Gladstone. Lord Derby also retired, and Benjamin Disraeli took over as leader of the Conservatives. With two new leaders, both with very definite views and an intense dislike of each other, the stage was set for conflict and drama as both struggled to lead the country.

Gladstone and the Liberal Party

Who made up the parliamentary Liberal Party?

The parliamentary Liberal Party was not a political party in the modern sense of the word – a solid body of people elected to fulfil a specific manifesto and voting almost as one in support of policies determined by the leadership – but it was beginning to develop as such. In the years to 1885, it was more of a loose body of individuals with certain shared attitudes and, within a few years of 1867, united in its admiration of Gladstone. Members of the parliamentary Liberal Party could be divided roughly into three groups, as follows.

1   The old, traditional Whigs whose attitudes lay far to the right, but who were open to reform provided its benefits could be clearly demonstrated. Although a large group in the House of Lords, they were a relatively small one in the Commons, where their influence greatly outweighed their numbers because they held virtually all the key posts in all the Liberal ministries. As a group, they were held in considerable esteem by other members of the parliamentary party.

2 Radicals made up a similarly small group to the far left of the party, committed to political, social and economic reform. On any specific issue, though, they could depend on the support of many more Liberals. The most important element of this group were the Nonconformist manufacturing interest – men like John Bright, Samuel Morley, William Rathbone and Titus Salt, whose passion for reform was backed by intellectual members such as Henry Fawcett and John Stuart Mill.

3 The vast bulk of the parliamentary party was made up of middle-of-the-road Liberals, landowners, bankers and lawyers, inclined by their nature to be cautious but open to persuasion and inclined to be loyal followers of the party leaders.

Question

Read Source B. If Paul Adelman is correct, what are (a) the strengths and (b) the weaknesses of this hierarchy?

Source B

This was the major purpose of the parliamentary party as a whole: to sustain the power of a leadership which, in a rough and ready way, skimmed the cream of the administrative talent available in the Liberal ranks in both Houses of Parliament. It was this belief that Administration was the highest form of politics – the greatest legacy of the Peelites to the Liberals – that helped to make the governing hierarchy of the Liberal Party in the age of Gladstone something of a distinct group within, but also apart from, the parliamentary party; a group with its own traditions, its own loyalties, and its own code of disinterested, efficient and high-minded service.

From Paul Adelman, *Gladstone, Disraeli and Later Victorian* Politics, published in 1997 (third edition)

New areas of support

Three new social forces were developing that looked to the Liberal Party for support and gave it in return.

1 The abolition of stamp and paper duties between 1855 and 1861, combined with the development of the railways and the telegraph, led to the growth in newspapers which were, by and large, owned by men of Liberal Party persuasion. Edward Baines and the *Leeds Chronicle,* Joseph Cowens and the *Newcastle Chronicle*, and Robert Leader and the *Sheffield Independent*, for example, used their papers to spread Liberal views and opinions, and in doing so built up a provincial following that both prepared the ground for, and also linked in well with, the growth and establishment of local political party organisations.

2 The Conservative Party had traditionally been staunch upholders of the Anglican Church, whereas the Liberals, with their reformist tendencies, had been far more sympathetic towards Nonconformity. The Nonconformists felt themselves, in the religious sense, to be second-class citizens: they resented having to pay a Church rate to the Anglican Church, objected to the Anglican domination of the universities of

Oxford and Cambridge and argued against the Anglican dominance of the school system. Some even wanted the disestablishment of the Church of England, and the journal the *Non-Conformist,* edited by Edward Miall who was also a Liberal MP, pressed for it. By the mid-1860s, the Nonconformists were a growing, increasingly powerful community. Indeed, the 1851 Religious Census showed that about half of those going to church on a specific Sunday in that year went to a Nonconformist chapel. Nonconformity was strongest in the north of England and in Wales, and the 1865 election resulted in some 87 Nonconformist MPs being elected to the Commons – all of whom brought with them the full weight of Nonconformity provincial support.

3   The newly emerging skilled artisans and trade union leaders, the elite of the newly enfranchised 'respectable' working class, had strong reasons to support the Liberal Party. There was much to gain, economically, from supporting a party of reform when the payback may be an improvement in their living and working conditions. There was also the opportunity to combine against the traditional Conservative and landowning interests, and much working-class Liberal support was the result of local alliances and allegiances.

Throughout the years to 1885, therefore, the parliamentary Liberal Party became of major political importance throughout the country, largely because it had established sound links with the new, dynamic forces that were emerging in the provinces. It was Gladstone who perceived their importance and who was particularly adept at communicating with this new electorate and carrying them with him by way of his oratorical skills, developing and enhancing his reputation as 'the people's William'.

Disraeli and the Conservative Party

Benjamin Disraeli had no such place in the hearts of Conservatives. Having out-manoeuvred Gladstone over parliamentary reform in 1867, he was left with a party that seemingly quickly forgot its gratitude and with grandees who were alarmed at the prospect of having to appeal to a working-class electorate. Disraeli's job therefore was similar to Gladstone's in that he had to hold his party together, but quite different in that he was not universally revered as party leader and did not, and indeed could not, relate to the new social forces that were emerging.

Who made up the parliamentary Conservative Party?

Traditionally, the old Tory Party was strongly associated with land, the landed interest and with innate conservatism. Despite the growing numbers of industrialists and the addition of a bookseller (W.H. Smith) to the Cabinet in 1874, nothing really changed after 1867. The Conservative Party remained one dominated by the landowning class and the country gentry. Of the 350 Conservative MPs returned in the general election of 1874, for example, over 200 had connections to the land.

What tensions were there within the party?

The dominance of the landed interest created specific tensions within the party, as outlined below.

- The landed gentry made up the bulk of Conservative Party members, and so it was their attitudes and beliefs that dominated the party. They tended to be suspicious of centralisation and firmly opposed anything that challenged the traditional way of life in the rural counties, where there was a strong tradition of paternalism, which went hand in hand with a belief in an hierarchical society based on mutual obligation.

- In order to attract working-class votes, the Conservative Party had to be seen to embrace reform in working and living conditions, and social reforms were not attractive to the landed gentry.

- Many middle-class voters, alarmed by Gladstone's overtures to the new working-class half of the electorate, began to find the more traditional Conservative values and attitudes more attractive. The Conservative leadership, therefore, had to create and find support for policies that wouldn't frighten away the middle class while simultaneously proving attractive to the 'respectable' working class. In reality, it was the middle class they needed more in order to be able to place provincial organisations in safe hands. Indeed, in 1868 and 1874 there was a Conservative break-through in Lancashire. However, in reality, overall the Conservatives did not have the ready constituency grass roots support that was available to the Liberals. The Conservatives had to create it.

- Disraeli himself was not a natural leader of the Conservative Party. Born a Jew and baptised an Anglican, he had no bedrock of support among the country gentry that would automatically be given to someone with a landed interest background. He became Conservative leader in the Commons only because of the party split over the abolition of the Corn Laws (see pages 124–126) and when the Duke of Newcastle famously intoned: 'We must of necessity choose the cleverest man we possess.' Disraeli's personal position as leader of the party was by no means secure. Inevitably, and unlike Gladstone, he needed to be aware of this when initiating any legislation.

How did the political parties gain support in the constituencies?

Before 1867, there was relatively little structured party organisation in the constituencies, and what there was tended only to spring into life when general elections loomed. The electorate was small, not many elections were contested and treating was common. Central organisation was in the hands of the whips, whose parliamentary job was to ensure attendance, discipline and correct voting among members of a particular political party. Beyond this, they raised money for constituency work, found appropriate candidates and generally kept in touch with the local party agents out in

Question

In no more than 100 words, sum up the essential differences between the Conservative and Liberal parties at this time.

the provinces. But this was very haphazard work and generally done on a response to need basis, rather than a proactive one. Additionally, links were made between the two great London clubs, the Carlton (Conservative) and the Reform (Liberal) and their agents in the constituencies but these were not formalised in any way. Local organisations grew up and some flourished while others collapsed, and this was very much dependent on the enthusiasm of local organisers and local need rather than any concerted central direction.

Source C

He was broadminded in all his views, an able platform speaker and well-versed in all the chicanery of election plots and devices. He was agent for Sir Robert Clifton when he first stood for Nottingham, and he told me what difficulties he had in coaching Sir Robert in politics. But he was equal to any emergency. At the first meeting he placed a man in the back part of the room, and when the candidate faltered, stammered and got into a muddle, the man cried out: 'Damn politics, Sir Robert, tell us who is going to win the Derby.' Sir Robert was at home, he could talk about horses, he became popular and was elected by a 1,400 majority. Acland's motto was to win the election – never mind the expense: a defeat, he would say, is the most expensive of all contests.

Mr Acland dabbled in all sorts of election work. He was an adept at election addresses. He knew how to say nothing and to say it well. None of his candidates could be convicted of breaking election pledges after their election. He was free and generous to a fault. He could never save money, however much he earned. He was a willing helper without fee or reward when the person wanting help was too poor to pay. But as regards the rich candidate, who had his own game to play, he felt justified in using their wealth. But he never sold his candidate; never relaxed his efforts to get him returned. The system was corrupt; that was not his fault. He advocated a better system. Parliament refused it. The candidates liked the system. Why should he complain?

George Howell, who became secretary of the Reform League in 1865, wrote this pen-portrait of James Acland; Acland had been a Methodist minister and a journalist as well as an Anti-Corn Law lecturer, before becoming an election agent for a Liberal candidate

The 1867 Reform Act changed all this. While the need for voter registration after 1832 had generated some constituency activity, this was nothing compared to the flurry of activity generated by the 1867 Act. The enlargement of the borough franchise made efficient voter registration essential; it also made sustained party political presences in the constituencies imperative. Registering voters was one thing, actually getting them to the polls and to vote for the right party was quite another!

Two major developments took place.

1 Both Conservatives and Liberals established a central office in London and party organisation became both centralised and more efficient.

2 Local party organisations were set up throughout the country. These eventually combined under the umbrella organisations of the Conservative National Union and the National Liberal Federation. Working parallel to these great umbrella organisations were smaller ginger groups – for example, the Liberal Liberation Society and the Conservative Primrose League.

Source D

'The claims upon a Fund' are as follows:

1st Registration. We have an office in London with a secretary in communication with all the local agents, giving them advice, etc. and also doing most important work at an election in looking up voters. This is supposed to be kept alive by annual subscriptions, but I find that £300 a year is all I get towards an expense of near £1500. I have kept this up this year as it would be most foolish to lose all this perfect machinery (the only basis of organisation which we have) upon the eve of a general election. I am sure we have saved thousands of votes by the information and instructions sent to local agents from our headquarters.

The 2nd expense is The Office here, which is needful to have for some months before an election. If one sees how the daily work here runs, the visits of candidates and agents and the correspondence and telegraphs upon candidates' matters, the necessity for such a 'house of call' could not be doubted.

The fund is needed 3rdly for aid in some cases towards local registration and, to some degree, for expenses of meetings etc., to rouse popular feeling which can only be done by sending men down to aid candidates etc. etc.

4thly for direct assistance to candidates and of course here, when the money is gone, I cannot tell exactly how it goes but it is given to the candidates and upon the understanding that it is in aid of legitimate expenditure. There are many places where special men are necessary and sometimes such men may have a little less money to spend than the place will fairly cost . . . I don't think it possible to manage properly without say £10,000 to £15,000.

From a letter by George Glyn, the Liberal Party Chief Whip, to Gladstone, dated 12 September 1867

Source E

ORDINARY WORK OF CONSERVATIVE CENTRAL OFFICE

Registration. Enquiries are made as to the residence and qualifications of the outvoters of all the counties in England & Wales. Forms, instructions & advice are furnished to both counties and boroughs.

Elections. Local leaders are assisted in finding suitable candidates. Forms, instructions and election literature are supplied. County outvoters are canvassed.

Organisation. Formation of new Associations is promoted and assisted. Model rules etc. are supplied. An annual list of clubs and associations is compiled.

Meetings. The continual holding of small meetings is advised and encouraged. Speakers and hints for speeches are provided. Special meetings (as for example on the Irish question) are from time to time recommended and promoted.

Publications. Pamphlets and leaflets on current political topics are issued: important speeches are reprinted and circulated. A weekly publication, called the 'Editors' Handysheet' is issued to provide materials for political articles to the Conservative Provincial Press. Political telegrams are sent from the Lobby to several provincial papers.

Parliamentary. All Bills affecting the interests of the party are circulated among local leaders. Petitions are from time to time promoted.

Statistics. Facts respecting elections, parliamentary and municipal, are collected and tabulated. An index of political events during the past 10 years is in course of formation.

Correspondence. Enquiries are answered upon such subjects as Finance, Foreign Affairs, Army and navy administration, Election statistics & interviews, India, Irish affairs, Licensing, Education, Friendly Societies etc., etc.

Interviews. People of every class call at the office on political business, and every endeavour is made to treat them with courtesy & consideration.

Visits. Constituencies are visited by emissaries from the Central Office of two sorts: (1) Experienced agents to advise on the electoral and registration machinery; (2) Gentlemen to stir up dormant constituencies, & recommend local organisation & effort.

Correspondence from J.A. Gorst to Disraeli, dated 24 February 1881;
Gorst was the first professional party business manager

SKILLS BUILDER

1 Read Sources C–E. All three are concerned with party organisation in the constituencies. What were the main characteristics of party organisation in the provinces as described in Source C?

2 George Glyn (Source D) seems to have encountered problems as he tried to organise the Liberal Party so that it had maximum impact in the regions. What are these problems?

3 What impression of Conservative Party organisation does Source E give you?

4 Read these three sources again. How could these three sources be used to show how party political organisation in the constituencies changed over time?

How effective was the Conservative Party's organisation?

In the 1860s, the Conservative Party lacked the ready support from the newly emerging forces in the constituencies that were enjoyed by the Liberals. It was therefore essential, after the passing of the 1867 Act, that the Conservative Party established itself outside Westminster. It was here that problems began. Once discussions began as to the form these provincial organisations should take, these tensions rose to the surface. Specifically:

- should the local organisations be 'bottom up' ones, arising from the needs of local communities and involving middle and working classes in setting them up and running them, or
- should the local organisations be 'top down' ones, directed from Westminster?

Given the structure and attitudes of the parliamentary Conservative Party, it isn't really surprising that they adopted the 'top down' approach.

Conservative Central Office and John Gorst

The Conservative Central Office (see Source E) was set up in London in 1870, pushing the Carlton Club (see page 131) into the background, and John Gorst was employed as the first national party agent. Realising that the Conservatives had to attract the working-class vote in the boroughs, he was highly successful in establishing Conservative associations in urban constituencies. By the end of 1873, 69 new associations had been founded, making a total of over 400 throughout the country, including 33 in the 49 largest boroughs. Indeed, by the time of the 1874 general election Conservative candidates had been found for every constituency in which they had a reasonable chance of success, and the Conservative victory in that election in many ways reflected Gorst's hard work and administrative skills. However, it is clear that this whole approach was 'top down'; while Gorst concentrated on winnable seats, the smaller associations in the marginal and Liberal-dominated constituencies were very much left to their own devices.

The Conservative National Union

Founded in 1867, the aim of the Conservative National Union was to unite all existing local Conservative working men's clubs under one umbrella organisation. Here, again, the Conservative 'top down' approach was clear. Not only did John Gorst chair the first, inaugural, meeting of the Union attended by 67 delegates from 55 cities, but the emphasis there was on electing men of substance as union officers rather than working-class men whom the Union was supposed to support and welcome into the Conservative Party.

Unsurprisingly, by 1871 the union was run from Gorst's office in London and became, in effect, an organisation for the distribution of pamphlets, fliers and other forms of propaganda. Its status within the Conservative Party was understandably weak until, in 1872, Disraeli decided to use the Union's conferences as providing him with a platform from which to make major policy speeches.

Local clubs and associations

Large numbers of working men became more or less politically active through their membership of Conservative working men's clubs. Although originally intended as political clubs, there was a strong social aspect to their activities, with outings and other gatherings organised for members. Given the 'top down' approach adopted by the central Conservative Party, it is hardly surprising that these groups did not act as 'ginger groups' in the ways in which the Liberal Birmingham **caucus** did: their opinions were neither sought nor expected.

The Primrose League

One of the more influential groups to emerge from the Conservative Party organisation was the Primrose League. It was set up in 1883 to promote the Conservative Party and to support aspiring Conservative MPs. Unsurprisingly, its membership was strictly hierarchical: there was one class of membership, with an expensive subscription, for the rich and well-to-do, and a second, cheaper associate membership for the rest. What it did do, though, was to admit men and women on equal terms. Local Primrose groups were called 'habituations'. Within these habituations, women were heavily involved on the social side, organising fetes and garden parties, and other fund-raising events. On the political side, they delivered leaflets and helped bring Conservative voters into the polls on election days – an essential but somewhat subservient role! Indeed, the Primrose League didn't, in the 1880s or later, campaign on behalf of female suffrage. Many of its members were suffragists, but they were not able to influence the policy of the Ladies Grand Council, who firmly maintained that members were free to support votes for women but that it was not, and never would be, one of the policy aims of the Primrose League.

> **Definition**
>
> **Caucus**
>
> A group of people who unite to promote a particular policy or interest.

Source F

They obviously corroborate the impressionistic evidence of the Primrose League as an organisation which catered for women: but what is more striking is that they show the League as a body which incorporated men and women rather than segregating them. Moreover, they suggest that the Primrose League – uniquely for a Victorian institution – must have included hundreds of thousands of women in its ranks.

From Martin Pugh, *The Tories and the People 1880–1935*, published in 1985; here he is describing what he found when he analysed the early membership records of the Primrose League

> **SKILLS BUILDER**
>
> Read Source F and use your own knowledge. To what extent are you surprised that the Primrose League 'contained hundreds of thousands of women' in its ranks?

What were the dangers of a 'top down' approach to constituency organisation?

The dangers of using this 'top down' approach were demonstrated in 1875 when Gorst's contract as party agent came to an end. Party leaders allowed Gorst's carefully established party organisation to run down, and control of the party organisation passed back to the whips, traditionalists to a man and who tended to represent the aristocratic element in the party. Alarmed by defeat in 1880 (see pages 154–155), Gorst was again employed as a party agent working with a reconstituted Central Committee. Despite his undoubted skill and vision, he was unable effectively to counter the attempts of the Tory traditionalists to assert control. Gorst's successor, G.C.T. Bartley, met with similar problems and, along with the **Chief Whip**, resigned in 1877. It was not until the electoral legislation of the 1880s (see pages 106–112) that the Conservative Central Office was really able to assert itself over the more traditional elements in the party.

Source G

If the Tory Party is to continue to exist as a power in the State, it must become a popular party. A mere coalition with the Whig aristocracy might delay, but cannot avert its downfall. The days are past when an exclusive class, however great its ability, wealth and energy, can command a majority in the electorate. The liberties and interests of the people at large are the only things which it is now possible to conserve: the rights of property, the Established Church, the House of Lords, and the Crown itself must be defended on the grounds that they are institutions necessary or useful for the preservation of civil and religious liberty and securities for personal freedom, and can be maintained only so far as the people take this view too.

Unfortunately for Conservatism, its leaders belong solely to one class; they are a clique composed of members of the aristocracy, landowners and adherents whose chief merit is subserviency. The party chiefs live in an atmosphere in which a sense of their own importance and of the importance of their class interests and privileges is exaggerated and to which the opinions of the common people can scarcely penetrate. They are surrounded by sycophants who continually offer up the incense of personal flattery under the pretext of conveying political information. They half fear and half despise the common people, whom they see only through this deceptive medium; they regard them more as dangerous allies to be coaxed and cajoled rather than as comrades fighting for a common cause.

From an article by J.A. Gorst, 'Conservative Disorganisation', published in *The Fortnightly Review*, 1882

SKILLS BUILDER

Read Source G and use your own knowledge. How far, in your opinion, are the criticisms of the Conservative Party made by Gorst in Source G valid ones?

How effective was the Liberal Party's organisation?

The Liberal Party made no great changes to its central organisation as a result of the 1867 Reform Act, and so the party whips continued to run the organisation. Indeed, they did good, solid work in building up links between local Liberal organisations and the central party in Westminster. This lack of change at the centre was partly because the Liberals had no one of the calibre of John Gorst to take on the role of party manager, but was mainly because the constituencies themselves took the lead in party organisation outside Westminster. For the Liberals, it was changes at the grass roots that were of major importance. Thus change, for the Liberals, was 'bottom up' as opposed to the Conservative 'top down' approach.

Clubs and associations

The Liberals, as the Conservatives, founded a wide range of working men's clubs, and by the 1880s every sizeable town had its own local Liberal Association, some of which were exclusively for women. They ran a wide range of social events, intended to attract and retain middle- and working-class Liberals: there were picnics and outings, cycling clubs and educational lectures – and even a Wild West show! The aim, of course, was to support Liberal MPs and potential Liberal MPs and to build up solid support for Liberal policies in the country at large. The focus was not only on general elections, but on local ones, too: school board elections, elections of Poor Law guardians and parish and district elections.

Joseph Chamberlain and the Birmingham Caucus

There were many different kinds of Liberal Associations in the provinces, but the most well known and the most influential was that which became known as the Birmingham Caucus.

Birmingham had long had a tradition of co-operation between middle and working classes when it came to reform. It was thus no surprise that, following the 1867 Reform Act, this co-operation became even more intense. **Joseph Chamberlain** (who was then just a leading local Liberal) worked out an electoral system of persuading electors to vote according to advice and guidance provided by the local Liberal organisation and as a result Nonconformists were able to form a majority on the Birmingham School Board. Working with Francis Schandhorst, Chamberlain developed this technique and applied it to local and general elections. In this way, Birmingham was able to outwit Disraeli's cunning plan. Disraeli had inserted a clause in the 1867 Act whereby voters in boroughs with three MPs had two votes. In this way he had hoped to diminish the impact of Liberal influence in the boroughs. However, by building an efficient party organisation with accurate lists of supporters, and 'advising' Liberal voters as to which two candidates they should vote for, Schandhorst and Chamberlain ensured Liberal votes were spread evenly between all three Liberal candidates and the Conservatives were squeezed out. Many boroughs subsequently adopted the Birmingham model.

Biography

Joseph Chamberlain (1836–1914)

Joseph Chamberlain made his fortune as a screw manufacturer in Birmingham. This enabled him to retire at the age of 38 and devote his life to politics. As mayor of Birmingham (1873–76) he introduced and carried through many reforms (including sewerage and drainage as well as slum clearance) and encouraged the public acquisition of land and ownership of gas and water utilities. In 1876 he was elected MP for Birmingham and, through the National Liberal Foundation, tried to commit the Liberal Party to a programme of social reform. Gladstone, however, refused to be drawn into a programme that would involve both cost and state intervention. Despite his somewhat frosty relationship with Gladstone, in 1880 he joined Gladstone's Cabinet as President of the Board of Trade. A staunch imperialist, he was uneasy with Gladstone's policies regarding South Africa and Egypt, and resigned in 1886 over Irish Home Rule. He eventually allied with the Conservatives and became Colonial Secretary in Salisbury's Cabinet of 1895. He split the Conservatives over his views on tariff reform (Chamberlain favoured Imperial preference), and in doing so helped to create the Liberal landslide of 1906.

What were the dangers of a 'bottom up' approach to constituency organisation?

In 1877, Chamberlain was instrumental in creating the National Federation of Liberal Associations, with a central office in Birmingham; Chamberlain was elected president with Francis Schandhorst its paid secretary. By 1879, Schandhorst had brought over 100 provincial Liberal Associations under the umbrella of the Federation. This powerful re-organisation seemed justified by the Liberal victory in 1880, where the Liberals gained or retained over 60 constituencies where such associations existed, and Joseph Chamberlain (elected MP for Birmingham in 1876) was appointed to the Cabinet. However, there were those who worried. With such a powerful provincial organisation, when would it start devising a party programme and imposing it on the Central Office? What, indeed, was to be the relationship, now, between central and provincial Liberalism?

Source H

The Federation is designed to assist the formation of Liberal Associations, on a popular representative basis, throughout the country; to bring such organisations into union, so that by this means the opinions of Liberals, on measures to be supported or resisted, may be readily and authoritatively ascertained; and to aid in concentrating upon the promotion of reforms found to be generally desired, the whole force, strength and resources of the Liberal Party.

The essential feature of the proposed Federation is the principle which must henceforth govern the actions of Liberals as a political party – namely, the direct participation of all members of the party in the direction of its policy, and in the selection of those particular measures of reform and of progress to which priority shall be given. This object can be secured only by the organisation of the party upon a representative basis; that is, by popularly elected committees of local associations, and by the union of such local associations, by means of their freely chosen representatives, in a general federation.

From the *Proceedings Attending the Formation of the National Federation of Liberal Associations*, published in 1877 in Birmingham

Source I

I do not feel at all certain that we ought to give our support to this federation scheme. The Birmingham plan is perhaps the only one on which the Liberal Party can be sufficiently organised in a great constituency; and I do not know whether there is much, or any objection to its being extended to others. But it is almost certain to put the management into the hands of the most advanced men, because they are the most active. And when we come to a federation of these associations, it seems to me that it will come before long to placing the chief control and direction of the party in the hands of these men, to the exclusion of the more moderate and easy-going Liberals. There is a good deal of the American caucus system about it, which I think is not much liked here; and though we have all been preaching organisation, I think we may sacrifice too much to it.

From a letter by Lord Hartington to Lord Granville, dated 23 November 1877; at the time, Lord Hartington was leader of the Liberal Party

Source J

The opponents of the Caucus are not to be convinced – they hate it for its virtues – because it puts aside and utterly confounds all that club management and Pall Mall selection which has been going on for so long and which has made of the Liberal Party the boneless, nerveless thing it is. The Caucus is force, enthusiasm, zeal, activity, movement, popular will and the rule of the majority – the Seven Deadly Sins, in fact.

From a letter by Joseph Chamberlain to John Morley, dated 29 September 1878

SKILLS BUILDER

1 Read Source H. What is the declared aim of the National Federation of Liberal Associations?

2 Read Sources I and J. How far are Lord Hartington's worries borne out by what Joseph Chamberlain wrote in his letter to John Morley?

Source K

Political parties after 1867 undoubtedly grew in size, in number and in complexity; they developed an increased sense of their own importance, and certain individuals within them had major ambitions both for themselves and for party organisations. However, above all, in both the Conservative and Liberal parties, the leadership was usually able to keep the grass roots party out of policy and decision making.

From Sean Lang, *Parliamentary Reform 1785–1928*, published in 1999

How did the parties try to win the support of the electors?

Organising political parties so that they established a presence in the constituencies and developed voter loyalties was one thing; turning this into victory in the general elections could be quite another. Both political parties, after 1867, acknowledged the need to attract, and retain, the loyalty of the newly enfranchised working classes in order to turn this loyalty into electoral victory. But how successfully did they adapt their policies to enable them to do this?

Source L

Year	Date	Prime Minister	Party	Majority
1868	10 December	Gladstone	Liberal	115
1874	5 March	Disraeli	Conservative	49
1880	29 April	Gladstone	Liberal	51

Elected governments 1868–1880

The 1868 general election

A general election was bound to follow soon after the 1867 Reform Act. Disraeli could not forever hold together a Conservative Party that, once the excitement of out-manoeuvring Gladstone had worn off, was more than a little alarmed at what it had achieved. It was Gladstone, however, who forced the issue. In April 1868 he succeeded in getting the Commons to approve a resolution that the Irish Church must be disestablished. Disraeli declared that he would ask the Queen to dissolve parliament in the autumn, by which time the new electoral registers would have been prepared. Gladstone had found a new personal mission, Ireland, and a new rallying cry for the Liberal Party that conveniently combined political expediency with a sincere belief that the Irish 'problem' had to be solved.

The main issue in the general election, therefore, was the disestablishment of the Irish Church; social reform remained very much in the background. Indeed, neither party made much of an effort to attract the support of the working-class voter so newly enfranchised. The parties had scarcely had time to begin to understand the implications of the new political landscape.

It would seem that, unsurprisingly, the Conservatives failed to attract the new urban voters. They gained only 25 seats in the 114 largest boroughs and were thus still heavily dependent on the landed interest, with 60 per cent of their seats coming from the counties.

The Liberal Party swept into power and, as a consequence, Disraeli ended his flirtation with democracy and turned again to the traditional power-base of the Conservative Party: the landed interest. But what of the Liberals, now in power with a massive majority? Traditionally regarded as the reforming party, how would they woo the new electorate?

Source M

When the propertied classes became frightened by Gladstone's attacks on vested interests after 1868, by trade unionism and by Nonconformist radicalism, they looked to the Tories to defend the status quo. Disraeli was prepared for the flight into the Conservative Party of sections of the middle class, a process assisted by large increases in the numbers of white-collar workers and the separation of classes in urban and suburban areas as a consequence of cheap railway travel.

He realised that the future of the party lay in the direction which Peel had indicated in the 1840s: an alliance between landed property and industrial and commercial wealth. Disraeli was, therefore, obliged to woo the propertied middle classes rather than the new voters. Tories were too anxious to maintain the existing social order, too involved with landed property, capitalist enterprise and traditional institutions to welcome working men into genuine political partnership.

From D.G. Wright, *Democracy and Reform 1815–85*, published in 1970

Question

How sensible was it for Disraeli to abandon his attempts to woo the working classes?

1868–74: working-class Liberalism

Trade unions

The majority of the new voters, as you have seen, were Liberal by inclination. Mainly Nonconformists, they supported free trade, low taxation and limited reform to the franchise and to education. But many were also members of trade unions, and it was here that Gladstone needed to focus if he was to be sure of their continued support. Indeed, in 1869 Liberal trade unionists had established the Labour Representation League not as a separate political party but as a ginger group within the Liberal Party aimed at giving the needs of the trade unions a higher profile. Gladstone did give a nod in their direction with the passing of the Trade Union Act in 1871, which recognised unions as legal bodies with the right to own property and funds, and, importantly, recognised their right to strike. However, any goodwill gained was almost completely nullified by the Criminal Law Amendment Act, passed almost immediately afterwards in the same year.

Question

Why do you think that Gladstone, having supported the passage of the Trade Union Act in 1871, supported also the Criminal Law Amendment Act that was passed by parliament immediately afterwards?

Source N

[The Act] inflicted a punishment of three months' imprisonment, with hard labour, on any one who attempts to coerce another for trade purposes by the use of personal violence; by such threats as would justify a magistrate in binding a man to keep the peace; or by persistently following a person about from place to place, hiding his tools, clothes, or other property, watching and besetting his house, or following him along any street or road with two or more other persons in a disorderly manner. These last clauses were directed against the practice of **picketing**.

From William Edward Hartpole Lecky, *Democracy and Liberty: vol II*, published in 1981

Definitinon

Picketing

The act, by striking workers, of standing outside a workplace to try to prevent or dissuade others from going to work.

Working-class candidates

Efforts by the Labour Representation League to encourage Liberal selection of working-class candidates for election to parliament met with little success. For example, in the Bristol by-election of 1870, where there was one wealthy businessman candidate (Samuel Morley – who had trade union support), the Liberal Party resolutely refused to contemplate putting up a working-class candidate for this two-seat constituency, selecting instead another leading local employer. Indeed, during this period only two working men were elected to parliament: Thomas Burt (a Northumberland coalminer elected to represent Morpeth) and Alexander MacDonald (leader of the Miners' Union, who represented Stafford). It was no accident that these two men were from mining areas where union pressure on local Liberal organisations was strong.

Disillusionment by 1874?

By 1874, many working- and middle-class Liberal supporters had become disillusioned. The trade unions had reason to be furious, but so too had other sections of traditional Liberal supporters.

The Nonconformist revolt

Nonconformists, from whose ranks Liberals drew considerable support were alienated by the 1870 Education Act. In 1869 Joseph Chamberlain and a group of radicals had founded the National Education League to press for a national, free and **secular** system of education. Yet the 1870 Education Act, while extending the schooling provided by the Church authorities by setting up secular school boards and schools in areas not covered by the Church, also seemed to be favouring Anglican Church schools by extending their grants and allowing them some measure of help from the rates as well.

Definition

Secular

Not involved with religion, or religious bodies, in any way.

Source O

They have deliberately chosen to pursue a retrograde policy, and although we have cherished a hearty loyalty to the old leaders of the Liberal Party, our loyalty to the principles which both they and we are called to defend is stronger, more intense and deeper than loyalty to them. We are at last thrown upon ourselves; for a time, perhaps, for a few years, we shall have to act independently of the recognised leaders of the Liberal Party. The old union between us and them is now dissolved. I do not regard that dissolution with any degree of satisfaction.

From R.W. Dale, *The Education Act (1870) Amendment Bill and the Political Policy of Nonconformists*, published in 1873

The rift between Nonconformists and government over education was worsened by a national campaign for the disestablishment of the Church of England (see page 117) launched by the Liberation Society early in 1871. This was seen as a direct response to the successful (1869) disestablishment of the Church of Ireland. Although the motion was lost in the Commons by 374 votes to 89, with both Gladstone and Disraeli voting against it, it was nevertheless significant that a large minority of Liberal Nonconformists and radicals voted in favour.

The brewers' revolt

The Licensing Act of 1872 was another blow to the working class. It created the offences of being drunk in public with a maximum fine of £200; of propelling a horse, a cow (or other cattle), a steam engine or a loaded firearm when drunk, with a possible penalty of a fine of up to £200 or 51 weeks in prison. It restricted the closing times in public houses to midnight in towns and 11 pm in country areas; regulated the content of beer (one of the most common practices was to add salt to the beer, which increased the thirst and therefore sales); laid down that licensing hours were to be determined by local authorities and gave boroughs the option of becoming completely 'dry', i.e. banning all alcohol.

These policies were enforced by the police, and there were a number of near riots when they tried to enforce closing hours. Brewers resented what they saw as an attack on their independence and profits; others disliked the Act because it interfered with personal liberty. However, Nonconformists, always suspicious of the sale and consumption of alcohol, might have been expected to have been satisfied with the Act; instead, strict Nonconformists were upset at what seemed to them to be government legitimisation of the sale of drink. 'We have been borne down,' Gladstone declared, 'in a torrent of gin and beer.'

Unsurprisingly the Liberals lost the 1874 general election (see Source L). In considering the elements of working-class discontent that contributed to the Liberal defeat, historian Paul Adelman takes a wider view.

SKILLS BUILDER

Read Sources N and O and use your own knowledge. How far would you regard these sources as evidence of a serious failure on the part of the Liberal Party to gain and to retain the allegiance of its supporters?

Source P

These issues are best seen, perhaps, as evidence of a wider, middle-class disenchantment with Gladstonian Liberalism. For the most important reason of all for the Liberal defeat was, quite simply, the swing of the middle-class voter, alarmed by the rise of the working classes in strength and influence, and increasingly conscious of his own status as a 'man of property', to the Conservative Party, particularly in suburbia, as all sections of political society recognised. And all these factors were worsened for the disunited Liberal Party by the raggedness of its party organisation compared with that of its opponents.

From Paul Adelman, *Gladstone, Disraeli and later Victorian Politics*, published in 1997 (third edition)

The 'defection' of the middle classes

Is Paul Adelman correct (Source P)? Did the disillusioned and afraid middle classes really turn from the Liberal Party in sufficient numbers to ensure a Conservative victory in 1874? While it is the case that the middle classes supported the Liberals in 1868, ensuring a resounding victory for Gladstone and his party, there had been significance straws in the wind by 1874. By-elections showed Conservatives gaining a small number of seats in urban constituencies, and an analysis of the poll books shows that this was almost entirely due to the middle classes switching their support to the Conservative Party. For example, in 1859 and 1865 the Conservatives failed to win a single seat in London; in 1868 they won three, and in 1874, ten.

This trend was not limited to London; it could be detected, too, in towns like Salisbury and Cheltenham. While the Liberals still had more MPs with industrial and commercial backgrounds, and the Conservatives still drew their support from the English counties, the Conservatives were beginning to gain ground in the larger towns and were forging links with industry and trade.

Why was this middle class swing happening?

The great reforms of Gladstone's first administration had, for many new 'men of property' seemed too radical. Despite civil service and army reforms opening the way to men of talent, middle-class Nonconformists had been alarmed by the reforms to education, the regularisation of the brewing trade and still more Liberals by what seemed to them highly radical trade union legislation.

Read Sources P and Q. How far do they agree about the reaction of the middle classes to Gladstonian Liberalism?

Source Q

The middle classes began to feel that a Conservative government would do more to check the political advance of the working classes than the Liberals. Under Disraeli's leadership the Conservatives had quietly dropped their policy of trade protection, thereby removing a major obstacle to middle-class support. As many of the middle classes became wealthier, they tended to move into the suburbs, become less attached to the Nonconformist faith of their parents and grandparents, and to identify more closely with the landed classes. The basis for a Conservative Party built on an alliance of property interests was being laid in the 1860s and 1870s.

From Bob Whitfield, *The Extension of the Franchise 1832–1931*, published in 2001

1874–80: the Conservatives in power – wooing the electorate?

Working-class conservatism

It is clear that about one-third of working-class voters supported the Conservative Party after 1867, spread throughout the country, but being particularly strong in the east end of London and in Liverpool.

It would seem that this support was based less on Conservative policies, but more on perceptions of patriotism (Disraeli, as you will see, was making a good job of presenting the Conservatives as the party of Empire) and on the habit of deference, which was particularly strong in rural areas. However, for Disraeli and the Conservatives the dilemma in the 1870s was clear: how to produce policies that would prove attractive to the working classes and so increase their level of support, and yet at the same time not frighten the middle classes, who were beginning to find the Conservatives a safer proposition than the Liberal Party.

Disraeli's conservatism

The 1867 battles for parliamentary reform may well have seemed to have presented Disraeli to the electorate as a reforming Prime Minister. Far from it. His one aim, as you have seen (pages 98–100), was to outwit Gladstone and in doing so provide some credibility for the Conservative Party that had been out of office for so long. A speech made by Disraeli in 1872 gives some very strong indications as to where his priorities lay.

Source R

Gentlemen, I have referred to what I look upon as the first object of the Tory Party – namely, to maintain the institutions of the country, and reviewing what has occurred, and referring to the present temper of the times upon these subjects, I think that the Tory Party, or, as I will venture to call it, the National party, has everything to encourage it. I think that the nation, tested by many and severe trials, has arrived at the conclusion which we have always maintained, that it is the first duty to maintain its institutions, because to them we principally ascribe the power and prosperity.

Gentlemen, there is another and second great object of the Tory Party. If the first is to maintain the institutions of the country, the second is, in my opinion, to uphold the Empire of England. If you look to the history of this country since the advent of Liberalism – 40 years ago – you will find that there has been no effort so continuous, so subtle, supported by so much energy, and carried on with so much ability and acumen, as the attempts of Liberalism to effect the disintegration of the Empire of England.

Gentlemen, another great object of the Tory Party, and one not so inferior to the maintenance of the Empire, or the upholding of our institutions, is the elevation of the condition of the people.

From a speech by Benjamin Disraeli at the Crystal Palace, 2 June 1872

Conservative social reforms

Disraeli's ministry began by introducing a range of social reforms, but it is important to appreciate that these reforms were not part of a coherent Conservative social policy. Rather, they were forms 'left over' from the ministries of Russell and Derby, and would probably have been put in place no matter which party was in power. Furthermore, they were 'safe' reforms, dealing with, for example, public health, working hours, merchant shipping and paupers. None of these reforms posed any kind of threat to the existing social order, and issues that did pose such a threat, such as trade unions and education, were avoided. After 1876, there were no Conservative social reforms.

Definition

Queen's speech

The monarch always opens a session of parliament by making a speech outlining the government's work for that session. From the nineteenth century onwards, the monarch didn't write the speech; it was always written by the Prime Minister.

Source S

When the Cabinet came to discuss the **Queen's speech**, I was, I confess, disappointed at the lack of originality shown by the Prime Minister. From all his speeches, I had quite expected that his mind was full of legislative schemes, but such did not prove to be the case; on the contrary, he had to rely on the various suggestions of his colleagues, and as they themselves had only just come into office, and suddenly, there was some difficulty in framing the Queen's speech.

Comments by R.A. Cross on Disraeli's attitude to social reforms immediately after the 1874 general election; Cross was Conservative Home Secretary 1874–80 and responsible for piloting social reforms through the Commons

SKILLS BUILDER

1 Read Source R. What does Disraeli believe should be Conservative Party priorities?

2 Now read Source S. How far are these comments about Disraeli's attitude to social reform reflected in the speech he made at the Crystal Palace in 1872 (Source R)?

The Conservatives and Empire

By shifting the focus of the Conservative Party from reform to Empire, Disraeli was playing a clever hand. By identifying the Conservatives with patriotism and national interest, he was appealing to both working and middle classes. It was also difficult for the Liberals to argue against support for Empire. The Conservatives had, or so it seemed, successfully captured the ground previously occupied by Palmerston and the Liberals. Furthermore, Disraeli's appeal to patriotism went down particularly well in constituencies where the voters depended on the defence industry for their livelihood: the armaments industry of the Midlands, for example, as well as constituencies that were home to naval dockyards.

Source T

"NEW CROWNS FOR OLD ONES!"

SKILLS BUILDER

1 Look carefully at Source T. What point is the cartoonist making?

2 Use your own knowledge to explain how this cartoon helps to explain Disraeli's attraction to the electorate.

Cartoon by John Tenniel, published in *Punch* magazine on 15 April 1876; Disraeli (left), dressed as Aladdin, is offering the crown of India to Queen Victoria

The general election of 1880

In February 1880, the Conservatives won an unexpected victory in the Southwark by-election, and Disraeli decided the time was right for him to call a general election. It was a complete misjudgement. The Conservative Party lost more than 100 seats and all the 1874 gains were wiped out. They lost most heavily in the large boroughs, where out of an original 114 seats they held only 24 but they also lost 27 county seats. In the end, the Liberals had an overall majority of about 50. It would have been considerably more if there had not been so many uncontested seats. What had happened? How had the Conservatives' appeal to tradition, stability and Empire gone so badly wrong?

Why did the Conservatives' appeal to the electorate fail?

There were a number of electoral factors that combined to bring about Conservative defeat, and leave them facing the reality that their period in power was just a blip in the onward march of Liberalism.

- Disraeli delayed calling the election until the 'feel good' factor of a successful foreign policy – culminating in the 1878 Treaty of Berlin, which, among other things, gave Britain almost unlimited access to the Black Sea – had worn off.

- An economic depression resulted in some businesses facing ruin; the level of unemployment rose from 1–2 per cent to around 11 per cent in 1879.

- The Farmers' Alliance, an independent movement formed because of the Conservatives' negative attitude to helping them weather the depression, put up successful candidates in the counties, which resulted in a slump in Conservative votes.

- The lack of a coherent Conservative policy on Ireland caused the Home Rule Party to redouble their efforts to obstruct parliamentary business.

- A powerful nationwide campaign for social reform was begun in Birmingham by Schnadhorst and Chamberlain, which created a lot of support for Gladstone in the Midlands and North.

Important though these issues were, they paled into insignificance when compared to the impact of Gladstone's Midlothian campaign.

The Midlothian campaign

Having retired from the Liberal Party's leadership, and unhappy with his Greenwich constituency, Gladstone accepted the invitation in May 1878 to contest the Midlothian constituency and stand against the Conservative candidate Lord Dalkeith, son of the Duke of Buccleuch. He accepted, and made a series of highly effective, nationally reported, campaign speeches attacking Disraeli's imperial policies, which he called 'Beaconsfieldism', parodying Disraeli's elevation to Lord Beaconsfield. In doing this, Gladstone brought issues directly to the attention of the public with his emphasis on the immorality of Disraeli's whole foreign and imperial policy. Indeed, Gladstone was one of the first national figures to run such a high profile campaign, speaking directly to the people. Gladstone won the seat with ease and returned to lead the Liberal Party.

This sort of campaigning had never been done before and in a very real sense, as never before, the electors had chosen the leader of the Liberal Party and their Prime Minister.

Source U

Go from South Africa to the mountains of Central Asia. Go into the lofty hills of Afghanistan, as they were last winter, and what do we there see? I fear a yet sadder sight than was to be seen in the land of the Zulus. You have seen during last winter from time to time that from such and such a village attacks had been made upon the British forces, and that in consequence the village had been burned. Have you ever reflected on the meaning of those words? Those hill tribes had committed no real offence against us. We, in the pursuit of our political objects, chose to establish military positions in their country. If they resisted, would not you have done the same? And when, going back and forth from their villages they had resisted, what you find is this, that those who went forth were slain, and that the village is burned. Again, I say, have you considered the meaning of these words? The meaning of the burning of the village is, that the women and the children were driven forth to perish in the snows of winter. Is that not a terrible supposition? Is not that a fact that rouses in you a sentiment of horror and grief, to think that the name of England, under no political necessity, but for a war as frivolous as never was waged in the history of man, should be associated with consequences such as these?

Remember the rights of the savage, as we call him. Remember that the happiness of his humble home, remember that the sanctity of life in the hill villages of Afghanistan among the winter snows, as inviolable in the eye of Almighty God as can be your own.

From a speech by Gladstone at the Forsters Hall, Dalkeith, 26 November 1879

SKILLS BUILDER

1 Carefully read Source U. What arguments is Gladstone making to counter Disraeli's imperialism?

2 How appealing and convincing do you think voters would find this style of oratory?

Unit summary

What have you learned in this unit?

By doubling the electorate to include most of the 'respectable' working class, the 1867 Reform Act created new challenges for the two main political parties. Both Conservatives and Liberals had to adapt their policies and organisation in order to attract the new electors while at the same time keeping the loyalty of their existing supporters. This was a difficult balancing act.

Both Conservatives and Liberals established a central office in London and local organisations throughout the county. However, the organising ability of John Gorst, combined with the natural inclinations of the Conservatives, meant that the Conservatives adopted a 'top down' approach, whereby the Conservative Central Office was in control of the local organisations. This meant that focus and attention was given to those organisation in 'winnable' seats, while others were left to struggle. The Liberal Party, on the other hand, encouraged a 'bottom up' approach, whereby local organisations grew from grass roots' demand. This resulted in some powerful organisations, such as the Birmingham Caucus under Joseph

Chamberlain, and fears that the localities could have a huge influence on party policy.

Both political parties had problems in attracting the new working-class vote; Gladstone managed to alienate traditional Liberal supporters by his somewhat radical Education Act and trade union legislation; Disraeli focused more on attracting the middle-class voters and, by presenting the Conservative Party as one of supporting traditional institutions and Empire, attracted both middle- and working-class votes. This was, however, to rebound on him in Gladstone's great Midlothian campaign, where he attacked the 'immorality' of Disraeli's foreign policy and began to develop a new kind of campaigning, taking issues directly to the people.

What skills have you used in this unit?

You have worked with a range of primary, contemporary and secondary sources in order to explore and analyse the impact the 1867 Reform Act had on the Conservative and Liberal parties as they grappled with the implications of an electorate that had doubled in size to include the 'respectable' working class. You have explored the reasons why the Liberal and Conservative parties adopted different styles of approach to attracting support in the constituencies, and you have considered and evaluated the complexity of the relationships between parliamentary parties and the regions, and how this was translated into success at the polls.

Exam tips

Below is the sort of question you will find appearing on examination papers as a (b) question.

Study Sources E, I and K, and use your own knowledge. How far would you agree with the view that both Liberal and Conservative grassroots organisations were of little importance to the parliamentary parties?

You tackled (b) questions at the end of Units 3, 4 and 5. Look back at the tips you were given then and apply them to this question. This time, however, remember that the 'view' isn't specifically contained within the secondary Source K, but is one inference that could be made from that source.

RESEARCH TOPIC

What do historians mean by 'Gladstonian Liberalism' and 'Tory democracy'?

Thematic review: source-based debate and evaluation

It is important, especially when dealing with a topic that addresses change over time, to stand back and review the period you have been studying. You need to ask yourself not only what happened, but why it happened and why it happened then and not, say, 100 years earlier or twenty years later. What had driven change? Which factors were significant and which were not? Were there any events that were critical turning points? Thematic review questions, spanning the whole time period, will help to focus your thinking. These are the thematic review questions that relate to 'Britain 1830-85: Representation and Reform'. You can probably think of more, but for the moment these are the ones with which you will be working.

- How far would you agree with the view that it was the 1867 Parliamentary Reform Act that brought about the greatest change to the representation of the British people?

- In considering the process of change to the electoral system in the years 1830-85, how significant was the role of individuals?

- How effective was protest in bringing about change to the electoral system in the years 1830-85??

- To what extent would you agree with the view that continuity, rather than change, characterised the Liberal and Conservative parties in the years 1830-85?

Choose one of these thematic review questions that you plan to answer. Working through this section will make much more sense if you have an actual question in mind.

Answering a thematic review question

There are two keys to answering a thematic review question: **select** and **deploy.**

Select   You need to select appropriate source material

    You need to select appropriate knowledge

Deploy   You need to deploy what you have selected so that you answer the question in as direct a way as possible.

Unpacking 'Select'

You will see that all the thematic review questions are asking for an evaluation. They ask 'How far ...' 'To what extent ...' which means that you will have to weigh up the evidence given by the sources you have selected. You will, therefore, have to select sources that will give you a range of evidence. Six diary entries, for example, will not give you the range you want. You will also need to select sources that seem to provide evidence that pulls in different directions. Eight sources saying more or less the same thing but in different ways will not help you weigh up the significance of different sorts of evidence and reach a reasoned, supported conclusion.

So now go ahead.

(i) Look back through this book and select the sources, primary and secondary, that you think will give you the appropriate range, balance and evidence.

(ii) Make notes of the knowledge you will need to use to contextualise the sources and create an argument.

You can't, of course, simply put some sources into an answer and hope that whoever is reading what you have written can sort things out for themselves. You need to evaluate the sources you have selected and use that evaluation to create the argument you will be making when you answer the question. You have already had practice of doing this in the Exam Zone section of this book, but here is a reminder of some of the questions you will need to ask of a source before you can turn it into evidence:

- Is the **content** appropriate for the question I am answering?

- Can I supply the appropriate **context** for the source?

- How **reliable** is the source as evidence? Was the author or artist **in a position to know** what he or she was talking / painting about?

- What was the intended **audience** of the source? What was the **purpose** of the source?

- If the source is a photograph, did the photographer **pose** the people in the picture? Was the photographer **selective** in what he or she chose to photograph?

- If the source is a **painting**, why did the artist choose to spend time on that particular view?

- If the source is a **cartoon**, what point was the cartoonist making and how far did that **reflect** current attitudes in society?

- How **useful** is this source in developing an answer to the question? Remember that a source that is unreliable can still be useful.

Now you have your selection of source material, you need to think about it as a package. Does it do the job you want it to do? Does it supply you with enough evidence to argue your case, while at the same time providing you with enough evidence of different points of view so that you can show you have considered what weight the evidence will bear in reaching a reasoned, supported conclusion? In other words, can you effectively **cross-reference** between the sources, showing where they support and where they challenge each other?

Unpacking 'deploy'

The key to successful deployment of evidence and knowledge in answering a question like the one you have selected is always to keep the question in the forefront of your mind, Keep focused! Don't be tempted to go off into interesting by-ways. Make every paragraph count as you build your argument.

You have already had a lot of practice in essay planning and writing as you have worked through the Exam Zone, so this is just a reminder of the main things you need to bear in mind.

Plan carefully how you are going to construct your answer and make out your case.

Structure your answer, and you could use this framework as a guide.

- **Introduction**: Here you 'set out your stall' briefly outlining your argument and approach

- **Paragraphs**: These should develop your argument, using the evidence you have created by questioning the sources. As you create the case you are making, remember to cross-reference between the sources you are using so as to weigh the evidence, showing on which you place the greater weight.

- **Conclusion**: Here you should pull your case together, giving a supported summary of the arguments you have made and coming to a reasoned, supported judgement.

In other words, say what you are going to do, do it, and show that you have done it.

You do not, of course, have to respond to these thematic review questions by writing an essay all by yourself. You could work collaboratively in a small group, or you could use one or more of the questions to prepare for a class debate. In whatever way you are going to use these thematic review questions, the approach will be the same: select, deploy and keep to the point.

Good luck!

Exam zone

1 Relax and Prepare

Hot Tips

From GCSE to AS level

- I really enjoyed studying modern world History at GCSE but I am glad that I had the chance to look at some nineteenth century English history at AS level. It has been challenging but enjoyable to study a different period.

- Many of the skills that I learned at GCSE were built upon at AS level, especially in Unit 2 where the skills of source evaluation and analysis are very important.

- AS level History seems like a big step up at first with more demands made on independent reading and more complex source passages to cope with. However by the end of the first term I felt as if my written work had improved considerably.

- The more practice source based questions I attempted, the more confident I became, and quite quickly I picked up the necessary style and technique required for success.

- I found it really helpful to look at the mark schemes in the textbook. It was reassuring to see what the examiners were looking for and how I could gain top marks.

What I wish I had known at the start of the year

- I used the textbook a lot during the revision period to learn the key facts and practice key skills. I really wished that I had used it from the beginning of the course in order to consolidate my class notes.

- I wished that I had taken more time reading and noting other material such as the photocopied handouts issued by my teacher. Reading around the subject and undertaking independent research would have made my understanding more complete and made the whole topic more interesting.

- AS History is not just about learning the relevant material but also developing the skills to use it effectively. I wish that I had spent more time throughout the year practising source questions to improve my style and technique.

- I wish I had paid more attention to the advice and comments made by my teacher on the written work I had done. This would have helped me to improve my scores throughout the year.

How to Revise

- I started my revision by buying a new folder and some dividers. I put all my revision work into this folder and used the dividers to separate the different topics. I really took pride in my revision notes and made them as thorough and effective as I could manage.

- Before I started the revision process, I found it helpful to plan out my history revision. I used the Edexcel Specification given to me by my teacher as a guideline of which topics to revise and I ticked off each one as I covered it.

- I found it useful to revise in short, sharp bursts. I would set myself a target of revising one particular topic in an hour and a half. I would spend one hour taking revision notes, and then half an hour testing myself with a short practice question or a facts test.

- I found it useful to always include some practice work in my revision. If I could get that work to my teacher to mark all the better, but just attempting questions to time helped me improve my technique.

- Sometimes I found it helpful to revise with a friend. We might spend 45 minutes revising by ourselves, and then half an hour testing each other. Often we were able to sort out any problems between us and it was reassuring to see that someone else had the same worries and pressures at that time.

2 Refresh

Revision Checklist

1 The old order challenged: from repression to reform

- The system of government, elections and electorate before 1832
- Government repression of early reform movements, 1815-20
- Pressure outside parliament for reform, 1825–32
- The struggle in parliament for the reform bill.

2 'Reform that you may preserve.' Change and continuity after 1832

- Changes made by the 1832 Reform Act to the franchise and the distribution of seats
- The impact of the changes on political life in boroughs and counties
- The impact of the changes on the development of political parties.
- The extent of continuity with the pre-1832 system.

3 Aftermath: the emergence of Chartism 1837–40

- Why did Chartism emerge as a working class movement in the 1830s?
- For what different reasons did people join the Chartists?
- How did the Chartists put their ideas into action?

- How serious was the Chartist challenge to government in the years 1837–40?

4 Challenges and Consequences: Chartism 1841–58

- The reasons for the failure of the second and third Chartist petitions
- How serious was the threat of revolution in 1848?
- Chartist leadership and the failure of Chartists to achieve their objectives
- Alternative activities undertaken by the Chartists to empower working people

5 The Triumph of Democracy?

- Changes in the country indicating the need for further parliamentary reform
- Political manoeuvrings at Westminster: the role of Russell and Gladstone
- Political manoeuvrings at Westminster: the role of Disraeli
- Why was the 1867 Act not enough? Further measures.

6 Parliament, Party and People 1832–67

- The Tamworth Manifesto and the emergence of the parliamentary Tory/Conservative Party
- The Lichfield House Compact and the emergence of the parliamentary Whig/Liberal Party
- The significance of Sir Robert Peel
- The organisation of politics in the constituencies.

7 Landing in Daylight? Party reform 1868–85

- What were the characteristics of the Conservative and Liberal parties at this time?
- How did the Liberal Party appeal to the enlarged electorate?
- How did the Conservative Party appeal to the enlarged electorate?
- How effective was Party organisation in the constituencies?

This revision check-list looks very knowledge based. The examination, however, will test your source-based skills as well. So remember that when dealing with sources you must be able to:

- Comprehend a source and break it down into key points

- Interpret a source, drawing inferences and deductions from it rather than treating it as a source of information. This may involve considering the language and tone used as well.

- Cross-reference points of evidence between sources to reinforce and challenge.

- Evaluate the evidence by assessing its quality and its reliability in terms of how much weight it will bear and how secure are the conclusions that can be drawn from it. This may include considering the provenance of the source.

- Deal with the sources as a set to build a body of evidence

3 Result

You have spent a lot of time working on plans and constructing answers to the (a) and (b) questions. In units 1, 2 and 6 you worked with (a) questions; in units 3, 4, 5 and 7 you worked with (b) questions. So you now have a pretty good idea about how to plan an answer and write a response to the question of the examination paper. But what are the examiners looking for? And what marks will you get?

What will the exam paper look like?

There will be three questions on the paper.

(a) Compulsory: everyone has to do this.

(b) (i) and (b) (ii) You will have a choice here and will only have to answer one (b) question.

Sources There will be nine sources on the examination paper. But don't worry: you won't have to deal with them all! You'll only need to deal with six sources – three for each of the questions you will be answering. And here is the good news. So far, you have worked with very long sources, some of which were complicated. In the

examination, because you will only have one hour and twenty minutes to answer the two questions, the sources will be much shorter. You'll probably be dealing with no more than around 550 words altogether.

Question (a)

What will you have to do, and what marks will you get for doing it?

You will have to focus on reaching a judgement by analysis, cross-referencing and evaluation of source material. The maximum number of marks you can get is 20. You will be working at any one of four levels. Try to get as high up in the levels as you can. Remember that the only knowledge, outside of that which you can find in the sources, is what examiners call 'contextual' knowledge. This means you can write enough to enable you to interpret the source, but no more. For example, if one of the three sources is by William Gladstone and the focus of the question is on the 1867 Reform Act, you will need to show the examiners that you know about his political manoeuvrings with Disraeli at this time, but you do not need to go into detail about, for example, his Midlothian campaign unless this information helps the understanding of a particular source.

Level 1   Have you shown that you understand the surface features of the sources, and have you shown that you have selected material relevant to the question? Does your response consist mainly of direct quotations from the sources?

1–5 marks   This is what you will score.

Level 2   Have you identified points of similarity and difference in the sources in relation to the question asked? Have you made a least one developed comparison or a range of undeveloped ones? Have you summarised the information you have found in the sources? Have you noted the provenance of at least one of the sources?

6–10 marks   This is what you will score

Level 3   Have you cross-referenced between the sources, making detailed comparisons supported by evidence from the sources? Have you shown that you understand you have to weigh the evidence by looking at the nature, origins, purpose and audience of the sources? Have you shown you have thought about considering 'How far' by trying to use the sources as a set?

11–15 marks   This is what you will score

Level 4   Have you reached a judgement in relation to the issue posed by the question? Is this judgement supported by careful examination of the evidence of the sources? Have you cross-referenced between the sources and analysed the points of similarity and disagreement? Have you taken account of the different qualities of the sources in order to establish what weight the evidence will bear? Have you used the sources as a set when addressing 'How far' in the question?

16–20 marks   This is what you will score.

Now try this (a) question

(a)   Study sources 1, 2 and 3. How far do sources 2 and 3 support the claim made by Lord Grey in Source 1, that failure to respond to the demand for parliamentary reform would lead to revolution?

Now use the marking criteria to assess your response.

How did you do?

What could you have done to have achieved a better mark?

Source 1

(From a letter written to King William IV in 1830 by Lord Grey, arguing in favour of parliamentary reform.)

There is a universal feeling that reform is necessary. I am myself convinced that public opinion is so strongly directed to this question, and so general, that it cannot be resisted. Failure to reform would leave the government deprived of all authority and strength and unable to deal with popular outrage. In short, we would face a revolution.

Source 2

(From a letter written to Francis Place by his fellow London radical, William Bowyer. He is referring to violence in London in October 1831, which accompanied popular demonstrations in favour of parliamentary reform after the Reform Bill had been rejected by the House of Lords.)

The violence came from a group who followed the main procession and were beyond our control. The main procession was perfectly peaceable, consisting of shopkeepers and skilled craftsmen. We intended to create, if possible, an impression that popular violence would be provoked if the Reform Bill were any longer obstructed. There was scarcely a cheer, or a groan, except by word of command.

Source 3

(From the diaries of Charles Greville, a well-informed observer of political life. This entry was written during the May days of 1832, when the Duke of Wellington was trying to form a government)

There is so much wonder and curiosity and expectation around that there is less abuse and exasperation than might have been expected. But it will all burst forth if the Duke succeeds.

Question (b)

What will you have to do and what marks will you get for doing it?

You will have to analyse and evaluate a historical view or claim using two sources and your own knowledge. There are 40 marks for this question. You will get 24 marks for your own knowledge and 16 marks for your source evaluation. You can be working at any one of four levels. Try to get as high up in the levels as you can. The examiners will be marking your answer twice: once for knowledge and a second time for source evaluation.

This is what the examiners will be looking for as they mark the ways in which you have selected and used your knowledge to answer the question:

Level 1   Have you written in simple sentences without making any links between them? Have you provided only limited support for the points you are making? Have you written what you know separately from the sources? Is what you have written mostly generalised and not really directed at the focus of the question? Have you made a lot of spelling mistakes and is your answer disorganised?

1–6 marks   This is what you will score

Level 2   Have you produced a series of statements that are supported by mostly accurate and relevant factual material? Have you make some limited links between the statements you have written? Is your answer mainly 'telling the story' and not really analysing what happened? Have you kept your own knowledge and the sources separate? Have you made a judgement that isn't supported by facts? Is your answer a bit disorganised with some spelling and grammatical mistakes?

7–12 marks   This is what you will score

Level 3   Is your answer focused on the question? Have you shown that you understand the key issues involved? Have you included a lot of descriptive material along with your analysis of the issues? Is your material factually accurate but a bit lacking in depth and/or relevance? Have you

begun to integrate your own knowledge with the source material? Have you made a few spelling and grammatical mistakes? Is your work mostly well organised?

13–18 marks   This is what you will score.

Level 4   Does your answer relate well to the question focus? Have you shown that you understand the issues involved? Have you analysed the key issues? Is the material you have used relevant to the question and factually accurate? Have you begun to integrate what you know with the evidence you have gleaned from the source material? Is the material you have selected balanced? Is the way you have expressed your answer clear and coherent? Is your spelling and grammar mostly accurate?

19–24 marks   This is what you will score.

This is what the examiners are looking for as they mark your source evaluation skills.

Level 1   Have you shown that you understand the sources? Is the material you have selected from them relevant to the question? Is your answer mostly direct quotations from the sources or re-writes of them in your own words?

1–4 marks   This is what you will score.

Level 2   Have you shown that you understand the sources? Have you selected from them in order to support or challenge from the view given in the question? Have you used the sources mainly as sources of information?

5–8 marks   This is what you will score

Level 3   Have you analysed the sources, drawing from them points of challenge and/or support for the view contained in the question? Have you developed these points, using the source material? Have you shown that you realise you are dealing with just one viewpoint and that the sources point to other, perhaps equally valid ones? Have you reached a judgement? Have you supported that judgement with evidence from the sources?

9–12 marks   This is what you will score

Level 4 Have you analysed the sources, raising issues from them? Have you discussed the viewpoint in the question by relating it to the issues raised by your analysis of the source material? Have you weighed the evidence in order to reach a judgement? Is your judgement fully explained and supported by carefully selected evidence?

13–16 marks This is what you will score.

Now try this (b) question.

(b) Read sources 4, 5 and 6 and use your own knowledge.

Do you agree with the view that Disraeli's support for the 1867 Reform Act was motivated mainly by personal ambition?

Explain your answer, using the evidence of Sources 4, 5 and 6 and your own knowledge.

Now use the marking criteria to assess your response.

How did you do?

What could you have done to have achieved higher marks?

The examiners will not be nit-picking their way through your answer, ticking things off as they go. Rather, they will be looking to see which levels best fit the response you have written to the question, and you should do the same when assessing your own responses.

Source 4

(From a letter written by Disraeli to the Prime Minister, Lord Derby, in February 1867, arguing in favour of amendments to the Reform Bill that would greatly extend the right to vote.)

What are called the 'working classes' in the small boroughs are under the patronage of the Upper classes and depend on them for employment and existence. The Liberals will win the big boroughs, but the Conservatives can win the small ones. Of which there are many.

Source 5

(From Robert Blake *Disraeli* published 1966)

It is often believed that, in 1867, Disraeli forsaw that household suffrage would enfranchise a basically conservative class and aimed for this throughout the struggle for the Bill. He persuaded Derby and educated the rest of his party in the process. Therefore, the argument goes, the Conservative breakthrough in the election of 1874 was the result of Disraeli's vision of the new social forces at work. Disraeli encouraged this impression, declaring that household suffrage had been his objective all along.

More accurately, however, Derby later described the Bill in its final form as a 'leap in the dark' and never really denied that its main objective was to 'dish the Whigs' and take credit for electoral reform.

Source 6

(From Paul Adelman *Gladstone, Disraeli and later Victorian Politics* published 1970)

It is now clear that. During the 1867 Reform Crisis, Disraeli was simply seizing an unexpected opportunity. He did not seek to 'educate his party'. Nor did he display either firm principles or consistency of purpose in his support for 'democracy'. Indeed, during these months, Disraeli had one major aim: to destroy Gladstone's leadership over a united Liberal Party, and by seizing the initiative in reform himself, to consolidate his own leadership of the Conservative Party.

How will I time my responses?

You have 1 hour 20 minutes to answer two questions. Remember that the (a) question is compulsory and that you will have a choice of one from two (b) questions. Take time, say, five minutes, to read through the paper and think about your choice of (b) question. The (a) question is worth half the marks of the (b) question, so you should aim to spend twice the time on the (b) question. This means that, including planning time, you should spend about 25 minutes on the (a) question and about 50 minutes (again, including planning) on the (b) question.

You have now had a lot of practice in planning, writing and assessing your responses to the sort of questions you can expect to find on the examination paper. You are well prepared and you should be able to tackle the examination with confidence.

Good luck!

Bibliography

Adams, W.E. *Memoirs of a Social Atom* (1903)

Adelman, P. *Peel and the Conservative Party 1830–50* 3rd ed (1990)

Adelman, P. *Gladstone, Disraeli and Later Victorian Politics* 3rd ed (1997)

Culpin, C. and Evans, E. *The Birth of Modern Britain 1780–1914* (1997)

Epstein, J. *The Lion of Freedom: Feargus O'Connor and the Chartist Movement* (1982)

Evans, E.J. *Forging of the Modern State* 3rd ed (2001)

Evans, E.J. *Political Parties in Britain 1783–1867* (1985)

Evans, E.J. *The Great Reform Act of 1832*

Evans, E.J. *Chartism* (2000)

Evans, E.J *Chartism Revisited* (1999)

Finn, J. *Chartists and Chartism* (1992)

Gammage, R. *History of the Chartist Movement* (1854)

Gash, N. *The Age of Peel: Documents of Modern History* (1968)

Gash, N. 'Wellington and Peel' published in D. Southgate (ed) *The Conservative Leadership 1832–1932* (1974)

Hilton, B. *A Mad, Bad and Dangerous people* (2006)

Hovell, M. *The Chartist Movement* (1970)

Kebbel, T.E. (ed) *Selected Speeches of the Earl of Beaconsfield* vol II (1882)

Lang, S. *Parliamentary Reform 1785–1928* (1999)

Large, D. *London in the Year of Revolutions* (1977)

Lecky, W.E.H. *Democracy and Liberty* vol II (1981)

Lovett, W. *Life and Struggles of William Lovett* (1876)

Newbould, I. *Sir Robert Peel and the Conservative Party: A Study in Failure?* (1983)

Pearce, R. and Stearn, R. *Government and Reform 1815–1918* (1994)

Pugh, M. *The Tories and the People 1880–1935* (1985)

Read, D. 'Chartism in Manchester' published in A. Briggs (ed) *Chartist Studies* (1959)

Royle, E. *Chartism* 2nd ed (1986)

Royle, E. *Revolutionary Britannia* (2000)

Smythe, H.R. *Parliamentary Reform Reconsidered* (1853)

Thompson, D. *The Chartists: Popular Politics in the Industrial Revolution* (1984)

Walsh, Sir J.B. *Chapters of Contemporary History* (1836)

Whitfield, B. *The Extension of the Franchise 1832–1931* (2001)

Wilson, A. 'Chartism' published in J. T. Ward (ed) *Popular Movements* (1970)

Wilson, B. *The Struggles of an Old Chartist* (1887)

Wright, D.G. *Democracy and Reform 1815–1885* (1970)

Wright, D.G. *Popular Radicalism* (1988)

Glossary

Adullamite   Those MPs who had opposed the 1866 Liberal Reform Bill.

Amendment   An amendment to a parliamentary Bill is a change that an MP, or group of MPs, would like to make to a Bill. Then, as now, MPs vote on the amendments before they vote on the actual Bill.

Anti-Corn Law League   A middle-class radical movement that gained tremendous popularity. Dissatisfied with the tinkering via 'sliding scales' that had taken place since 1828, the League campaigned for total repeal. It was well funded and highly organised, employing various techniques such as public meetings, pamphlets, newspaper articles and campaigns in support of pro-repeal MPs. Beyond the specific target of repealing the Corn Laws, the League also promoted the ideology of free trade.

Arlington Street Compact 1884   The agreement between Salisbury (Conservative) and Gladstone (Liberal), whereby Salisbury got the redistribution he sought and Gladstone the extension of the franchise he wanted.

Borough   A borough was a town that, at some point, had been given a royal charter. These charters allowed the town to levy tolls at their market, to hold a court that dealt with civil and some criminal matters, and send a representative to the House of Commons. Most boroughs sent two MPs to Westminster. So boroughs were contained within counties. Some boroughs, known as 'rotten boroughs', had so few voters that they were easily bought or bribed to vote for a particular candidate. Other boroughs were also under the control of a single powerful person or family. These 'pocket boroughs' would nearly always return the influential person's choice of candidate.

Boroughmonger (Boromonger)   A person who buys or sells parliamentary seats in a borough.

Carlton Club   Founded in 1832 in response to the Tory defeat in the wake of reform, the Carlton Club aimed to rally support by encouraging voter registration and co-ordinating propaganda in the press.

Catholic Emancipation   In 1829, the Roman Catholic Relief Act gave Roman Catholics the right to vote in British general elections and to stand for election to the House of Commons.

Caucus   A group of people who unite to promote a particular policy or interest.

Chandos clause   This was a clause inserted into the 1832 Reform Act by Lord Chandos. It gave the vote to tenants-at-will paying an annual rent of £50. Tenants-at-will could have their tenancy ended at any time by their landlord, and so they were highly likely to vote the same way as their Tory landlords.

Charlatan   Someone who falsely claims a special skill or expertise.

Chief Whip and whips   A parliamentary Chief Whip was responsible for a team of whips whose work was to ensure attendance, discipline and correct voting among members of a particular political party.

Compounder   A person who paid rent and rates together, to his landlord.

Corn Laws   Controversial legislation introduced in 1815, and variously amended until finally abolished in 1846. The Corn Laws were designed to protect the price of British wheat and other types of 'corn' against foreign competition. For radicals, both middle class and working class, the Corn Laws represented a great evil of the unreformed system. The landed interest was, it was argued, using its parliamentary influence to protect itself against cheaper imported corn that would otherwise benefit the rising urban population. Such blatant aristocratic self-interest aroused intense resentment, leading to the formation of the Anti-Corn Law League in 1838.

County   Britain is divided into counties. Until 1832, each English county sent two MPs. The exception was Yorkshire, which returned four.

'Deserving' and 'undeserving' poor   The deserving poor were those who were poor through no fault of their own – e.g. widows and orphans, the sick and the old. The undeserving poor were the able-bodied poor who, though fit enough, were unwilling or unable to work or find work.

Disestablishment of the Church of England The ending of official and legal links between the Church of England and the state.

Dissenter   A person who refuses to accept the authority, doctrines or practices of the Church of England, preferring instead to belong to a noconformist church such as the Methodists or Presbyterians.

Free trade   International trade not limited by interference from government, regulations or tariffs intended to restrict foreign imports. It is the exact opposite of protectionism.

Ginger group   A small pressure group within a larger organisation that strongly presses for action on a particular issue.

Habeas Corpus Act   This is still a very important law. It literally means 'to have the body produced' and meant that everyone imprisoned had to be brought to trial within a certain length of time. It prevents people from being imprisoned indefinitely without being charged of a crime.

Household suffrage   Giving the vote to the male head of a household.

Humbuggery   A hoax, fraud or sham meant to deceive or cheat.

Hustings   A platform from which parliamentary candidates were nominated and addressed electors, and on which voters shouted out the name of the person for whom they were voting.

Interests   An influential and powerful group of people who have the same aims, or support the same causes, the success of which is important to them personally or professionally.

Irish Famine   Between 1845 and 1851 at least a million Irish people died of starvation and disease. The famine was triggered by a fungal infection that destroyed most of the potato crop in 1845. This subsistence food had taken on an enormous significance because of exploitation of the peasantry through subdivision of landholdings. Potato blight was therefore the immediate but not the underlying cause of Irish distress. The government response was inadequate; but the crisis provided further grounds for repealing the Corn Laws in order to make it cheaper to import foreign grain.

Irish Home Rule   Self-government for Ireland.

Lichfield House Compact   An unwritten agreement made at Lichfield House in February 1835 between the Whigs, led by Lord John Russell, and a group of Irish MPs, led by Daniel O'Connell, whereby the Whigs could depend on Irish support in the Commons in return for promising to consider some reforming legislation for Ireland.

Marplot   A person who spoils something by meddling or interfering.

'Outdoor' and 'Indoor' relief   'Outdoor' relief was help given to the poor in their own homes. 'Indoor' relief was help given to the poor inside a workhouse.

Outworker   A person who works at home and is supplied with the raw materials by a manufacturer.

Nonconformists   Nonconformists were Protestants, of various denominations, who refused to conform to the Anglican Church. They had gained a degree of civil equality after 1828, when the Test and Corporation Acts were repealed, but still suffered discrimination. There was a longstanding tradition of Whig support for civil and religious liberty. The Municipal Corporations Act boosted the influence of Nonconformists and helped to create a strong link with the emerging Liberal Party.

Picketing The act, by striking workers, of standing outside a workplace to try to prevent or dissuade others from going to work.

Poor rates A parish tax levied on property and landowners in order to provide for parish paupers.

Poor relief Help given by the parish to people who did not have enough money to feed and clothe themselves. People who received poor relief were called paupers.

Preamble The opening section of an Act, which sets out the purpose of the legislation.

Protectionism Protectionism consisted of policies to defend national economic interests. This was to be achieved by imposing duties on foreign imports in order to safeguard domestic production. Protectionism was attractive to some politicians because it provided revenue and appeared patriotic. It also appealed to those domestic producers who were guaranteed artificially inflated prices.

Queen's speech The monarch always opens a session of parliament by making a speech outlining the government's work for that session. From the nineteenth century onwards, the monarch didn't write the speech; it was always written by the Prime Minister.

Radical A person who wanted to change the whole political system right from its roots.

Reform Club The Reform Club was founded in 1836, by a combination of Whigs and middle-class radicals, in response to the Carlton Club. Like its rival, the Reform Club aimed to combine sociability with better political organisation, enjoying also the added attraction of a renowned French chef.

Satire The use of humour, sarcasm and ridicule to attack institutions and individuals.

Secular Not involved with religion, or religious bodies, in any way.

Split voting Electors in a constituency with two seats had two votes. This double-vote system, which was recorded in poll books, has provided valuable evidence that has been subjected to computer analysis. The politicisation of voters can be inferred by examining whether they 'split' – by voting for candidates of opposing political views – or 'plumped' – by voting for two candidates on the same side or by throwing away their second vote if there was no suitable second candidate instead of 'splitting'.

Stamp duty A tax imposed by the government on newspapers. It was first levied in 1712 and gradually increased until in 1815 the tax was 4d a copy. This put the price of newspapers out of reach of ordinary people.

Temperance Not drinking any alcohol whatsoever.

Tolpuddle Martyrs In 1834 six agricultural labourers from the Dorset village of Tolpuddle were sentenced to seven years' transportation for using 'unlawful oaths' to establish a trade union.

Treating The practice of giving 'treats' to electors, usually in the form of meals and alcohol, in the hope of persuading them to vote for a certain candidate.

Ulterior measures These were the actions the Chartists suggested could be undertaken if their Petition was rejected by parliament. These included withdrawing all their money from the banks at the same time, converting their paper money to gold or silver all at the same time, holding a general strike (called a 'sacred month') and supporting only pro-Chartist candidates at the next general election.

Unenfranchised A person who doesn't have the right to vote.

Yeomanry Militia recruited from local businessmen, farmers and lesser gentry.

Index